🦁 *Gender and Language in Chaucer*

Gender and Language in Chaucer

Catherine S. Cox

University Press of Florida
Gainesville/Tallhassee/Tampa/Boca Raton
Pensacola/Orlando/Miami/Jacksonville

Copyright 1997 by the Board of Regents of the State of Florida
Printed in the United States of America on acid-free paper
All rights reserved

LIBRARY OF CONGRESS CATALOGING-IN-PUBLICATION DATA
Cox, Catherine S., 1962–
Gender and language in Chaucer / Catherine S. Cox.
   p.   cm.
Includes bibliographical references and index.
ISBN 0-8130-1861-7
1. Chaucer, Geoffrey, d. 1400—Characters—Women. 2. English language—Middle English, 1100–1500—Lexicology. 3. Women—England—History—Middle Ages, 500–1500. 4. Civilization, Medieval, in literature. 5. Chaucer, Geoffrey, d. 1400—Language. 6. Gender identity in literature. 7. Sex role in literature. 8. Women in literature. I. Title.
PR1928.W64C69   1997
821'.1—dc21   97-9730

The University Press of Florida is the scholarly publishing agency for the State University System of Florida, comprised of Florida A & M University, Florida Atlantic University, Florida International University, Florida State University, University of Central Florida, University of Florida, University of North Florida, University of South Florida, and University of West Florida.

University Press of Florida
15 NW 15th Street
Gainesville, FL 32611

To the memory of my sister
Diana Stallworth
1967–1992

Contents

Preface ix

Abbreviations xi

Introduction: Gender and the Craft of Making 1

1 Promiscuous Glossing and Virgin Words 18

2 The Text of Criseyde 39

3 "Wreched Engendrynge" and (wo)Mankynde 53

4 Marks of Womanhood in the Ballades 76

5 The Jangler's "Bourde" 97

6 The Summoner's Subversive Erotics 113

Notes 133

Works Cited 166

Index 187

❧ Preface

This study considers the significance of gender construction in Chaucer's work. My intention is to demonstrate the complex and ambivalent relation of Chaucerian texts to orthodox codes of gender, and to this end I consider the texts both within their cultural contexts (theology, epistemology, poetics) and in light of contemporary feminist and poststructuralist theories. It is my hope in writing this study that readers will find it informative and provocative, perhaps an impetus for their own pursuits. The book's intended audience, therefore, includes not only veteran Chaucerians but also scholars, teachers, and students interested in medieval literature and culture, feminist critical theory, and gender studies.

My work has benefited from the advice, criticism, and enthusiasm of a number of readers and colleagues whom I am pleased to acknowledge. I would like to thank in particular R. A. Shoaf, whose guidance has been invaluable. Special thanks go to Karen S. Robinson and Michael W. Cox. My thanks also to Ira Clark, Dan Cottom, Jack Perlette, Carol Lansing, Marie Nelson, John Taggart, Judy Shoaf, Bonnie Baker, Chauncey Wood, and the late Richard Hamilton Green; to the anonymous readers for *Exemplaria*, *South Atlantic Review*, and the University Press of Florida; and to Walda Metcalf, acquisitions editor for the press. I am grateful to have had the opportunity to present portions of my work at a number of conferences, including the 1993 and 1995 South Atlantic Modern Language Association, the 1994 Northeast Modern Language Association, the 1993 Medieval Congress in Kalamazoo, and the 1993 Citadel Conference on Medieval and Renaissance Studies. Local debts of fact and scholarship have been acknowledged in the notes, but, as a medievalist working in gender studies, I wish to acknowledge here a general indebtedness to Carolyn Dinshaw's groundbreaking work. Finally, I would like to thank the University of Pittsburgh at Johnstown for a Faculty Scholarship Grant awarded to me in 1994 and for the opportunity to teach Chaucer to interested and enthusiastic students—students Aimee Bouch, Shannon

Kelly, Chris Sedlmeyer, Jodie Nicotra, and Lynn Berry warrant special mention.

An early version of Chapter 1, now substantially revised and retitled, appeared in *Exemplaria* 5 (1993); a shorter version of Chapter 5 in *South Atlantic Review* 61 (1996); and Chapter 6, revised and retitled, in *Exemplaria* 7 (1995). Used by permission.

Abbreviations

CCSL	Corpus christianorum series latina
EETS, e.s.	Early English Text Society, extra series
EETS, o.s.	Early English Text Society, original series
ELH	*English Literary History*
MED	*Middle English Dictionary*
OED	Oxford English Dictionary
PG	Patrologiae cursus completus, series graeca, ed. Migne (volume and column cited)
PL	Patrologiae cursus completus, series latina, ed. Migne (volume and column cited)
PMLA	*Publications of the Modern Language Association*

❧ *Introduction*

Gender and the Craft of Making

"Diverse folk diversely they seyde, / But for the moore part they loughe and pleyde" (I.3857–58),¹ observes the *Canterbury Tales* narrator as the "folk" respond to the Miller's "nyce cas." Here we find a striking instance of narrative reflexivity,² where Chaucer acknowledges the diversity of interpretation expressed by an audience comprising diverse pilgrims. While their specific comments go unreported (with the exception of the Reeve, who personalizes the story and feels compelled to "quite" it),³ we may surmise, based on the detailed portraits "[o]f sondry folk" (I.25) reported by the narrator in the *General Prologue*, that the diversity of interpretation is informed to some extent by the personal "condicioun" and "degree" of each pilgrim—such characteristics as occupation and economic status, social position, physical appearance, intelligence, age, and gender (I.38, 40). By including this observation of diversity in the narrative frame of the *Canterbury Tales*, Chaucer overtly and reflexively relinquishes control over interpretation(s) of his text, thereby respecting its capacity to evoke many senses (polysemy)⁴ of meaning and to provoke varying interpretations from its audiences, both within and without the text.

❧ 1

This observation of diversity calls attention to Chaucer's recurring concern with the verity of representation and textuality. Throughout Chaucer's texts there is evident an anxious realization that a text circulates largely outside its author's own control. In "Chaucers Wordes Unto Adam, His Owne Scriveyn," for instance, Chaucer chides his scribe for carelessness— "But after my makyng thow wryte more trewe; / So ofte adaye I mot thy werk renewe" (4–5)—and acknowledges that a text, his own "makyng," may be corrupted by the "negligence and rape" (7) of the scribe.[5] Chaucer's "makyng" is the subject of his self-reflexive text, underscored by an acknowledgment that no control may be ensured over the finished product: the text is subject to scribal mutability or mutilation, and the author can only hope that its integrity might remain intact—indeed, as the narrator of *Troilus and Criseyde* concedes, "for ther is so gret diversite / In Englissh and in writyng of oure tonge, / So prey I God that non myswrite the" (5.1793–95).[6] Just as a text eludes an author's or narrator's control over its integrity once in circulation, so too it resists an author's attempted control over its inevitably diverse perceptions by the "diverse folk" that constitute its audience; "diverse folk" will indeed read and interpret individually and hence idiosyncratically, and they will do so independent of an author's wishes, whether these interests and intentions be known.

An analogy may thus be drawn between the scribal corruption of a physical manuscript and an audience's "corruption" (interpretation) of the literal text: both manifest the subjectivity of textuality, and both, in effect, usurp the author's role.[7] The physical activities of (mis)copying or corrupting correspond to literary acts of interpretation in that these activities are manifestations of appropriation; the scribe who disfigures the manuscript in effect transforms it into his own, just as hermeneutically minded readers, in subjecting the text to analysis and interpretation, transform the original author's text into personal readings, investing them with a significance that supercedes the literal text. Chaucer frequently addresses activities germane to author and audience such as manipulation, transmission, and reception, and his texts frequently demonstrate the further applicability of these and related issues to other categories of literary and cultural activity. Such is the texts' reflexive dimension, for "reflexivity" describes a text's property of self-conscious attention to its own processes; the term denotes what might be called a "metatextual" critical commentary, the properties of which contribute to a semantics of appropriation (to be described more fully below). In calling attention to its own textual status, then, a text at once reiterates and destabilizes its own subjectivity.

To appreciate how such attention articulates a self-reflexive subjectivity, some contextualizing of the poet's role as "maker" will be useful. "Makyng" is the label used by medieval poets to describe the activity of vernacular, common poetic construction; "makyng" is distinct from "poesye," which largely privileges Latin language and classical, permanent themes, and is clearly posited as the subordinate or inferior term.[8] As J. S. P. Tatlock noted, "makyng" describes the work of Chaucer and his contemporaries, while "poetrie" designates the work of the ancients and the few moderns deemed worthy of the label, namely, Dante, Petrarch.[9] One of the more self-conscious and elucidating articulations of this distinction is found in a concluding stanza of Chaucer's *Troilus:*

> Go, litel bok, go, litel myn tragedye,
> Ther God thi makere yet, er that he dye,
> So sende myght to make in some comedye!
> But litel book, no makyng thow n'envie,
> But subgit be to alle poesye;
> And kis the steppes where as thow seest pace
> Virgile, Ovide, Omer, Lucan, and Stace.   5.1786–92

Chaucer, who identifies his own work as "makyng," makes clear the narrator's hope that the *Troilus* need not "envie" other "makyng," that it might represent the best of its kind even as it accepts a subordinate position in relation to the classical poets. The poetry of the "makers" is self-consciously distinguished from that of the Latin "poets."

Although, as Lisa Kiser has demonstrated, the "makyng"/"poesye" distinction is not as distinct an opposition as it may seem, the medieval vernacular poets still considered themselves *makers*.[10] Chaucer, as we have seen, returns to the label throughout his work, and we could consider many more examples, such as the G Prologue to the *Legend of Good Women*, a text infused with references to "makyng."[11] Chaucer's two most accomplished English contemporaries, the *Pearl*-poet and Langland, share Chaucer's interest in the practice or craft of "makyng."[12] Henryson, too, speaks of his work in terms of its being made,[13] and Dunbar's *Lament for the Makars*, a roll call of fourteenth- and fifteenth-century "makars," identifies Chaucer and his contemporaries as such without apology and with respect: "He has done petously devour, / The noble Chaucer, of makaris flour" (49–50). Chaucer, "of makaris flour," is a "makar" nonetheless.

Of course, no contemporary critic would argue that Chaucer, Langland, the *Pearl*-poet, or Henryson should not legitimately be labeled "poet." But the medieval labels "maker" and "makyng" are evocative in suggesting the process of the vernacular poet's work and in elucidating the poets' metacritical sense of narrative textuality. To *make,* according to the *MED,* is "[t]o write or compose (a book, poem, song, letter, etc.)," a definition that evokes the word's sense of creating or engendering, of bringing into existence (the sense frequently associated with God, the Creator or Maker).[14] In making poetry, the medieval poet/maker exploits the instrumentality of language to produce something more than the materials it comprises. In addition, a Middle English pun may be determined in connection with two forms of "make": the form described above, which corresponds to creation and production—textual engendering—and an additional form designating "match," "mate," "peer," "equal."[15] The latter sense, while etymologically distinct from and unrelated to the former, underscores the connectedness of textual and sexual en/gendering; it is representative of sexual engendering, pro/creation and re/production. The generation of texts, like the generation of progeny, entails making/mating in order to produce something new, something more than its origins. When I speak of *making* and *en/gendering,* I am therefore using terms that for the fourteenth and fifteenth centuries are subtly fraught with sexual connotations figuratively connected to the act of textual production.

When Langland, for example, refers to the "gendre of a generacion" (*Piers Plowman* B.16.222), or when Chaucer's narrator expresses a wish "To know of hir signifiaunce / The gendres" (*House of Fame* 17–18), the generative properties of language are evoked and a sense of gender as category is implied. "Gender," "genre," "gendre," and "engendryng" derive from *generare,* to beget,[16] and these terms and other derivatives retain a twofold sense of textual/sexual implications. "Gender" as a critical and cultural category is distinct from, though obviously informed by, "sex"; "gender" corresponds to social and cultural identifications and ideologies pertaining to or derived from biological, chromosomal "sex," often interpreted quite loosely or even, as it might seem, arbitrarily. Eve Kosofsky Sedgwick theorizes, "Gender, then, is the far more elaborated, more fully and rigidly dichotomized social production and reproduction of male and female identities and behaviors—of male and female persons—in a cultural system for which 'male/female' functions as a primary and perhaps model binarism affecting the structure and meaning of many, many other binarisms whose apparent connection to chromosomal sex will often be exiguous or nonexistent."[17] As Sedgwick further points out, we may speak of "opposite" genders, given that "masculine" and "feminine" are cultural constructs, defined in relation to each other.[18] While "sex" is relatively fixed and represents a largely recognized irreducible difference, "gender" is not biologically determined and is therefore negotiable, subject to both the influence of and resistance to normative presuppositions. Gender and gender identity are thus complex and flexible, deriving from and yet not limited to the core "male"/"female" differential.[19]

Medieval attitudes toward gender/sex distinctions are not far removed from such contemporary thinking. As we shall see, medieval thinkers and writers invested "masculine" and "feminine" with characteristics and properties having nothing to do with chromosomal sex per se. And the flexibility in gender identity that constitutes a foundation for current thinking on gender—the recognition that a gender position may be taken up, that is to say, appropriated, by someone of either sex—is, I shall argue, part of Chaucer's own depictions of gender identity. Consider, for example, the prominence of descriptive gender designation in narrative expressions of praise and blame: Donegild of the *Man of Law's Tale*, for instance, is said to exhibit "traitorie . . . mannysh" (II.781–82); no woman, the *Troilus* narrator insists, is "lasse mannyssh in semynge" than Criseyde (1.284); the Host likens the Clerk to a "mayde" in his riding behavior (IV.2–3). This brief sampling calls attention not only to the ubiquitous and omnipresent attention to gender in Chaucer's texts but also to the social, political, and cultural implications of gender identities.

Gender construction is coincidental with cultural definition, particularly those junctures where social and political considerations intersect. Here again contemporary gender theories can help elucidate these cultural imperatives and enable us to look on gender construction in Chaucer's day as part of a larger, continuous process.[20] Gender identity, its perception, and its contexts constitute an important aspect of Chaucer's work, particularly as gender is a subjective concept that in effect articulates its own processes of conceptualization and reconfiguration. In connection with the metatextual, or self-reflexive, dimension of Chaucer's work, evocations of gendered textuality may be understood as en/gendered reflexions, that is, as metacritical representations of the gendered process of textual production.

How Chaucer uses manifestations of gender to articulate a metapoetics is a focus of this study, and I want particularly to consider in what ways and to what effect a text en/genders its epistemological permutations, what significance the interconnectedness of gender and textuality has in relation to the construction of self-reflexive subjectivity. In opening up a text's metacritical dimension for analysis, I do not purport to determine what Chaucer the poet wants to do but rather what the text does or might be doing, for Chaucer operates within an environment of cultural and literary production beyond his control, and his work is clearly a product of intersecting cultural forces.[21] How Chaucer's work might be understood in relation to these contexts can help us appreciate his work in new light, even if the extent to which the author might himself desire to embrace or resist cultural influences remains speculative at best.

2

Gender identification for Chaucer's literary environment largely derives from a twofold tradition of the Christian and the classical, both of which characterize the feminine negatively in relation to the masculine. In medieval Christian theology's antifeminist tenets, "feminine" and "carnal" are linked; all that is perceived as negative and threatening about carnality is ascribed to the feminine, equating the feminine with flesh and hence corruption, sin, and filth. Woman is identified as the cause of Man's fall, and antifeminist behaviors are justified through a curious illogic of collateral responsibility and perpetual obligation. To catalog the biblical and theological writings associated with misogyny would of course require far more space than can be justified here, but a few illustrations should suffice for contextual demonstration. Consider, for example, St. Paul's admonition:

> Mulier in silentio discat cum omni subiectione. Docere autem mulierem non permitto, neque dominari in virum: sed esse in silentio. Adam enim primus formatus est: deinde Eva: et Adam non est seductus: mulier autem seducta in praevaricatione fuit. Salvabitur autem per filiorum generationem, si permanserit in fide, et dilectione, et sanctificatione cum sobrietate.[22]

> [Let the woman learn in silence with all subjection. To teach however I suffer not a woman, nor to use authority over the man: but to be in silence. For Adam was first formed: then Eve. And Adam was not seduced: the woman however being seduced was in the transgression. Yet she shall be saved through the generation of children if she abides in faith, and love, and sanctification with sobriety.]

Paul advocates that Woman be denied voice, and insists that the female body's capacity for procreation in marriage remains its sole redeeming feature. The argument for salvation through childbearing furthermore usurps what women accomplish by transferring the maternal contribution to a wholly patriarchal design, as Augustine notes in *De civitate Dei:* "nec mater, quae conceptum portat et partum nutrit, est aliquid, sed qui incrementum dat Deus" [It is not the mother, who conceives, carries, brings forth and nourishes, who is significant, but it is God who gives growth].[23]

The institutionalized subjection of women and the onerous endorsement of redemption through childbearing are authorized further by Paul's analogy of women and the church:

> Mulieres viris suis subditae sint, sicut Domino: quoniam vir caput est mulieris: sicut Christus caput est Ecclesiae: ipse, salvator corporis eius. Sed sicut Ecclesia subiecta est Christo, ita et mulieres viris suis in omnibus.   Eph 5.22–24
>
> [Women be subject to their husbands, as to the Lord, because the husband is the head of the wife, just as Christ is the head of the church, exactly the saviour of his body. Therefore as the church is subject to Christ, so also let the wives be to their husbands in all things.][24]

Frequently articulated through metaphors of the body, the feminine flesh is subjugated by hierarchical protocols to an inferior, disdained position and regarded with revulsion by patristic theologians and by those who embrace their tenets.[25]

In addition, the feminine is accorded a negativeness connected to epistemology and textuality. Because of the definitive associations of carnal and literal, carnal and feminine, a third association—of literal and feminine—operates as a subtext of much critical commentary on the theological interpretations of body and spirit, flesh and reason. The "carnal" is "literal" in Pauline theology, and hence the feminine, as carnal, is both literal and deadly. Paul's famous dictum "littera enim occidit, Spiritus autem vivificat" (2 Cor 3.6) [for the letter kills but the spirit quickens] and its companion verse "Nam prudentia carnis, mors est" (Rom 8.6) [For the wisdom of the carnal is death] helped found Augustine's influential concern with letter and spirit. Augustine writes in *De doctrina christiana,* "Cum enim figurate dictum sic accipitur, tamquam proprie dictum sit, carnaliter sapitur. Neque ulla mors animae congruentius appellatur, quam . . . intellegentia carni subicitur requendo litteram" [Nor can anything be more correspondingly called the death of the spirit than . . . understanding (being) subjected to the flesh in search of the letter].[26] The ideal woman in patristic theology represents the feminine carnal subjected to masculine control, while the overtly sexual woman suggests the threat of unleashed carnality, the potential of the feminine to corrupt inherently vulnerable patriarchal decorums.[27] Corruption owing to feminine sexuality finds representation in images, for example, of the temptress—"aliena quae verba sua dulcia facit" (Prv 7.5) [the stranger who makes her words sweet][28]—who lures the unwary man away from the path to God. This stereotype further reinforces the correlation of flesh and language, for the carnal woman is said to corrupt man's appreciation of the spiritual Word by enticing him to the flesh, thereby obstructing his course toward the spirit.

The medieval correlation of feminine and flesh and the patriarchal tenets of marriage and subordination described above point to a norm that obviously fails to account for every behavior and status. Yet—with the exception of virgins—most childless women, women who resist marriage, and men who are said to act like women represent in this context, according to the Christian perspective, such perceived deficiencies as unnaturalness, sterility, wasted potential and language abused.[29]

Within medieval intellectual and theological systems, however, the strictures of patriarchal tenets and their applications had to compete with other, provocatively contradictory, models. From the perspective of classical epistemology, within the Aristotelian/Pythagorean antifeminist tradition, the feminine is "unlimited" as well. According to the Aristotelian paradigm, which Aristotle attributes to Pythagoras, epistemological duals define and schematize meaning: "limit and unlimited, odd and even, one and plurality, right and left, male and female, resting and moving, straight and curved, light and darkness, good and bad, square and oblong."[30] Those terms listed first in each pairing correspond to masculine attributes, the subsequent term to the feminine. The feminine is characterized as passive, bad, plural, and the like, while the ostensibly more desirable traits are gendered masculine. R. Howard Bloch further comments: "This association translates into what might be thought of as a medieval metaphysics of number, according to which, under the Platonic and Pythagorean schema, all created things express either the principle of self-identity (*principium ejusdem*) or of continuous self-alteration (*principium alterius*). The first is associated with unity, the monad; the second with multiplicity, dyadic structures. Also they are specifically gendered, the monad being male, the dyad female."[31] The feminine is associated with instability, mutability, and unpredictability, characteristics appropriated by Christian writers to intensify the construction of feminine stereotypes, particularly regarding speech. As Bloch observes, "The assumption is, of course, that woman is the equivalent of the deception of which language is capable, a prejudice so deeply rooted in the medieval discourse on gender that it often even passes unnoticed."[32] The Christian and classical epistemologies—however contradictory they appear—are often merged, as we shall see, and yet they expose the contradictory directions in which medieval interpretations and representations of gender may be traced. Thus Christian writers associate the feminine with both silence (submissive, marginal) and loquaciousness (immodest, excessive); one decorum emphasizes a controlled subject, the other a rationale for imposing control, and in both cases, the masculine is purported to remedy the feminine, to keep Woman in line.

The negativeness accorded the feminine is manifest in the hierarchical value structure attached to conventional ideologies of gender difference, since the asymmetrical value structure of gendered ideology has conventionally devalued the feminine. Hélène Cixous, in her "Sorties" critique of binary structures, observes of the gender dual, "Always the same metaphor: we follow it, it carries us, beneath all figures, wherever discourse is organized. If we read or speak, the same thread or double braid is leading us through-out literature, philosophy, criticism, centuries of representation and reflection"; and addressing Cixous's argument, Toril Moi notes, "It doesn't matter which 'couple' one chooses to highlight: the male/female opposition and its inevitable positive/negative evaluation can always be traced as the underlying paradigm."[33] Medieval antifeminism may indeed be traced to the classical paradigm of contraries, which was furthered by Christianity's applications until the influence of the underlying antifeminist male/female, superior/inferior paradigm became ubiquitous in the Middle Ages: "*Male* and *female* were contrasted and asymmetrically valued as intellect/body, active/passive, rational/irrational, reason/emotion, self-control/lust, judgment/mercy, and order/disorder."[34]

Thus in accordance with antifeminist decorums, feminine flesh and feminine mutability are usually depicted in medieval poetry as negatives. By unremittingly inscribing anything culturally construed as negative to be feminine, early Christian and medieval patriarchal discourses ensured that the negativity of the feminine would be culturally perpetuated, though patronizing assertions of compassion and respect obscured much of the blatancy. In both theological and epistemological representations, the feminine is used to privilege the masculine, though theology paradoxically valorizes the feminine through virginity directives.³⁵ Codes of decorum are thus designed to valorize virginity and to condemn those who resist constraint. Indeed, patristic theologians express a desire to deny gender difference in its entirety, echoing Paul, who declares that in an ideal Christian environment, "non est masculus neque femina" (Gal 3.28) [there is no masculine nor feminine]. The most influential misogynist of all,³⁶ Jerome, overtly attempts to blur gender distinctions by seeking to deny the feminine even as he valorizes the masculine; conflating polysemous gender with a kind of unisex ideal, Jerome rewards women who deny their identity as women with the honorary title "man":

> [Q]uandiu mulier partui servit et liberis, hanc habet ad virum differentiam, quam corpus ad animam. Sin autem Christo magis voluerit servire quam saeculo, mulier esse cessabit, et dicetur vir.
>
> [As long as woman is for birth and children, she has difference from man, as body from soul. But if she wishes to serve Christ more than the world, then she will cease to be woman and will be called man.]³⁷

It is hardly surprising, then, as Bloch notes, that "in the misogynistic thinking of the Middle Ages there can be no distinction between the theological and the sexual."³⁸ Such bizarre statements as Jerome's indicate that for Jerome—and for other Christian misogynists—the problem that Woman poses is how the theologian is to exclude women, the objects of revulsion, from patriarchal hegemony while simultaneously purporting to embrace all of God's creation.³⁹ In the Middle Ages, then, antifeminism, deriving from paradigmatic epistemology, often took the form of outright misogyny.

The conflicting implications of the classical and Christian associations of the feminine with the unlimited and with the flesh inform various debates of contemporary feminist theory as well. A connection between the multiple and the feminine, for example, is articulated in *This Sex Which Is Not One* by Luce Irigaray, who finds that "women's speaking lips/ écriture féminine metonymically suggest plurality, multiplicity, and the dissolution of bounds."⁴⁰ Irigaray argues, from a perspective that borders upon a sexual essentialism, for a "multiplicity of female desire and female language," noting that "[f]emale sexuality has always been conceptualized on the basis of masculine parameters."⁴¹ Irigaray—who addresses the complex, unpredictable, and mutable nature of the feminine as defined by the polemical antecedents put forth by the ubiquitous binary epistemology—is concerned that the feminine has been conventionally understood in relation to the masculine, that is, it has been used "to mark difference from a masculine universal."[42] In this sense, the masculine/feminine dichotomy operates within the ancient epistemology-by-contraries system; epistemologically, comparison is used to determine difference, and hence definition, though in practice a hierarchical divestment of value is effected.[43] One might argue that the devaluation of one item of the pair in relation to the other does not negate the utility of binarism as an epistemological model, even as its ideological implications and cultural applications are problematic. But the parity suggested by the inocuous label of "duality" is a false one, and we shall see just how insidiously this devaluation operates.

While it is beyond the scope of my analyses to engage the feminist/ psychoanalytic debate on the origins of desire and the priority of difference, I do wish to emphasize the risk of essentialism—a metaphysics of presence—that informs Irigaray's theorizing of gender and sexual difference, an essentialism whose presence informs medieval interpretations of gender as well. For Irigaray, as for medieval constructions of gender epistemology and representation, a morphology of the body is used metaphorically; the body of Woman is not only the empirical corpus but also the origin of selectively representational flesh-metaphoricity connotations. In this respect, the "essentialism" debate is largely a quibbling over terminology, for any representational apparatus may be reduced to its "essential" foundation—and either privileged or denigrated as a result. While many feminists wish to reject the masculine/feminine contingency owing to its insistence on an essentializing of Woman,[44] it is important to recognize its historical and conventional contexts, for in order to appreciate the feminine in medieval poetry and poetics, one cannot isolate the feminine from its place in binary structures.[45] While addressing the contingency of masculine and feminine as cultural constructions perceived in binary form, I should note here also that while contemporary gender studies, including my own, frequently concentrate disproportionately on the feminine, an evocation of one gender necessarily evokes the other as well, at least as a point of reference and contrast. Hence while my analyses focus more on the role of the feminine than the masculine, it should be understood that I am addressing the relationship between the two as well. My own analyses of textual gender correspond, therefore, not to the presence of an *écriture féminine* but to a medieval epistemological metaphor of paradigmatic distinction.

In evoking a twofold tradition of metaphorized representations of flesh and mutability,[46] Chaucer, we shall see, exploits the discrepancies between the two components in relation to language; there is, it should be clear, no monolithic "otherness" inhabiting medieval discourses of gender. Medieval Woman is not only the carnal or only the passive, or submissive, or whatever; complex and multiple, often contradictory and paradoxical, Woman is representative textually not only of the carnal—the feminine flesh from which further meaning might be conceived, predicated as this medieval model is on a heterosexual orthodoxy—but also of the potential multiplicity of meaning that gives rise to the polysemy necessary for language to transcend literal constraints. Woman may be understood to represent not only the body of the text—as Carolyn Dinshaw has so effectively argued—but also its figurative capacity to generate and articulate meaning; Woman corresponds to both form and process. Representations of the "feminine" as a gendered component of epistemological constructions and hermeneutic processes are manifest in figurative representations, and Chaucer supplies his texts with complex and reflexive tropes that call attention to these gendered relationships. Because Middle English lacks the overt gendered identifications of Latin—which makes possible the elaborate grammatical puns of, say, Alan of Lille's *De planctu Naturae*[47]—gender is presented by means of tropic representation that takes us beyond the level of superficial images to metaphoric representations and epistemological constructions that operate in cognitive, literary, and cultural spheres.

3

This relationship of the feminine to language incorporates a medieval poetics that identifies language in terms of property and decorum, which I sketch here, the particulars to be detailed in the chapters that follow. Figurative meaning is imposed, "improper"; such meanings are not the literal, "proper" (*proprium*, one's own) definitions of words (inasmuch as there can be a truly literal or proper sense) but rather are extraliteral, additions that are neither property nor proper. In *Contra mendacium* Augustine posits his fundamental epistemological definition of appropriation and transfer: "quae appellatur metaphora, hoc est de re propria ad rem non proprium verbi alicujus usurpata translatio" (10.24) [which is named metaphor, that is, the usurped transfer of any word from a thing proper to a thing not proper].[48] While the *signum proprium* represents proper association, the *signum translatum* suggests improper, erring senses[49] effected by usurpative, transgressive, and arbitrary transfer ("usurpata translatio," according to Augustine and Isidore of Seville, "translata in eum" to Quintilian, "ornatus difficilis" to Geoffrey of Vinsauf).[50]

The designation "proper" evokes a twofold set of semantic parameters, corresponding to both decorum and property; that is, the word operates within a set of parameters designating appropriate usage, and it calls attention to ownership and identity, its sense of belonging to someone or something. Property, as identity, is marked by contingencies—the interrelationships that occur within socially and politically delineated parameters—and cannot be fixed even as, paradoxically, appropriation supplies a sense of location and relativity. When we make something "proper," when we insist that it is our property, available to us owing to our appropriation of it, we are in effect asserting our belief that we have made something truly our own while exposing our anxiety that we have not. As "property," language operates within a semantic economy of exchange, a system of linguistic quid pro quo that defies certainty and invites manipulation, and which also assimilates the erotic dimension of textuality manifest in gendered acts of reading and writing. The pleasure of the text—of the hermeneutic enterprise, *impositio ad placitum*—is predicated upon a synthesis of appropriation and exchange.[51] Medieval theologians and poets caution against appropriation that insists on too extensive a personalization, for to make language too personal—too much one's own property—is to render it wholly literal and exclusive, to deny the spiritual sense that might otherwise be known.

As the carnal flesh, the feminine would be presumably limited; but as the unlimited *translatio*, the feminine sense of language is its errancy, its extraliteral, improper senses. As I hope to demonstrate throughout the chapters that follow, the feminine *translatio* inscribes the capacity of signification to challenge—or violate—proper decorum in order that multiple senses (*poly / seme*) obtain. The feminine *signa*, as improper, are frequently articulated in conjunction with sexual metaphors since the unlimited sense of the epistemological feminine is, in effect, promiscuous (*pro / miscere*, mixed, confused, indiscriminate), for *signa translata* resist constraint and challenge masculine insistence on ordered decorum. The language of contraries inscribes the feminine difference in terms of plurality, in contrast to the stability, consistency, and certainty implied by a masculine universal, and the governing concept in patriarchal definitions of Woman is mutability; Woman recuperates the potential of multiplicity to defy decorum and hence to resist control and so is almost universally subjected to textual/sexual parameters imposed by masculine codes.

Woman, then, may be understood to represent the feminine text that challenges the limitedness of proper masculine stability and the oppressive rigidity of patriarchal propriety. Hence medieval feminine associations are used pejoratively because feminine *signa* necessarily violate masculine decorum in their poetic instrumentality; there is no *usurpata translatio* without impropriety, and accordingly the "improper" woman is the subject of masculine scorn. But in poetic terms the correspondence of the feminine to language, problematized by the inhering contradiction of theological and epistemological origins, is itself figurative; hence metaphorized feminine representations are both unstable and destablizing. The unlimited/improper feminine is checked by the propriety of masculine parameters but would seem otherwise free-playing and unpredictable, indeed promiscuous. Thus while the female association with "unlimitedness" is largely negative owing to the positive/negative valuation of the pairings, medieval poetics' emphasis on the polysemy of "improper" signification enables the unlimitedness of the feminine to be understood as representative of polysemy and hence of poetic language itself, with all its ambiguities and uncertainties and with all its capacity to facilitate the construction of meaning. There is therefore a maneuverable space inhering in the tension between antifeminist decorums, which Chaucer arguably appropriates to negotiate gendered tropes of discursive investiture.

Couching language in terms of property and appropriation leads us to consider the tenuousness of meaning and propriety. If appropriation describes a gesture of possessive identification, it follows that the threat of potential reversal—the dismantling of possession and authority—underlies any linguistic transfer. Appropriation as a descriptive epistemology foregrounds both the tenuousness of meaning and the sense of loss that underlies language and representation. In a recent essay on origin and loss, Gayle Margherita critiques the problematics of literary origins and questions the degree to which history and mourning are themselves a problem of language, arguing that medieval studies, like psychoanalytic discourse, has "an obsession with the problem of origins, an obsession that in both cases is linked to a traumatic loss" and underscoring the "difficulty and contradiction inherent in conceptualizing what can only be known in terms of absence or lack."[52] The linguistic transfer of property operates in a discursive system that conceptualizes loss while seeking to restore an image of its shape and meaning; traces of what is lost make their presence known and call attention to their contextual absence. In his study of memory and presence, *Memoires for Paul de Man*, Derrida argues that we are involved with "an absolute past, not reducible to any form of presence: the dead being that will never itself return, never again be there, present to answer to or to share this faith [in the fidelity of memory]"; what we cannot bring back, we can only try to recall through image (*eidolon*).[53] If we consider the substance of the body—the flesh—as the origin of the *eidolon* of gender, we may come to recognize the subtle, and not so subtle, presence of the flesh in the gendered nuances of language and textuality. We may trace the presence of gender, how it constitutes and is constituted by interpretive paradigms, how it is situated in an imagined space that renegotiates the flesh as a site of textual production.[54] The gendered sense of language evokes the originary flesh that gives definition to meaning; inhering in language is a recollection, a memoir as it were, of the flesh, and to trace the metaphoric operations of gender in language is to recognize the paradoxical presence of what is absent.

What I have described here is an epistemological framework for gender that I believe can further our understanding of Chaucer's texts. It is important to note, however, that each text dictates its own sense of gender and gendering. Conventional patterns and associations form the basis of gendered expressions; owing to the contradictory multiplicity of these very decorums, however, there are no universals, even for a historical era so uniformly associated with antifeminist tradition. But it is not enough merely to identify poetry as misogynistic (or not so). In order to consider the place of misogyny in relation to gendered poetics and to recuperate the feminine as a legitimate agent of hermeneutic representation, we will also need to determine how misogyny informs the texts' articulation of their own subjectivity. Subjectivity—a text's qualitative treatment of its own "subject" and its manifestation of subjective presentation—is articulated reflexively by the texts' voice, mediated by voice characterizations and representations; thus the relationship of character, narrator, and author is crucial to the texts' articulation. As an illustration, it will be useful to recall that all of the *Canterbury Tales* are "rehallowed" by the pilgrim-narrator "Chaucer": "Whoso shal telle a tale after a man, / He moot reherce as ny as evere he kan" (I.731–32).[55] No one speaks in his/her "own" voice but rather in the voice the narrator-Chaucer assigns in his own recollective narration—there is one self-described narrator of the *Canterbury Tales*, and he supplies the illusion of many character-narrators. The narrator here expresses a concern with the accuracy of his recollections—juxtaposing Plato and Christ, the classical and the Christian, in the process—and insists on the efficacy of "ful brode" language, even as he articulates these concerns in the language of poetry. And he is himself a rhetorical construct, a narrator used by Chaucer to articulate the text, to give it a voice that is itself reflexively a fiction. Bakhtin's argument that there are two narrative levels operating simultaneously in the text, "one, the level of the narrator, a belief system filled with his objects, meanings, and emotional expressions, and the other, the level of the author, who speaks (albeit in a refracted way) by means of this story and through this story,"[56] seems fitting in this respect. Accordingly, narrator and poet are divided, even as the poet uses the narrator to shape the text.

Within the frame, Chaucer's Canterbury pilgrims are both narrators and characters participating in the articulation and the fiction of the text, as are the narrators of the *Legend, Troilus and Criseyde,* and others, who recall and report the dialogue and events as they ostensibly wish the experiences to be told. Through these voices the poet articulates his concern with the narrative line that gives existence, moment by moment, to the texts. Narrators and characters may be understood as mimetic representations, as having a history and psychology beyond that specifically depicted in a given text; characters are also clearly fictive constructs whose reality is defined by the parameters of the text in which they appear. (As Milan Kundera wittily asserts, "It would be senseless for the author to try to convince the reader that his characters once acutally lived. They were not born of a mother's womb; they were born of a stimulating phrase or two or from a basic situation.")[57] But the two need not be mutually exclusive, and we should therefore consider the characters in the analyses to follow as both, with the necessary distinctions and simultaneity to be addressed where significant throughout the chapters.

Chaucer's narrators thus *recall* speakers and stories, evoking the presence of that which is lost and offering the text as memoir. Briefly, then, let us note Derrida's theorizing of narrative and its connection to memory. Derrida asserts that narrative evokes something lost, something that can never again be fully present, and yet narrative comes as close as is possible to recuperating the loss: "Who can really tell a story? Is narrative possible? Who can claim to know what a narrative entails? Or, before that, the memory it lays claim to? What is memory? If the essence of memory maneuvers between Being and the law, what sense does it make to wonder about the being and the law of memory? These are questions that cannot be posed outside of language, questions that cannot be formulated without entrusting them to transference and translation above the abyss."[58] The ineffable link between memory and narrative accentuates the emotional aspects of telling and making, for coinciding with the theoretically sophisticated dimension of Chaucer's work is an equally emphatic appreciation of human vitality and evanescence—passion, joy, grief, and pain. It is neither naive nor sentimental to address these issues in the significant work of an accomplished poet, and indeed Chaucer's poetics are never too far removed from their human origins. The poetry is not a history of "real life" but rather a history of how those experiences are remembered and interpreted. That the history of humanity resides in the flesh is a reality that Chaucer never lets us forget.[59]

My purpose throughout the chapters that follow is to explore the interconnectedness of gender, epistemology, and poetics in Chaucer's texts by focusing on idioms of gender that attend narrative protocols of reflexivity and appropriation. I do not claim to trace a single image or ideology; rather, I wish to address issues of gender and textuality as they inform the making of poetry and the process of interpretation for specific texts, though I shall address the connections among them as well. Chaucer's work covers a wide range of topics and techniques, but the manner by which gender and narrative are articulated metaphorically is frequently an overt concern or an underlying motive for various narrative occasions—characters, narrators, and texts take up and relinquish gendered positions throughout the Chaucerian canon. Chaucer's texts are about gender and, therefore, about language—or, we could say, that because about language, therefore about gender—for the two are coexistent and coincidental. By considering how these relationships operate and are articulated in various texts, we can get a sense of how the texts recall gendered epistemological foundations, and how their applications may be traced through the texts as gestures of appropriation that underscore both the foundations and their conflicts.

In the Preface to his *Mervelous Signals*, Eugene Vance reminds us that "[n]o important medieval literary text lacks an awareness of language, whether as a medium of consciousness or as the living expression of the social order. . . . [A] poet such as Dante or Chaucer is concerned with the personal, ethical, and historical consequences of choosing words to express (or conceal) our thoughts and deeds."[60] It is my aim throughout the following chapters to locate and elucidate the complex and powerful textual operations of such expressions as they coincide with the language of gender.

🎋 *Chapter One*

Promiscuous Glossing and Virgin Words

The Wife of Bath seems a likely starting point for an analysis of Chaucerian gender, for she continues to be Chaucer's best-known and most controversial "feminine" construction. Indeed the popularity of the character has given rise to a sense among readers that she is somehow an autonomous, self-determined, real voice. No other Chaucerian narrator has been attributed the same degree of self-determination, it would seem, as the Wife; readers continue to define her, as Elaine Hansen notes, "as speaker, agent, and, most recently, reader of texts."[1] And yet as a character within a fictional frame, the Wife of course exists as words of narrative; her existence is a textual reality. And as a fictional voice articulated from moment to moment by narrative structures, the Wife does not control the agency of her own narrative, her "own" voice, even as the narrative voice constructs the illusion of character. As Marshall Leicester notes, "What we call the Wife of Bath exists in the text as a set of unresolvable tensions between self-revelation and self-presentation, repentance and rebellion, determinism and freedom, the individual and the institution, Venus and Mars, past and present. In each of these cases the opposition is both necessary and unsustainable, and the terms ceaselessly turn into one another. Of course the Wife is a construction, an interpretation."[2] Although without the mimetic portrait there would be no "Wife," Chaucer's concern lies more clearly with the Wife as textual fiction, and my own remarks attend primarily to the Wife as the narrative/discursive construct that Chaucer uses to delineate his own discovering of the limits of discourse. While the Wife ultimately does not replace or supplant the masculine with what could be construed as an *écriture féminine*, her characterization nonetheless challenges patriarchal orthodoxy in its evocation of the feminine component of epistemological dualism and in the text's grappling with the tensions thereby introduced.

1

Although the Wife of Bath, in her Prologue, argues in a quasi-feminist voice for the validity of her own experience and authority,[3] her narrative seems ambiguously—and ambivalently—both feminist and antifeminist.[4] This sense of the narrative becomes clearer when we consider the Wife to be a textual "feminine" representation, one constructed within the parameters of "masculine" discourse and articulated in masculine terms, even as specific components of the construction may be identified as feminine. The feminine may be understood as an engendered epistemological construct existing *within* the parameters of an ostensibly masculine discourse. The Wife, herself a textual construct, does not produce what could be described as a feminine discourse; rather, she is produced by and reiterates an ostensibly masculine discourse, though as I hope to demonstrate, her narrative calls attention to an ambivalent feminine poetics within those parameters.

The Wife's narrative foregrounds its treatment of gender positions—including those of reading and writing—in relation to the body, establishing a contextual frame of morphological essentialism in which to situate idioms of femininity and masculinity:

> Glose whoso wole, and seye bothe up and doun
> That [thynges smale] were maked for purgacioun
> Of uryne, and oure bothe thynges smale
> Were eek to knowe a femele from a male,
> And for noon oother cause—say ye no?
> The experience woot wel it is noght so.   III.119–24

Here the Wife argues that "thynges smale" of both female and male are intended not only for procreation and identity but also, as she goes on to insist, for "ese," for pleasure. Moreover, this "ese" is produced by bodily interaction, the engagement of their "instruments"; the Wife notes that the bodies of the two sexes are different, but she uses the same word to describe them together. The narrative thus evinces an awareness of the critical distinction between sex and gender—humans have bodies and bodies have sex, but gender is subjectively constructed and situationally occupied, subject to both the dictates of cultural "auctoritee" and the parameters of personal "experience."

That said, I want to consider the linguistic, discursive, and sexual ambiguities of the Wife's attention to "glossing," which I shall eventually connect to the narrative's articulation of an appropriative gendered poetics. This poetics in turn inscribes Chaucer's concern with his own glossing, his own sense of the equivocalness of discursive investiture. To gloss a word, phrase, or passage is to supply a new and more readily accessible interpretation or annotation, ostensibly for clarification or explanation. Owing to the word's etymology, however, an underlying erotic sense informs its use in the Wife's discourse.[5] For example, the Wife's description of glossing—"Men may devyne and glosen up and doun," "Glose whoso wole, and seye bothe up and doun" (III.26, 119)—not only suggests a thorough attempt at interpretation, covering both ends and everything between, but also hints at erotic activity, of the connotations of which the Wife is no doubt aware and, indeed, in which the character delights. It is important, too, to note the shift in gender identification: first, the Wife insists that "men" may gloss (III.26), using a noun that, while signifying a general sense of "people," is nonetheless masculine; she then uses "whoso" (III.119), signifying "anyone," masculine or feminine.[6] Thus what is initially described as a masculine activity is subsequently assigned to—or appropriated by—the feminine. Both men and women may "gloss," be it sexually or textually; as the Wife clearly demonstrates in her own ambiguous "glossing," the tongue is, in effect, bisexual, belonging to and representative of both the masculine and the feminine.[7]

Glossing informs the role of the text as mediation of desire, underscored throughout the Prologue by the Wife's articulation of sexualized language "pleye": "But yet I praye to al this compaignye, / If that I speke after my fantasye, / As taketh not agrief of that I seye; / For myn entente nys but for to pleye" (III.189–92), claims the Wife, using a disclaimer typical of Chaucerian narrators (that likewise reminds us not to "make ernest of game" [I.3186], not to impart to the text such seriousness that it is stripped of its wit and pleasure).[8] Glossing is connected to sexualized textuality[9] in the Wife's description of the episode involving Jankyn's "book of wikked wyves" (III.685), for example, an episode demonstrating that this particular text serves as an instrument of seduction.[10] It is, after all, the book that prompts the confrontation that in turn leads to reconciliation (according to the Wife's narrative of events). Jankyn is described as preferring the book to his wife, substituting the eros of the text for the eros of the marital relationship. The Wife notes that he amuses himself with the book, reading it "gladly, nyght and day" (III.669). The confrontation between Jankyn and the Wife is provoked by the Wife's apparent jealousy over her husband's preferring to spend his evenings with his book rather than with her. Thus the book substitutes for desire (for Jankyn) and then effects desire's mediation, ultimately bringing together Jankyn and the Wife. Indeed, the Wife notes that he gave her "of his tonge, and of his hond also" (III.815), again suggesting the correlation of eros and language in her controlling of his "tonge."[11] The Wife's narrative insists on an alignment of the two—eros and language—and indeed the Prologue itself "glosses" one in terms of the other.

There is, then, a crucial connection between eros and language that the Wife draws on throughout her narrative; her attention to sex may be understood as attention to language and vice versa, for her discourse on marriage is not only a commentary on marriage as institution but also on the discourse of that institution and, indeed, on discourse itself. Further, as the Wife embodies the textuality of the framing narrative, her textuality is sexualized just as her body is textualized. The relationship of textuality and sexuality is underscored by attention to the abuse of each component in that the abuse of eros—perversion—serves as a commentary on or metaphor of the abuse of language. As Eugene Vance comments, "The equation between idolatry, including idolatry of the letter, and sexual perversion became a subtle force in medieval poetics,"[12] informing sexual metaphors that call attention to their own signification processes in addition to thematic considerations of the activities described. The Wife's inclusion of fairly explicit double entendres, then, provides an incessant, though erratic, reminder throughout the Prologue that the character is commenting on both medium and message, that the narrative addresses concerns of both textual representation and normative presuppositions in the narrative's moral dimension. Chaucer sets out the Wife as a kind of narrative decoy in order to confront normative/narrative presuppositions and to test the dangers of glossing in relation to his own poetic appropriation. He demonstrates the inevitability of discursive promiscuity—an inhering insistence on the resistance of language to unmitigated subjection.

Whereas moralizing readings that fault the Wife's behavior or find her wanting—usually conventional masculine readings—are clearly supported by the text's own emphases,[13] the Wife, as a narrative construct, as a textual representation of Woman, also supports a reading that challenges this perspective without ignoring the unfavorable details included in the

Wife's construction. In other words, to find a feminine valorization inhering in the Wife's narrative is not—and need not be—to ignore the reality of the portrait. That said, the Wife delights in *talking* about sexuality; the language of eros is, for the Wife, apparently far more appealing than is any active participation itself. Of course since the Wife is narrative, she can only talk; however, her apparent attitude toward her subject matter varies. Clearly she suggests delight when speaking of sexual matters, just as she clearly suggests anger when describing antifeminist sterotypes of women. With regard to her "olde" husband she notes, "For wynning wolde I al his lust endure, / And make me a feyned appetit; / And yet in bacon hadde I nevere delit" (III.416–18) she endures her husband's sexual demands in order to maintain her profit-making status as "wyf."[14] Moreover, she confesses outright that she feigns an appetite, that she fakes arousal and desire because she has no interest in nor derives enjoyment from "bacon." (She describes her older husband[s] sexually as "bacon," old meat, aged and dry, while her own female anatomy she identifies as *"bele chose,"* beautiful thing [III.447, 510].) Her comment suggests that for all her sexually charged banter and erotic "pleye," language is the medium of eros for her, and the excitement she does not find in active sexuality she finds in language, its substitute. The Wife participates in an eroticization of the letter, for the erotic sense of language apparently holds for the Wife far greater appeal than does participation in the activities to which the language refers. Her *"bele chose"* is her "pleye" of language, not the play of her female anatomy, and she apparently derives satisfaction from the reponse that her word-"pleye" elicits from her audience. To construct her "pleye," then, she imposes connotations not only according *to* her pleasure but *for* her pleasure as well.[15]

The Wife's use of "appetyt" to describe her desire for sexual/textual pleasure—*jouissance*—points to her true motive in speaking. The Wife desires to desire (to borrow the phrase made popular by Mary Anne Doane),[16] to elicit a response from her predominantly male audience, even if her narrative/rhetorical performance demands inconsistencies in the narrative/rhetorical line. "Rhetorical" here suggests that "desire" is constructed by the discourse; desire exists only as the rhetorical line suggests its existence; the rhetorical line is not informed by an a priori desire, but rather the line generates desire simultaneously with its articulation, even if the articulation contradicts itself. "Desire" is for the Wife rhetorical, for her desire to desire seems to be accompanied by a desire to be *recognized* as having desire; she seems to construct her narrative for the effect of eliciting approval from her audience of "lordynges" (III.4) and, as such, the narrative voice ventriloquizes, speaking their language—the language of the audience—rather than her "own." Hence her claims of sexual promiscuity ("I ne loved nevere by no discrecioun" [III.622]) and her impulse to talk about this alleged lack of discretion may be understood as an attempt to enhance the likelihood of acquiring this recognition from her masculine audience (comprising the "lordynges" whom she addresses overtly and the clerical women whom she largely ignores).

Indeed her very status as "wife" is wholly rhetorical, subject to the faith of the audience. No husband is present to corroborate her status and the discourse could just as easily be fanciful rantings or the sour grapes of a spinster ("For half so boldely kan ther no man / Swere and lyen, as a womman kan" [III.227–28]). The Wife's attempts to maintain audience interest render her a caricature, an exaggeration of a woman who not only desires to desire but who uses that desire as a rhetorical strategy, as a sexualized *captatio benevolentiae*. As a caricature of a feminine desire produced by the dominant masculine discourse, the Wife is not only made a spectacle but is shown as a conspirator in her own objectification.[17] Hence too her own narrative of desire continues despite interruption ("'Abyde!' quod she" [III.169]), while the subsequent telling of the formal tale is contingent on the audience's interest ("if ye wol heere" [III.828]; "right as yow lest" [III.854]; "If I have licence" [III.856]). The Wife privileges her Prologue, which reports her own desire, over her *Tale*, which merely narrates the desire of wholly fictive others (themselves produced by a fictive construct).

Moreover, in calling attention to her "appetit," the Wife calls attention to her desire as a desire to consume, be it sexually, textually, or otherwise. In effect, as she "glosses" she consumes both partners and texts, appropriating them for her own use and deriving from them whatever satisfaction she can find. Her warning—"For peril is bothe fyr and tow t'assemble— / Ye knowe what this ensample may resemble" (III.89–90)—uses the consumption metaphor of fire and fuel that suggests, or "resemble[s]," the consuming nature of sexuality.[18] The metaphor is reiterated later in the narrative—"The moore it brenneth, the moore it hath desir / To consume every thyng that brent wole be" (III.374–75)—essentially restating Prv 30.15–16 and its explication in Jerome's *Adversus Jovinianum:*

> Non hic de meretrice, non de adultera dicitur, sed amor mulieris generaliter accusatur, qui semper insatiabilis est, qui exstinctus

accenditur, et post copiam rursum inops est, animumque virilem effeminat, et excepta passione quam sustinet, aliud non sinit cogitare.¹⁹

[It is not of the harlot, or the adultress who is spoken, but the love of women in general is accused, which is always insatiable, which extinguished, bursts into flame, and after plenty, it is wanting, and it effeminizes a man's spirit, and except for the passion that it feeds, it does not permit any other thought to think.]

Her attention to consumption imagery therefore calls attention to the twofold manifestation of her ambivalent desire: it represents both lack and surplus. Louise Fradenburg comments: "The inability of the Wife's desire to find closure—the sense in which it is a desire for desire—is thus presented, on one level, as lack. But of course this characterization of her desire is meant to constrain the text's presentation, on another level, of desire as multiplicity, a supplement or surplus—*as always more than* its representations, and hence as always urged to remake the world."²⁰ Her glossing suggests a kind of excess that calls attention to its own vicariousness. In Derridian terms, the Wife's excess may be understood as supplement: "The supplement adds itself, it is a surplus, a plenitude enriching another plenitude, the *fullest measure* of presence. . . . But the supplement only supplements. It adds only to replace. It intervenes or insinuates itself *in-the-place-of-it;* if it fills, it is as if one fills a void."²¹ The process of consumption, as the Wife describes it, not only represents an attempt to fill in empty space, to satisfy some perceived lack, but also suggests the underlying almost paradoxical nature of desire as represented by the Wife: in her quest to fill the empty spaces, she is depicted as consuming far more than needed but remains necessarily unfulfilled by the vicariousness of her excessive supplementation. Thus Chaucer locates in the Wife his apparent angst about his own measure of supplementation and appropriation; he constructs and embodies in the Wife his own concern with excess.

It is therefore quite fitting that the Wife should be initially described as having "hipes large" (I.472), as having excessive flesh or girth, for she apparently fails to respect any boundary or limit of consumption. (Overconsumption of food and drink is obviously manifest in the kind of carnal evidence that cannot be negated through language alone.)²² Further, she aligns her excessive consumption of drink with other sumptuary interests:

"And after wyn on Venus moste I thynke, / For al so siker as cold engendreth hayl, / A likerous mouth moste han a likerous tayl" (III.464–66), suggesting that perhaps she must ply herself with alcohol to trigger a minimum erotic response or, additionally, that in her mind activities of consumption—carnal behaviors—are locked together. Her comment, too, erotically aligns "mouth" and "tayl," noting that both may be described as "likerous," that is, lustful, greedy, eager. Just as "likerous" suggests "gourmandizing—with food, drink, and licking," so, too, its connotations extend to "lechery," and here the Wife's alignment seems to emphasize the possible pun of "likerous" and "lecherous."[23] The Wife's "mouth" is as eager as her "tayl," indeed even more so, and calls attention to the Wife's carnal excesses, for the mouth is the point of intake for excesses of food and drink, and it is a vehicle for her excess of words, most of which are associated with her "tayl."

Further, the "mouth" and "tayl" may be likened in sexual terms—an analogy articulated in contemporary feminist theory by Luce Irigaray and discussed at length in Jane Burns's recent analysis of fabliaux[24]—in that the mouth not only resembles the "tayl" but serves as its substitute as well. Burns analyzes a fabliau that uses anal descriptions to identify female genitals: "To call a vagina an asshole is to characterize woman's lower orifice in terms of man's own singular hole, obscuring the fact that women have two distinct openings in the lower body" (87). The Wife, in using the ambiguous word "tayl," would seem to evoke a similar confusing of the masculine and the feminine, reducing the feminine plural to the masculine singular. For the Wife the mouth is instrumental in effecting not merely consumption but *excessive* consumption, both sexually and textually. Hence she describes herself as "Gat-tothed" (III.603), again associating her mouth with her sexual behavior and reiterating that consumption—effected by mouth—is for the Wife an erotic act.[25]

The mouth is the locus of sexuality for the Wife, for not only does it contain the teeth that conventionally signify erotic interests, but, more important, it houses the origin of speech—it is the location of the tongue of which the Wife seems so fond. Indeed, the tongue mediates the utility of both textuality and sexuality. Flesh and text cleave through the instrumentality of the tongue, and the two are united through the metaphoricity of "glossing." The tongue both covers and consumes; for the Wife, to "gloss" a text is to sexualize it, and, in turn, the sexualized text elicits erotic excitement. The tongue seduces as well, having potential use as an instrument of flattery and deception; the efficacy of flattery may be accorded to the tongue.[26] Along these lines the Wife notes that her husband could easily seduce her with his tongue: "And therwithal so wel koude he me glose / Whan that he wolde han my *bele chose*" (III.509–10). In this respect, "glossing" functions as erotic foreplay, as Carolyn Dinshaw argues: "But, curiously, it is the openly pejorated, carnal, ostentatiously masculine glossing by the clerk Jankyn that the Wife—the body of the text—finds so appealing, so effective, so irresistible. . . . Glossing here is unmistakably carnal, a masculine act performed on the feminine body, and it leads to pleasure for both husband and wife, both clerk and text."[27] While this particular instance of "glossing" represents a masculine act, here the Wife's treatment of "glossing" does not preclude the possibility of reciprocation; indeed, the Wife seems herself quite capable of "glossing"—one could argue that as the Wife usurps the masculine propriety of "glossing" in its textual sense, so too does she usurp its erotic sense.

The Wife exploits the etymology of "glossing" and the practice of glossing biblical texts to construct a sexual rhetoric. Her treatment of patristic authority in conjunction with her descriptions of her own experience results in a kind of "holy erotica," a scriptural glossing designed for titillation. Her quasi-holy erotic discourse represents a rhetorical mixing, for her sexual rhetoric comprises a mixing, or coupling, of two distinct registers, the theological and the erotic.[28] Erotica represents a "coupling" of textuality and sexuality, for it textualizes sex and sexualizes the text in its sexual instrumentality. Moreover, the instrumentality of erotica is autoerotic, for it serves the self and requires no other; it is narcissistic, an erotic exclusion of other-ness manifest in self-affection. (Though contemporary theorists—Luce Irigaray in particular—identify autoeroticism as a positive concept,[29] in a context of medieval language metaphor, autoeroticism is clearly negative in suggesting sterility, a point to which I shall return.) Glossing the Bible and its concomitant patristic directives is, for the Wife, an erotic act; she derives a kind of erotic excitement and satisfaction from her glossing and in conveying—or exhibiting—her glossing to an audience. The autoeroticism of the glossing is extended further in that the body as *textus* becomes a target for her own glossing as well; in effect she glosses herself.

Moreover, this sexual rhetoric is again a substitution, interchanging textuality and sexuality in a blurring of boundaries between the two. This substitution is of course not limited to the female alone, as the Wife notes, for Jankyn himself used the text as a substitute for eros (III.669–70). In addition, the Wife argues that such substitution by men is fairly commonplace:

> The clerk, whan he is oold, and may noght do
> Of Venus werkes worth his olde sho,
> Thanne sit he doun, and writ in his dotage
> That wommen kan nat kepe hir mariage!   III.707–10

But the major difference between masculine and feminine substitution, according to the Wife's demonstration, is that while men read and write about eros, women *talk* about it. Speaking to an audience provides the kind of direct, immediate response not possible through writing; while men derive satisfaction from the solitary act of writing about eros, women, the Wife suggests, desire active appreciation and response from an audience, an "other."[30] Erotic textuality is an active oral process for the Wife, delighting both speaker and audience through the instrumentality of the mouth and tongue.

2

Having identified the narrative's use of "gloss" as both a destabilizing erotic metaphor and a discursive operating feature of narrative errancy, I would now like to turn to the self-reflexive, or metatextual, "glossing" that underscores the narrative's attention to an engendered epistemology, beginning with the Wife's rambling treatise on the role of sex in marriage, wherein she argues in favor of unrestrained sexuality by suggesting that procreation justifies such behavior (though she acknowledges no offspring of her own):

> For hadde God comanded maydenhede,
> Thanne hadde he dampned weddyng with the dede.
> And certes, if ther were no seed ysowe,
> Virginitee, thanne wherof sholde it growe?   III.69–72

By first aligning the image of seed and sowing to "virginitee" as the desired fruits of that labor, the Wife extends the metaphor not only to evoke the relationship of seed and sowing to sexual reproduction but also to question the paradox inhering in what she has determined to be the scriptural privileging of virginity.[31] Human seed must be sown if procreation is to take place, and, according to widespread fourteenth-century explanations of physiology and reproduction, this sowing entails both male and female seed—the female contributes her own seed to the conception process even as she serves as the receptacle for the male seed.[32]

The Wife's assertion here is flawed by hyperbole, for she uses an extreme example and has lifted out of context the exegetical directives regarding marriage and procreation. One could of course argue that she is reacting to the views of Jerome, whose rigid and excessive advocation of virginity in *Adversus Jovinianum* and *Ad Eustochium* is coupled with an ambivalent attack on marriage in these and other texts, the most famous being *Ad Furiam*, in which Jerome counsels the widow against remarriage using fervently unappealing images:

> [A]marissimam choleram tuae sensere fauces. Egessisti acescentes et morbidos cibos: relevasti aestuantem stomachum. Quid vis rursum ingerere, quod tibi noxium fuit? *Canis revertens ad vomitum suum et sus ad volutabrum luti.* Bruta quoque animalia et vagae aves, in easdem pedicas retiaque non incidunt.[33]
>
> [The bitterest of gall your throat has tasted. You have voided the sour and disease-causing food: you have relieved a heaving stomach. Why would you wish to force back something that has been harmful to you? *The dog reverts to his own vomit and the sow to the slough to wallow.* Even brute animals and roving birds, into the same snares or nets do not fall twice.]

To this end, the Wife fulfills Jerome's realistic recognition that his virginity directive could hardly be met with widespread acceptance or successful implementation: "Noli metuere ne omnes virgines fiant: difficilis res est virginitas, et ideo rara, quia difficilis: *Multi vocati, pauci electi.* Incipere plurimorum est, perseverare paucorum" [Be not afraid that all will become virgins: a difficult thing is virginity , and therefore rare, because difficult: *Many are called, few chosen.* Many are to begin, few to persevere].[34] Her ironic, satiric treatment of marriage doctrine calls attention to the flawed structure of such directives, suggesting that "all pretensions to and regulations of marital affairs, all selective codes of behavior, are ludicrous because, as the Wife of Bath suggests, they come from precisely those people who know least about them."[35] Again the Wife privileges "experience" as "auctoritee." In addition, she hints at the unsuitability of Christian scriptural models—"Crist was a mayde and shapen as a man, / And many a seint, sith that the world bigan" (III.139–40)—suggesting a sense of puzzlement that masculine practitioners of patriarchal directives should set the standards for women as well.

The Wife's reponse to Jerome, however, is in part problematic because Jerome's views are hardly typical of the Wife's contemporary social context.[36] Moreover, the Augustinian argument that to praise Christian virginity need not be to denigrate Christian marriage marks a more realistic and acceptable stand for both the Church and those who follow the Church's directives.[37] Thus while the Wife shows off her knowledge of patriarchal "auctoritee," she simultaneously is shown to demonstrate her appropriation of anachronistic core issues, to avail herself of patriarchal orthodoxy in the construction of her rhetorical lines even as she mis/represents them by omission or exaggeration. And because virginity is too rigid a directive, the Wife accepts no directive, no restraint; she rejects the notion of continence in its entirety, observing no balance or moderation within the parameters of sexual behavior. It is hardly surprising that she who delights so in talking of sexuality would be aghast at what she perceives to be the virginity directive's rigid constraints and at the implicit repression that such a decorum represents.

But by casting sexuality in the radical division of virginity/promiscuity, the Wife leaves no middle ground for women. Her dichotomizing imposes on her social/political reality what might be described as patriarchal binary thought, "this endless series of hierarchical binary oppositions that always in the end come back to the fundamental 'couple' of male/female."[38] Virginity, as the patriarchal ideal, is privileged within this schema as the positive, male component of the dual, while promiscuity serves as the negative complement, ultimately the target of scorn. Here, then, the Wife subverts her ostensibly assertive stance to a pervasive and ultimately oppressive patriarchal context. And clearly, too, the Wife seems to invert the positive/negative valuation underlying her dichotomy—perhaps owing to her desire for audience approval—and identifies herself as promiscuous: "I ne loved nevere by no discrecioun" (III.622), she notes, boldly stating that she lacks discretion or discrimination in matters of "love"— love in its erotic, sexual sense, which the Wife herself equates with sin: "Allas, allas! That evere love was synne" (III.614), she exclaims, smugly identifying herself as a sinner. The either/or rigidity of the Wife's imposed identifications is as reductionistic and value-laden as the patriarchal "auctoritee" against which she ostensibly rails. Further, her identification calls attention to the problematic masculine nature of her stereotypical sexual boasting: she in essence speaks like a man about acting like a man, using a bullying sexuality to confront restrictive social and theological guidelines. Yet she seems to sacrifice her femininity in the process of adhering to the masculine dichotomy that she herself introduces to the rhetorical line.

The Wife's sexualized dichotomizing is further problematized by engendered tropes of fertility and propagation. In terms of the Pauline sowing metaphor, "seed" must be "sown" if the word is to propagate, and unsown seed represents unused potential. With regard to the command "to wexe and multiplye" (III.28), the Wife notes "[t]hat gentil text kan I wel understonde" (III.29).[39] The pleasures of the text are propagated by multiplication; therefore to deny multiplication is both to deny the pleasure of the text and to curtail further propagation. Following this analogy, "virginitee" may be understood not only as the physical state of sexual chastity but also, as the Wife suggests, as a state of unused capability, of wasted potential—of seed unsown. Literal and figurative manifestations of "seed" constitute a complex relationship of signification structures that underscores the Prologue's attention to poetic language, the language of the Prologue explicating what may be described as its own figurative mulitiplicity, its awareness of the crucial relationship between polysemy and poetry. The sexual wordplay in the Prologue may be understood as a commentary on the necessity of polysemy if poetic language is to have meaning. Through this garrulous, vulgar voice, Chaucer addresses his own apparent concerns about the complex dangers of discursive fertility/promiscuity, the paradoxical necessity of the author's appropriations of languge to his own task. Poetic language is necessarily promiscuous, no matter how the poet wishes to control his own words to limit their fertility; he proves by that very desire that language is too fertile, too promiscuous, beyond his control. The Wife exploits the polysemy of language in order to construct her sexual wordplay; she insists that many seeds be sown, that many shades of meaning inhere in the language of her discourse in order for the "pleye" to occur. The Wife as a representation of Woman is a caricature, an exaggeration that draws from an antifeminist tradition even as it ostensibly attacks that tradition. The Wife is shown to delight in the entertainment value of the potentially offensive word-"pleye," yet at the same time she seems oblivious to the contradictions inhering in her self-revelatory discourse, making unclear just what, in fact, she is advocating, though clearly the Wife couches her argument in sexual terms to an ostensibly feminist end.

The Wife seems similarly oblivious to the ramifications of those contradictions in terms of what many readers perceive to be the Prologue's valorization of the feminine. To this end, the Wife's discourse calls attention to an apparent and problematic alignment of the "feminine" and the "carnal." The pairing of "flesh" and "female" suggests a correlation of the feminine and the carnal, in that the seductive threat of the female to the male finds epistemological representation in the seductive threat of the carnal to the spiritual (indeed, many well-known instances of medieval misogyny can be traced to this analogy).[40] And in a positive sense, just as the literal carnal is, in terms of signification, the base starting point from which further spiritual meaning may be conceived, so, too, the feminine represents positive potential.[41] But to suggest that the feminine be equated wholly with the carnal as the Wife embodies carnality is to suggest that the Wife's limiting, restrictive, and rather hostile generalizations—the either/or dichotomy of virginity and promiscuity—are valid. The crux of this problematic of valorization is the Wife's appropriation, that is, her attempting to take possession—"assertively" and "knowingly," as Carolyn Dinshaw argues[42]—of the patriarchal language of which she presumably recognizes the efficacy, or at least the necessity. The Wife would arguably not need to appropriate patriarchal discourse if she had at her disposal an alternative discourse; nor would she appropriate the patriarchal if she were not confident of its efficacy and utility. In short, she usurps what she knows works—or, more accurately, what she knows should give the illusion of working—apparently hoping that the appropriation will supply her discourse with the authority, credibility, and efficacy that she herself finds lacking.

The Wife's appropriation may be understood, in terms of the medieval sign theory that designates language in terms of property, as a problematic dichotomizing of public and private (or, in Bakhtinian terms, as the public or social dimension rather than an authoritative or privileged system).[43] Medieval theologians, philosophers, and poets would have understood language in terms of the literal and figurative, proper and improper, as usurpative and polysemous. To use language figuratively is thus to usurp meaning and transfer it. Beyond the literal sense, language signifies according to usurpation and transfer, and transfer by usurpation allows for the Wife's bawdy and significant word-"pleye." Usurpative transfer allows for public access to private appropriation, *impositio ad placitum*, imposed according to the pleasure of the imposer;[44] the Wife, of course, is no stranger to the pleasures of textuality.

Further, the public/private semantic implications of the Wife's attention to glossing are framed by the aforementioned patriarchal binary thought, manifest in the ubiquitous medieval epistemology by contraries, asserting that comparison is the basis for all understanding and that definition is contingent on the difference identified by the process of comparison.[45] Clearly, the epistemology by contraries, in its construction of oppositional binarisms, dichotomizes. The dichotomizing of contraries within the epistemology, however, is not the rigid, exclusive dichotomizing evident in the Wife's demonstration. For while the Wife uses dichotomy to construct a valuated identification strategy of patriarchal labels, the epistemology uses dichotomy to *establish* difference, not to condemn it, and to use that difference as a means of freeing or enhancing thought, not to constrict or reduce it. If the Wife's narrative is interpreted within a context of this epistemology, her use of sexual language takes on additional connotations. Although infinite limitlessness would ultimately call into question the very possibility of meaning, the "unlimited" taken in conjunction with "plural" connotes a sense of polysemy, a choice of more than one even if some ultimate limit must be identified or assumed.

But the usurpative appropriation demonstrated in the Wife's narrative is problematic owing to the ostensibly feminine agency of the appropriation in relation to private discourse.[46] On the one hand, the excess of the Wife's glossing—culturally marked as feminine—underscores the Wife's insistence that the restrictive, oppressive signifying practices of the patriarchal "auctoritee" be opened up. The Wife invites further glossing even as she herself glosses, thereby challenging patriarchal claims of interpretive closure. As such, the Wife may be seen as challenging the propriety of private, self-serving glossing by exposing its underlying ideological exclusivity.[47]

And yet the Wife is herself shown as privatizing language. The Wife usurps patriarchal discourse, patriarchal "auctoritee," in an apparent attempt to challenge its dominance; and yet her usurpation effects an exclusivity not unlike that which she confronts. Just as she speaks like a man in challenging men's speech, so too she speaks the exclusive language of patriarchy in professing to speak out against patriarchal "auctoritee"; it is no less exclusive simply because it intends to confront exclusivity. The Wife's struggle with exclusivity marks Chaucer's own anxiety about appropriation: How is he to effect the usurpation necessary for polysemous signification without himself risking a personal exclusivity? Can the poet use language effectively and poetically without claiming it as his own? To retain possession to the exclusion of other possibilites is to render language problematic in that the possessive usurper not only denies language its proper—and thus accessible and universal—sense but also attempts to control how the language is understood. In short, exclusive appropriation denies language the very plurality that allows it to signify beyond the literal; attempting to privatize language shifts meaning to the private usurper.

The narrative's semantics of appropriation is in part played out through metaphors of the body that both concretize and destabilize language and flesh. That the Wife is aware of the male and female bodies and their differences is well established in the text; her attention to difference, however, seems coincidental with an attention to power and manipulation. The Wife's desire to control language is underscored throughout the narrative by a fervent attention to bodily manipulation, corresponding overtly to the body's sexual performance. For example, the Wife, echoing Paul out of context, declares that she will have her husband's "tribulacion withal / Upon his flessh, whil that I am his wyf" and that she will exercise "the power durynge al my lyf / Upon his propre body, and noght he" (III.156–59). She speaks of her husband's desire to be "maister of [her] body and of [her] good" (314). Her vitriolic demands do not go undetected or unchecked; the Pardoner responds to the oration on "instrument" usage, saying, "I was aboute to wedde a wyf; allas! / What sholde I bye it on my flessh so deere?" (166–67) and evincing an understanding that the dominance of one body is paid for by another. In fact the Wife's own body bears the scars, corporeal memoirs, of the struggle: the deaf ear (I.448, III.635–36, 795–96) and the sore ribs (III.505–7). The Wife's aversion to virginity is clearly informed by this connecting of sex and power—to forego sexual activity for the sake of virginity is to sacrifice the desired purchasing power of sex, even as the risk of "by[ing] it on [the] flessh" is thereby averted.

The Wife's desire to appropriate the flesh—the "propre body"—corresponds throughout the Wife's narrative to her appropriation of language. Assuming possession of the proper, carnal body is an act of what might be described as patriarchal literary activity, for such possession evokes the patristic suppressing of the flesh ostensibly effected in order to free and protect the spirit. The Wife's stated desire to control the flesh is therefore a statement of her desire to appropriate patriarchal power, and the Prologue tells the story of a struggle for power that circumscribes the flesh. But this desire is of course complicated by her status as a woman: the body of Woman is the site of the struggle, and as the Wife vacillates uneasily between rhetorically constructed parameters of victim and oppressor, she finds herself constrained by the very parameters that she wishes to breach. Her purported resistance to patriarchal decorum instead reifies its position of privilege. One senses anxiety and uncertainty in her supposedly bold statements that betray an apprehension. In effect the Wife embodies both the normative suppositions of patriarchal "auctoritee" and the personal "experience" that purports to subvert them—a twofold gesture of appropriation that threatens to negate itself.

The Wife professes to argue against virginity, the restricted sowing of seed, but in her attempt to usurp patriarchal language, she renders her language (as she possesses it) unisemous, not polysemous—in a sense, "virgin." In other words, in attempting to possess language that she cannot own, she harbors its meaning as a secret unto herself, attempting to control through possession the propriety of its signification. In fact, the Wife explicitly desires to mark her discourse as her "own," as having private meaning susceptible to misinterpretation by an audience: "If that I speke after my fantasye" (III.190). Her discourse is a subjective external articulation of an internal narrative, private and inaccessible even if partially, and willfully, exposed; it is a "queynte fantasye" (III.516) not unlike that which she says belongs to "wommen" (III.515). In attempting to appropriate language—in effect, "re-virginizing" it—she denies it the polysemy it would otherwise entail; the "virgin" word is unisemous. Moreover, the unisemy of the "virgin" word may be likened to the unisemy of the autoerotic word; both represent private appropriation—or retention—of ultimately wasted potential. A significant feature of the Wife's autoerotic textuality is in her female-ness. Although the metaphor of male auto-/homo-eroticism (what R. Howard Bloch terms "sterile perversions")[48] representing delight in one's own language is treated by Alan of Lille, Dante, and others,[49] Chaucer's treatment of the metaphor is given an interesting—and significant—twist in that the Wife's autoeroticism is female. While masculine metaphors of auto-/homo-eroticism call attention to the *spilling* of seed/language, the Wife's own autoeroticism emphasizes the *retention*, or privatization, of seed/language.[50] The Wife would seem to usurp from language its capacity to produce meaning outside of her own control, denying language its polysemous potential and rendering it with a sense of sterility akin to that of the unsown virgin seed.

If the "female" sense of language is "unlimited" and "plural," then virginity defeats that sense. Virginity hinders language because just as the virgin female represents wasted potential (as the Wife suggests), so, too, the "virgin" word—that is, the word devoid of its capacity for polysemy—lacks the sense of unlimited, plural signification. And although, as Hélène Cixous has argued, the binary epistemology inevitably reduces anything aligned with the female to a negative, inferior status within the hierarchy,[51] in poetic terms, the association of "feminine" and "plural" is significant. In attempting to deny the "unlimitedness" or "plurality" of language (that is, in attempting to control its signification), the Wife "re-virginizes" her language by denying its "unlimitedness" and "plurality"; she arguably denies it its "femaleness" as well. In short, the Wife reduces the unlimited to the limited, the plural to the one and, in essence, the female to the male, even as she seemingly attempts to valorize a new sense of the feminine. Thus while the Wife is sterile, her words are not; she wastes, but at the same time exploits and entertains, potential. Chaucer's impulse to re-virginize words, to appropriate them to limited, private use, in fact foregrounds their resistance to such appropriation. Bakhtin might consider them to have a public and social dimension, existing in a "dialogically agitated and tension-filled environment of alien words, value judgments, and accents," where a word "weaves in and out of complex interrelationships, merges with some, recoils from other," and where it "cannot fail to brush up against thousands of living dialogic threads."[52] The Wife, with every attempt to control words, instead empowers them to escape her control. Through the Wife's narrative Chaucer suggests that this desire for re-virginizing is essentially unappeasable; it exists as a kind of wishful thinking, an index of e(xc)lusive desire: "*if* that I speke after my fantasye," "*if* wommen had writen stories" (III.190, 693; emphasis mine).

But the Wife's appropriation of masculine discourse does not supply a newer "feminine" discourse; it merely supplies what could be labeled "the Wife of Bath's" discourse, an *écriture d'Alisoun*. The Wife's attempting to privatize language not only denies it the plurality necessary if her argument is to work within the context of her discourse but also provides commentary on the relationship between eros and language given attempts at privatization. Again, the Wife's attempt to make private that which is public may be understood in conjunction with her eroticization of the letter—her delight in talking about sexual issues—as an autoerotic act. Not only does the Wife find pleasure in words, in glossing, she finds pleasure in her *own* words, her *own* glossing. As a lover of her own words she is, in effect, her own lover. Her autoerotic textuality is private and exclusive, and although she may evoke a laugh from her audience through her "pleye," that laughter serves less to corroborate her complaints than to reinforce the autoerotic motivation for her sexual rhetoric. She supplies the object of her own delight and attempts to retain possession, even as such possession effects a sense of sterility through its exclusion of plurality. (The ambivalent nature of the Wife's appropriation is illustrated by her own framework: because the Wife insists on the rigid parameters of her own reductionistic dichotomizing—virgin/harlot, in particular—she effectively excludes even herself as *wyf*.)

To this end, the Wife's sexual representation is both paradoxical and ambivalent; she is sexual but not fertile, and, indeed, seems to advocate sterile sexuality. As a harborer of the autoerotic "virgin" word, the Wife represents a sexuality unwilling to participate within masculine parameters; it is, in a sense, uncorrupted by masculine seed yet corrupted by its own exclusiveness. In seeking satisfaction, the Wife instead generates it herself through autoerotic textuality—erotic glossing—and revels in the experience of her own delight. Ultimately, however, the narrative speaks to unrealized desire, for the Wife's "holy erotica" is not enough; the privatization of eros leaves her hungry for more, and she remains—both textually and sexually—isolated and constrained within the parameters of the masculine discourse. Hence her promiscuity: the Wife is depicted as continuously searching, grasping, mixing, seeking rhetorical satisfaction through a series of appropriations. Thus her self-proclaimed status of bullying sexuality, her own attempts to depict herself as an unattractively aggressive and indiscriminate woman, is balanced with the reality of her own frustration and unfulfillment; the apparent auto-/homo-erotic valorization is yet another cover or veil:

> We wommen han, if that I shal nat lye,
> In this matere a queynte fantasye:
> Wayte what thyng we may nat lightly have,
> Therafter wol we crie al day and crave.
> Forbede us thyng, and that desiren we;
> Preesse on us faste, and thanne wol we fle.   III.515–20

The Wife thus inscribes ambivalently the paradox of "re-virginized" language, implicating her author: the more the poet strives for the "virgin" word, the more he confirms the promiscuity of discourse.

The Wife herself provides a concrete example of what happens when meaning is made personal:

> Who peyntede the leon, tel me who?
> By God, if wommen hadde writen stories,
> As clerkes han withinne hire oratories,
> They wolde han writen of men moore wikkednesse
> Than al the mark of Adam may redresse.   III.692–96

Her reference to Aesop's lion does call into question the subjectivity inhering in any artistic representation, and the Wife uses the example effectively in this respect.[53] However, the bitter, angry words that follow the example undermine her apparent efforts to demonstrate a need for a feminine-sympathetic perspective by suggesting that she seeks to replicate the masculine crime of misrepresentation; the women's stories would merely supply an equally distorted view, framed by an opposing perspective. She advocates that the hegemonic patriarchal discourse be replaced by an equally hegemonic feminine one, thereby calling attention not only to the flawed, apparently self-serving nature of her diatribe but also to the confused relationships of masculine and feminine as put forth by her own mixing of the two. Rejecting or usurping the masculine does not constitute a feminine even as the Wife's inversion challenges the hegemony of the masculine. Hence the ambivalence of her narrative: her ostensibly profeminist arguments are betrayed by an articulation that supports what it professes to subvert.[54]

The Wife's narrative therefore comes across as an anti-antifeminist (rather than "feminist") misogamous discourse that may be read as a kind of antifeminist feminism. It attempts to refute the conventions of antifeminist textuality—laying the groundwork for ideological challenge—but supports those conventions through illustration that seems only to validate the stereotypes on which the conventions are based. She may claim to reject patriarchal decorum—"After thy text, ne after thy rubriche, / I wol nat wirche as muchel as a gnat" (III.346–47)—but her very act of articulating her resistance thwarts its own stated intentions. As Robert Hanning argues, "The Wife is lost in a world of words of which she is also a constituent. She exists as a literary creation of men, a system of texts and glosses which she repeatedly attacks but always ends up confirming."[55] Within the conventions of antifeminist textuality, the Wife does fight back—or talks back—using the only weapon she knows, that with which she has been assaulted; as Deborah Ellis notes, "Indeed, women who verbally attack men most successfully use not their 'own' language but rather that of the men they resist."[56] The Wife's appropriation of "men's" language serves to articulate her complaints but does little to effect a newer, "feminine" system of discourse.

"Deceite, wepyng, spynnyng God hath yive / To wommen kyndely, whil they may lyve" (III.401–2). The character of the Wife is associated with that of a weaver of fabric and, likewise, she is a weaver of texts, lifting and borrowing from even the most unlikely of sources to weave together a narrative web both self-promoting and self-incriminating; as she asserts specific argumentative points, she subsequently undermines them in a discourse that wanders from one idea to another, perhaps never really certain of its own purpose. And while the text of the Prologue is itself a fertile and provocative commentary on its own textual processes and the processes of engendered epistemological representation, the fictive character who voices those words is presented as a kind of caricature and is rendered oddly pathetic by her own role in the process. Unable to promote any single argument to any effective end, the Wife employs a sexual rhetoric that may indeed be described as promiscuous, that is, *pro/miscere*, "mixed" or "confused" as well as "indiscriminate." Just as the Wife cannot confine herself sexually to any single partner—"Welcome the sixte, whan that ever he shal" (III.45)—so, too, she cannot find rhetorical satisfaction in any single argumentative line.

If we return to Irigaray, we find a similar critical dynamic at work. Irigaray's attempts to destabilize the language of patriarchy likewise appropriate patriarchal language and therefore problematically reify its hegemony. In this respect the Wife's narrative anticipates Irigaray's own engagement with patriarchal epistemologies and arrives at a similar quandary—how can Woman find her own voice? Chaucer's depiction of the Wife's quasi-feminist appropriation invites further consideration in its necessary resistance to closure. Since any personal usurpation of the masculine hardly suffices as a feminine, her ineffectual promiscuous narrative would seem to underscore a need for some alternative. At a minimum, her futile usurpation calls into question the role of the feminine in a masculine hermeneutics, even if her ambivalent sexual textuality frustrates the reader's attempts to identify any potential resolution. Peggy Knapp comments, "Alisoun of Bath may become, then, a figure for the garrulous, incorrigible, inexplicable text, always *wandrynge by the weye*, always escaping from any centralizing authority that attempts to take over her story. She wants to be glossed and gives out a wealth of clues to reading her enigma, but no one reading will master the rest. And the glossing she invites is itself readable as the work of high intellect and spiritual insight, or the play of material forces and sexual cajolery, or both."[57] Indeed, the Wife's narrative calls attention to still unresolved problematic relationships of gender and language, and through its attention to the feminine utility of poetic polysemy it asserts a feminine valorization, albeit a problematic one: an ambivalent, paradoxical, and unresolved antifeminist feminism.

If the Wife leaves us with these unresolved problematic relationships of gender, language, and society, it is perhaps because through her we see the poet discovering the limits of poetry. She is, after all, his writing, and we read him both in her and through her. The unresolved issues are therefore crucial to readers' appreciation of Chaucer's narrative construction because they *are* unresolved, inviting further critical conversation and further debate—"Have thou ynogh, thee thar nat pleyne thee" (III.336).

Chapter Two

The Text of Criseyde

> Yef men blameth that ys noght worthy to be blamed,
> thanne hy buth to blame. Clerkes knoweth wel ynow that
> no synfol man doth so wel that he ne myghte do betre,
> nother maketh so good a translacyon that he ne myghte
> make a betre.
>
> —*John Trevisa*, Dialogue[1]

For Chaucer, Criseyde manifests literary activities—reading, glossing, writing, translating—and so the narrative that produces her, by extension, yields metatextual, or self-reflexive, commentary on its own manifestation of these and related activities.[2] The narrator of *Troilus* is a self-described reader and his narrative is situated overtly in relation to a predecessor, overtly complicated by the narrator's task of translating.[3] The narrator of *Troilus* concludes his work of translating "Lollius's" alleged source text by appending to the poem a prayer that incorporates a translation of Dante's *Paradiso* (14.28–30):

> Thow oon, and two, and thre, eterne on lyve,
> That regnest ay in thre, and two, and oon,
> Uncircumscript, and al maist circumscrive,[4]
> Us from visible and invisible foon
> Defende, and to thy mercy, everichon,
> So make us, Jesus, for thi mercy, digne,
> For love of mayde and moder thyn benigne.   5.1863–69

The prayer is, at first glance, a request for protection or defense; the phrase "visible and invisible foon" is comprehensive, accounting for both the overtly recognizable threats of the human world—e.g., enemy soldiers—as well as those more insidious foes (such as unfaithful women) whose evil is perpetrated under cover of their victims' ignorance or faith. Additionally, the prayer addresses the Virgin Mary—"mayde and moder"—thereby evoking the spiritual significance of a revered feminine icon by professing admiration and respect for the Virgin Mother, the truest and most laudable of women in the Christian tradition.

More than a typically generic reiteration of Christian orthodoxy, however, the prayer constitutes a remarkably self-reflexive gloss on the narrative preceding it. The text to which the prayer is appended obviously tells the story of "foon" both visible and unseen, for its various manifestations of human relationships, including war and romance, love and betrayal, are articulated in conjunction with the narrator's own stated concerns regarding the accuracy and propriety of his translation. I wish to argue that the text evinces an ambivalent position germane to its own literary activities by gendering these relationships: for the *Troilus* narrator, Woman is the "invisible foe" that troubles the translation. The exclusionary binarism of "mayde and moder" leaves no room for Criseyde within its nostalgic, naively fetishizing parameters. Criseyde's occupation of the feminine gender position is, the narrative insists, connected to her sexuality, and hence it is Criseyde as sexual Woman who fuels the narrator's problematic relationship to the matter of his text.

1

The character of Chaucer's Criseyde is mediated by layers of interpretation and perception; much of her history and profile are reported by the men of the narrative, and even "her" words are supplied by a narrator who, while claiming fidelity to his translation's source, nonetheless interjects with such frequency and zest that his professed ability to report without bias is obviously a fiction. Thus we find Criseyde introduced as an object of pathos and subservience who must plead, "with pitous vois" (1.111), for Hector's protection from those who would abuse her as a substitute for her traitorous father. Hector's promise to her—"youre body shal men save" (1.122)—is an act of compassion, but one that nonetheless foregrounds her corporeal objectification, that is, her staus as body rather than self. It introduces as well a pairing of promise and betrayal, one whose initiation and disintegration occur a step ahead of that involving Troilus and Criseyde; the two sets will intersect when the exchange for Antenor is made. Her introduction therefore foregrounds her identity as victim, a status never ameliorated by the narrative, despite the narrator's accentuated attempts to affirm otherwise.

I am aware that I may be positing the sort of argument often criticized for lacking humor and being too eager to exculpate a female character.[5] But feminists are too often silenced by the accusation of lacking humor, as if an unwillingness to overlook unpleasantries by veiling them in (masculine) humor warrants negation of a critical position. Thus it is important to understand why a reader might find in *Troilus* grounds for choosing not to condemn Criseyde. Clearly the text supports multiple readings, and, given the text's and the narrator's oscillating positions, determining in what ways and to what ends such equivocality operates can help us better to appreciate the text's gendered dynamics and its ambivalent presentation of its story and its telling.

The opening sequence of *Troilus* is curiously structured and articulated from a strikingly inconsonant narrative position. We are told from the start that this is a biased account—"The double sorwe of Troilus to tellen" (1.1), "In which ye may the double sorwes here / Of Troilus in lovynge of Criseyde, / And how she forsook hym er she deyde" (1.54–56)—for we are presented with the narrator's self-professed intention to tell, in retrospect, the story of Troilus's sorrow, how Troilus is betrayed, how Criseyde is to blame for his disappointment and hurt feelings. Clearly this narrative purports to elucidate a woman's act of betrayal by examining the events leading to and arising from her transgression, that is, her errant behavior apropos the decorum of romance; and although the narrator overtly emphasizes Troilus's perspective here, his narrative is much more Criseyde's story. Though framed as the transgressor, Criseyde is introduced in the narrative proper as having been subjected to prior misfortunes with rather dire consequences, continuing into the narrative present.

Hence the narrator's famous description points to her inevitably being manipulated, and it prepares for her being assigned blame by focusing on her physical attributes:

> Among thise othere folk was Criseyda,
> In widewes habit blak; but natheles,
> Right as oure first lettre is now an A,
> In beaute first so stood she, makeles.
> Hire goodly lokyng gladed al the prees.
> Nas nevere yet seyn thyng to ben preysed derre,
> Nor under cloude blak so bright a sterre.   1.169–75

She is a widow—"for bothe a widewe was she and allone" (1.97), apparently childless ("But wheither that she children hadde or noon, / I rede it naught, therfore I late it goon" [1.132–33])—and thus finds herself occupying the awkward social position of having no male protector in a culture known to victimize unprotected women, and, further, she is left behind to bear the brunt of Trojan society's gossip and desire for vengeance owing to her father's treason. It is hardly surprising, then, that her foremost emotional expression is shown to be fear, that she reiterates throughout the narrative sequence her anxiety and trepidation owing to her place in society and its structures. Disappointing her lover and causing him some emotional pain seem relatively minor compared to the harsh circumstances framing Criseyde's introduction.

Additionally, and overtly more troubling for the narrator, her status marks her as sexually experienced, yet without the obligation of child care or marriage. As noted above in connection with Chaucer's Wife of Bath, widows represent an ambiguous and troubling sexual status, and their presence is troubling for those who wish to conform to codes of patriarchal identification; like the widowed Wife, Criseyde has participated in sexual experiences and is yet unencumbered by the patristic sanction of childbirth. She is, the narrator emphasizes, "makeles"—without a match (an equal in beauty) and without a "make" (a mate, spouse). Hence the apparent contradiction in the continuation of the description: the narrator describes her as "Simple of atir and debonaire of chere, / With ful assured lokyng and manere" (1.181–82), after having just voiced his presumption that "she stood ful lowe and stille allone, / Byhynden other folk, in litel brede, / And neigh the dore, ay undre shames drede" (1.178–80). The narrator sets forth an image of a confident, gracious woman while simultaneously indicating that she has reason to wish to conceal shame from others; whether this is owing to her having had foisted upon her an identity of traitor's daughter or whether some personal experience motivates her shame, the narrator leaves ambiguous.

Criseyde's sexual status coupled with the narrator's comparison of her to the letter "A" defines her in relation to gender decorum and its epistemological connotations: as Carolyn Dinshaw, Elaine Hansen, and others have shown, she is perceived as the carnal letter, the feminine-body-as-text, a blank page to be inscribed by masculine agency in its numerous manifestations.[6] Dinshaw's argument demonstrates in particular the gendered dynamics of reading taking place in this text, explicating the "masculine" versus "feminine" readings posed by the narrator and Criseyde (the narrator's sometime doppelganger Pandarus complicates the sex/

gender association, Dinshaw argues, indicating that men need not read like men).[7] Further, the female-body-as-text metaphor is manifest in the text's recurring assertions of approval germane to the feminine being manipulated by the masculine, for she will reveal herself to be not the fixed, literal glyph (pointing to the *signum proprium* of decorum) to which the narrator compares her but instead a more complex and indefinite sequence of *signa translata*.[8] Criseyde thus embodies the "slydyng" text, subject to the manipulative manueverings of the men who would inscribe her. She is in effect the translated text of each reading, bearing the language that each imposes on her as each reader appropriates her as his or her own.

Troilus's initial attraction to Criseyde, for example, contributes to the text's reflexive theme of Woman-as-text, for the description of Troilus's incipient desire underscores not only the carnal/literal superficiality of visually incited desire—"And upon cas bifel that thorugh a route / His eye percede, and so depe it wente, / Til on Criseyde it smot, and ther it stente" (1.271–73)[9]—but also Troilus's own degree of complicity in the construction of his fantasy object/text:

Thus gan he make a mirour of his mynde
In which he saugh al holly hire figure,
And that he wel koude in his herte fynde.
It was to hym a right good aventure
To love swich oon, and if he dede his cure
To serven hir, yet myghte he falle in grace,
Or ellis for oon of hire servantz pace.   1.365–71

Gayle Margherita argues that such "specular pleasures become perilous precisely because of the potential slippage of desire into identification."[10] Troilus's imagination constructs a fantasy object whose origin is located in Troilus's singular desire; hence his narcissistic desire motivates his—and Pandarus's—pygmalionism, their attempt to force reality into compliance with the fantasy.[11] The manipulative, self-centered quality of Troilus's erotic interests is elided by their mode of articulation, which employs proper sentiment belonging to a conventional romance decorum and which therefore participates in the rather oxymoronic gesture of codifying that which resists codification.

It is thus fitting that the narrator interrupts Troilus's fantasy with a digression on the mechanics of translating and the difficulties of doing so with a missing text:

> And of his song naught only the sentence,
> As writ myn auctour called Lollius,
> But pleinly, save oure tonges difference,
> I dar wel seyn, in al, that Troilus
> Seyde in his song, loo, every word right thus
> As I shal seyn; and whoso list it here,
> Loo, next this vers he may it fynden here.   1.393–99

In a startling admission of invention, the narrator indicates that the *Canticus Troilii* he presents,[12] while deriving from the "sentence" of Lollius's text, is absent in its presented form from the supposed source—in other words, the narrator is "translating" an original that does not exist, or, to the point, he is writing the narrative himself.[13] For the narrator subsequently to claim total fidelity to Troilus's words then underscores his role as "maker"; it is he who constructs the fantasy of Troilus's fantasy at the level of its literal articulation. The narrator's interpolated commentary on language and fabrication gives further emphasis as well to Troilus's own process of "making," with this interruption jolting the narrative temporarily out of its romance mode, thereby calling attention to its own status as text. The narrator sharply juxtaposes the kitschy trappings of *fin' amors* convention with a pointed explication of the craft by which these conventions are brought to fictional life, as though the narrator—or Chaucer—does not want the reader to become too comfortable in the role of reading.

The narrator's exterior paternalistic role is taken up internally by Pandarus, who voyeuristically mediates the romantic exchanges like a vicariously adolescent father goading and applauding a son's initiation into active sexual manhood. To be sure, Troilus is as much a pawn in Pandarus's game as Criseyde, but for Troilus the stakes are much lower; Pandarus trifles with Troilus's affections using Criseyde as the prize object, but Criseyde's compliance connotes a sense of coercion. Pandarus expresses succinctly his self-designated role:

> That is to seye, for the am I bicomen,
> Bitwixen game and ernest, swich a meene
> As maken wommen unto men to comen;
> Al sey I nought, thow wost wel what I meene.   3.253–56

Clearly Pandarus derives vicarious excitement from orchestrating Criseyde's seduction; he is thereby able to experience erotic delight in the romance without having to invest personally in its consequences ("I dide al that the leste. . . . I kan namore seye" [5.1736, 1743], he responds in the aftermath of Troilus's dejection). Troilus, too, may be implicated in manipulative behavior, particularly as he determinedly adheres to the literal text of *fin' amors*, anxiously attempting to shape Criseyde according to a procrustean decorum that excludes the harsh political and social realities of a volatile and violent world. Thus the grandiose romance of the consummation scene is troubled by the ambiguous, subtle indications that it is Troilus and Pandarus whose desires are being fulfilled by Troilus and Criseyde. Consider, for instance, Troilus's seductive invitation, "Now yeldeth yow, for other bote is non!" (3.1208), which may be read as indicative of fantasy, rape-fantasy, or rape. In an insightful explication of the consummation episode, Louise Fradenburg argues that "the ambiguity cannot be resolved through interpretation; we cannot 'decide' whether Criseyde has consented or not, whether she has been raped or not."[14] Hence the impossible task of translation: ambiguity promotes slippage, uncertainty, and thus each reader translates the moment in a personal, appropriative gesture of interpretation.

The narrator's (and Pandarus's) exaggerated, voyeuristic, and vicarious delight in the conspicuously undetailed report of Troilus and Criseyde's much anticipated sex scene seems strikingly at odds with the troubling indications underlying the *fin' amors* clichés. Within the frame of the fiction, theirs is not a conventional, literary romance; it is complicated by outside forces, much as is the Paolo/Francesca literary romance that *Troilus and Criseyde* seems to evoke.[15] The masculine triumvirate (Troilus, Pandarus, the narrator) seems determined to shape the romance to fit the literary paradigm:

> O blisful nyght, of hem so longe isought,
> How blithe unto hem bothe two thow weere!
> Why nad I swich oon with my soule ybought,
> Ye, or the leeste joie that was theere?
> Awey, thow foule daunger and thow feere,
> And lat hem in this hevene blisse dwelle,
> That is so heigh that al ne kan I telle!   3.1317–23

Hence too the narrator's and Troilus's exaggerated response to Troilus's perceived betrayal; Troilus within the text and the narrator without both wish to write the story first as romance then as tragedy, even if the events being narrated betray their desires.

Thus the narrator's waxing romantic as he reports the consummation is quickly betrayed by the jarring contrast in tone as he prefaces Book 4. Lambasting Fortune in language remarkably similar to that subsequently used to condemn Criseyde, the narrator rehearses commonplaces of feminine mutability:

> But al to litel, weylaway the whyle,
> Lasteth swich joie, ythonked be Fortune,
> That semeth trewest whan she wol bygyle
> And kan to fooles so hire song entune
> That she hem hent and blent, traitour comune!
> And whan a wight is from hire whiel ythrowe,
> Than laugheth she, and maketh hym the mowe.   4.1–7

The conflation of Fortune and Woman is manifest most tellingly in the "traitor comune" label, not only owing to conventional associations but also because the phrase is used as part of a narrative that implicates a specific woman's analogous status. Traitorous mutability—"slydyng of corage" (5.825)—is identified as the ubiquitous, visible specter of Fortune; but Criseyde is to Troilus, the narrator regrets, an invisible foe. The narrator's oddly emphatic denouncing of Criseyde would seem to point to a larger displeasure with women and romance in general:

> For how Criseyde Troilus forsook—
> Or at the leeste, how that she was unkynde—
> Moot hennesforth ben matere of my book.   4.15–18
>
> ....
>
> This ilke ferthe book me helpeth fyne,
> So that the losse of lyf and love yfeere
> Of Troilus be fully shewed heere.   4.26–28

The vocative addresses, frantic exhortations, and personalized laments almost obscure the less than tragic quality of their underlying motivation: a woman takes up with a new lover. In fact the narrator admits to the relatively trivial nature of Criseyde's perceived transgression: "how that she was unkynde"; kindness and decorum are laudatory characteristics, but surely no act of mere unkindness warrants the text's obsessive laments, and thus the excess seems absurd. In the midst of war, death, injury, and other such devastation, the narrator finds the highest outrage, the greatest cause for grief, to be Troilus's feeling betrayed by the woman whom he let go. Granted, these other subjects provide context and are not themselves a significant part of the lovers' *aventure*. But the narrator's florid expressions nonetheless provide the text with a humorous irony generated by overstatement; the grandiose pretensions to high tragedy seem comical, the melodrama ironic.

The humor deriving from the narrator's ludicrous excesses, however, is quickly redressed by the central event of the *Troilus*, that of Criseyde's being sold to the Greeks.[16] Despite his professions of patronizing concern, the narrator, of course, goes ahead and blames Criseyde, as do Troilus, Pandarus, and the majority of *Troilus*'s critics. In this regard, one is reminded of Jerome's notorious condemnation of Helen—Criseyde's thematic counterpart—who is similarly victimized and blamed: "et propter unius mulierculae raptum, Europa atque Asia decennalia bella confligunt" [and on the account of the rape of one little woman, Europe and Asia clash in a ten-year war].[17] It is true, according to the narrator, that Criseyde readily finds a new protector in Diomede—"If that I sholde of any Grek han routhe, / It sholde be youreselven, by my trouthe!" (5.1000–1001)—presumably a necessity in enemy territory, though her Trojan protectors give her little reason for confidence: "I say nat therfore that I wol yow love, / N'y say nat nay; but in conclusioun, / I mene wel, by God that sit above!" (5.1002–4). It is true as well that Criseyde's retrospection of her night with Troilus does not correspond to her earlier professions; her telling Diomede, "I hadde a lord, to whom I wedded was, / The whos myn herte al was, til that he deyde; / And other love . . . ne nevere was" (5.975–78) is far removed from her recitation of romance clichés to Troilus after their consummation scene ("For I am thyn, by God and by my trouthe!" [3.1512]), though her love for her late husband comes across as sincere, an acute loss.

But while Criseyde's professed fidelity to Troilus is compromised once she belongs to the Greeks, it is Troilus who betrays Criseyde first. Consider, for example, Troilus's selfish desire to protect himself from mockery: "Bat natheles he no word to it seyde, / Lest men sholde his affeccioun espye" (4.152–53). Even while Hector attempts to protect Criseyde—"But on my part, ye may eftsone hem telle, / We usen here no wommen for to selle" (4.181–82)—Troilus is wholly ineffectual and passive—"Departed out of parlement echone, / This Troilus, withouten wordes mo" (4.218–19), and offers the weak excuse that to try to rescue Criseyde might result in her being slain (5.50–56). Further, Troilus sings of *his* woe with little regard for Criseyde (638–44), and his letter (1317–1421), full of *fin' amors* platitudes, blames *her* for going to the Greeks: "ye me lefte," "Whan that ye wente." Granted, Troilus does attempt to consult with Criseyde, to his credit, and he seems genuinely confused. But this is hardly the behavior of a hero, and thus while Troilus should be accorded some measure of compassion, even sympathy, by the reader, his inefficacy hardly exonerates him in relation to Criseyde's alleged betrayal.

To blame Criseyde without accounting for her dire circumstances is to legitimize misogynistic convention, to blame her for being both a woman and a victim. As Elaine Hansen observes, "Pandarus and Troilus make Criseyde the scapegoat for their own incapacities, and if we care to look, we see how and why misogyny works at one level."[18] Thus despite the narrator's overt attempts to implicate Criseyde as the betrayer, she is herself betrayed, in effect, by the men who fail her: her father, who deserts her in his traitorous movement to the Greeks (1.54–112) and who, like Pandarus, hints at incestuous attachment (4.1471–75, 1628–29); her husband, who dies and leaves her a widow (5.974–76); Pandarus, who orchestrates her seduction by exploiting her weaknesses (3.1563–68); Hector, who is unable to keep his promise to protect her (1.116–23, 4.176–96); Troilus, who passively relinquishes her (5.148–54, 218–19); and Diomede, who takes up where Pandarus and Troilus have left off (5.841–945). The narrator therefore betrays Criseyde most of all by naming her as the betrayer. Textualizing Criseyde's story ensures that her crime is perpetual; readers of *Troilus* who choose to blame Criseyde will find plenty of ammunition with which to attack her. The narrative invites alternative readings, but those who read literally—who, in Dinshaw's terms "read like men"— need not look beyond the narrative's superficial misogyny to find a cause to champion.

2

But what, then, we might ask, actually constitutes Criseyde's betrayal? And how does that betrayal correspond to the narrator's "translation" of Criseyde? Within the literal parameters of the fictional story, Criseyde's betrayal of Troilus is her neglecting to maintain the romantic fantasy after leaving Troy. Indeed her crime is her exposing their romance as the *fin' amors* cliché that it was; she violates the decorum by exposing it as decorum, and her errancy marks her as traitor within the literal paradigm. Troilus is unable to maintain the illusion of romance by himself, obviously, and certainly not when his fantasy-object is known to be associated with another man. It is no surprise that such a blow would be crushing to Troilus, given his reluctance to translate idealized fantasy into potentially disappointing reality—

"I have herd told, pardieux, of youre lyvyng,
Ye loveres, and youre lewed observaunces,
And which a labour folk han in wynnynge
Of love, and in the kepyng which doutaunces;
And whan youre prey is lost, woo and penaunces.
O veray fooles, nyce and blynde be ye!
Ther nys nat oon kan war by other be."   1.197–203

—and his deliberate attempts to make the romance fit his ideal, even speaking to *himself* in clichés, for instance: "O fool, now artow in the snare" (1.507). That Criseyde acclimates herself into the culture into which she has been sold is perceived by Troilus to be a personal rejection of such magnitude as to constitute a devastating betrayal. In fitting with the narrator's and Troilus's desire to force reality to fit literary decorum, Troilus finds in this unfortunate but relatively trivial incident the grounds for high tragedy and its grand expression. In order to present himself as the wronged party, Troilus blames Criseyde, thereby exonerating himself of any ethical shortcoming and enabling himself to indulge in self-pity (this from the "hero" who chose not to risk himself for the woman he purports to love): "But trewely, Criseyde, swete may, / Whom I have ay with al my myght yserved, / That ye thus doon, I have it nat deserved" (5.1720–23). The narrator, whose own rhetorical excesses supplementing the story parallel the melodramatic expressions within it, likewise indulges in excessive articulations that seem motivated not by factors present in the literal narrative but by some other source; the "Swich fyn" stanza, for example, exhibits a grandeur inappropriate for the story that contextualizes it ("Swich fyn hath, lo, this Troilus for love! / Swich fyn hath al his grete worthynesse! . . . Swich fyn hath false worldes brotelnesse!" [5.1828–32]).

As part of its larger explication of literary decorums and their artifice, the text considers the constraints imposed by decorum and exposes their insufficiency in the face of situational and contextual shifts. This is best exemplified, perhaps, by the text's treatment of exchange, whereby various decorums govern symbolic gestures subject to fluctuating interpretations. Thus the gift-giving exchange following the consummation—"As fel to purpos of this aventure, / And pleyinge entrechaungeden hire rynges" (3.1367–68)—though meaningful as part of the *fin' amors* decorum of appropriate romance behavior, loses its significance once *fin' amors* no longer obtains. Hence Criseyde's dream:

> And as she slep, anonright tho hire mette
> How that an egle, fethered whit as bon,
> Under hire brest his longe clawes sette,
> And out hire herte he rente, and that anon,
> And dide his herte into hire brest to gon—
> Of which she nought agroos, ne nothyng smerte—
> And forth he fleigh, with herte left for herte.   2.925–31

Because a dream, the "herte . . . for herte" exchange is painless, but, foreshadowing the reciprocal pain present in human relationships, the dream brings to the text the not-so-subtle message that there is no love without there being, ultimately, some pain, exchange, and loss. Thus the exchange of Criseyde for Antenor, which results in Criseyde's figuratively exchanging Troilus for Diomede, imposes a harsh reality on the romance decorum so fiercely held dear by Troilus and infuses their story with a realistic measure of pain and loss.

Criseyde is herself shown to be aware of what emotional and erotic entanglements entail. She has suffered one great loss before her introduction to Troilus, and she is well aware of the gender bias inhering in social decorums that perpetuate suffering: "Therto we wrecched wommen nothing konne, / Whan us is wo, but wepe and sitte and thinke; / Oure wrecche is this, oure owen wo to drynke" (2.782–84). Fradenburg observes: "But Crisede's lines about women's woe hint at that narrative paradigm wherein the coincidence of rescuer and tormentor in the same person turns the feminine subject's affect—her 'wo'—into body: she is language-less, somatized, and figured as the source of her own unpleasure: 'oure owen wo to drynke.'"[19] Criseyde's observation regarding gender and the origin of suffering follows shortly after her more famous "drynke," which she evokes figuratively to describe her reaction to the sight of Troilus's triumphant return from battle, "So lik a man of armes and a kynght / He was to seen, fulfilled of heigh prowesse" (2.631–32):

> Criseyda gan al his chere aspien,
> And leet it so softe in hire herte synke,
> That to hireself she seyde, "Who yaf me drynke?"
> For of hire owen thought she wex al reed.   2.649–52

The "drynke" that triggers her interest in showing Troilus "mercy and pitee" is the "wo" of which she later speaks. Criseyde correctly locates her own "wo" in her body, for it is her desired body that initiates her "wo"; Troilus desires her flesh, and the Greeks desire one body (hers) in exchange for another (Antenor). Passive, pathetic, and incapacitated by fear, Criseyde is obviously no heroine in the conventional sense—but that is precisely her point. She claims only to be human and to behave, however ineffectually or mistakenly, as a human and a woman.

Thus the text simultaneously reifies and destabilizes patriarchal order. At one level, Criseyde is the stereotypical fickle woman who betrays her good man, and her victimization points to the hegemonic and patriarchal social and literary codes that perpetually mark the feminine as errant; always subject to obsessive and conflicting desire and ideologies, Woman seems doomed to be measured as a manifestation of distance from a set of impossible masculine expectations and ideals. And yet, on another level, the narrative supplies so extensive a challenge to the patriarchal codes it ostensibly embraces that Criseyde-as-text destabilizes the system that condemns her. In connection with the text's metatextual dimension, Criseyde's betrayal points to far more than a naive young man's thwarted fantasies; it elucidates and is analogous to the narrator's translating of Lollius's text. To translate a text is to risk betraying it or being betrayed by the text, the translation, or the act of translating. Sources and authors share an uneasy relationship in which identities and labels are blurred: Boccaccio and Chaucer, Lollius and narrator, Criseyde and reader. The narrator's apparently naive desire that the integrity of his text be maintained—

> And for ther is so gret diversite
> In Englissh and in writyng of oure tonge,
> So prey I God that non myswrite the,
> Ne the mysmetre for defaute of tonge;
> And red wherso thow be, or elles songe,
> That thow be understonde, God I biseche!   5.1793–98

—is equally an ironic, reflexive observation that it will of course be subject to the corrupting (feminine) instrumentality of readers' diverse hermeneutics.

The narrator has overtly gone to great lengths to foreground Criseyde—Woman—as the corrupting, errant *translatio* and, as we have seen, the text obviously participates to a degree in reifying some conventional misogynistic associations. But that very participation invites its own dismantling, as Chaucer not only exploits the discrepancies between decorums but also points to the perilousness of rigidity and over-reliance on *signa propria* and codes of propriety and decorum. The denouement and peroration of Book 5 provide an instructive illustration of this metatextual trajectory. Criseyde's famous letter reiterates the figurative interconnectedness of gender, epistemology, and textuality:

> Yet preye ich yow, on yvel ye ne take
> That it is short which that I to yow write;
> I dar nat, ther I am, wel lettres make,
> Ne nevere yet ne koude I wel endite.
> Ek gret effect men write in place lite;
> Th'entente is al, and nat the lettres space.   5.1625–30

Criseyde recognizes the subjectivity of the text, that it is subject to interpretation and that interpretation and intent are frequently divided, beyond the author's control. In her reiteration of the polysemy of the text, she further underscores the subjectivity of the (feminine) letter: that its surface covers far more than is made apparent and that therefore the codified and formal articulation of the letter is betrayed by the invisible legions occupying its semantic space.

Hence the narrator's unwillingness to commit ultimately to a single opinion of his subjects, choosing instead an ambivalent oscillation that impugns even Troilus ("What nedeth feynede loves for to seke?" [5.1848]); excessive Christian rhetoric ends the text without concluding it, forcing the reader to contend with a jarring juxtaposition of the patriarchal security of Christian orthodoxy and the ambiguous uncertainty of the human world. This oddly situated closing gesture is further troubled, as are frequent occasions throughout the narrative, by a statement of its own unreliability: "Beth war of men and herkneth what I seye" (5.1785). There is no certainty or closure, Chaucer, through the narrator, insists, and those who seek it are, like Troilus, pursuing a fantasy.[20] Things unseen may be substantiated by faith—"Est autem fides sperandarum substantia rerum, argumentum non apparentium" (Heb 11.1) [Faith is moreover the substance of things to be hoped for, the argument for what is not apparent]—including a faith in the scapegoating of the "invisible foe," but the complex plurality with which Chaucer infuses *Troilus* belies such a convenience.

Chapter Three

"Wreched Engendrynge" and (wo)Mankynde

Although arguably the most provocative and fully developed of the women populating Chaucer's texts, the Wife of Bath and Criseyde are by no means Chaucer's only discursive exploration of cultural codes of sexuality and their textual manifestations. Despite the sense of strength and self-determination that many readers find in the Wife's narrative, the *pathos* that ultimately undermines the Wife's ostensibly aggressive words speaks, insidiously, to a more pervasive and more profound dimension of Chaucer's incorporation of gender decorums in his poetry, one I have argued complicates the theme of subjectivity and betrayal in *Troilus and Criseyde*—that of victimization.[1]

Feminists are often uneasy about Chaucer's interest in—indeed, obsession with—victimized women. Why is it that Chaucer, the "humanist" and "woman's friend,"[2] so frequently casts women in the role of victim? And why is it too that Chaucer seems to praise these women for their participation in cultural codes of suffering and subordination, thereby not only valorizing the necessity of women's suffering but seemingly absolving men of responsibility as well? Aside from the unlikely possibility that Chaucer is himself a misogynist whose depictions of women have been grossly misread as sympathetic by feminists and humanists alike, one could argue, as has Arlyn Diamond, that Chaucer, "unwilling to abandon the values and hierarchies he inherits, unable to reconcile them with what he has observed of human emotion and social realities ... accepts uneasily the medieval view of women as either better or worse than men, but never quite the same," that Chaucer himself participates, albeit uneasily, in the perpetuation of cultural codes of female pseudovalorization and submission.[3] To the extent that Chaucer's work is the product of a social system inextricably bound to institutionalized gender bias, suffering is an integral part of Chaucer's concern with gender, and it is situated in relation to convention. But, we might ask, to what end?

1

The *Legend of Good Women* is an appropriate starting point for analyzing Chaucer's attention to women's suffering, given the overt centrality of women's valorized suffering to the text's structure and theme. Ordered to perform a literary penance for his "shewing how that wemen han don mis" (G.266), the poet is instructed to make a "gloryous legende / Of goode women, maydenes and wyves" (G.473–74).[4] His task is to articulate a narrative memorial to exemplary women—to recall their stories and vivify their experiences, that their exceptional womanly goodness might be known and lauded. "[G]oode" is defined in context as both submissive and victimized, for the sequence of the ten legends that follow equates goodness with relativity and pain; more than half commit suicide, for instance, and many suffer horribly in the name of "love," e.g., Philomela's rape and mutilation: "she was served for hire sisters love" (2365). What makes the *Legend* so unnerving, in part, is that the tales recount the suffering of "goode" women—these are not the *topoi* of the despised harlot, wicked traitor, or insidious temptress so often inhabiting conventional misogynistic lore. And yet they are twice victimized: first in their situation of origin and second in the *Legend* narrator's re-telling, which reinforces the cultural codes that made possible, indeed inevitable, the original victimization. Apropos of this schema of valorization, to be a woman is to be subjected to suffering, and to be a "goode" woman is to accept it passively; "goode" women are replications of a masculine ideal, void of individuality as articulated within the constraints of the hagiographic paradigm.

In addition, women are grouped according to labels of social/sexual status according to a masculine ideal: "maydenes and wyves." Woman's social identity is determined by the sexual role she occupies in relation to men. Thisbe, for example, is one of the "Maydenes . . . ykept, for jelosye, / Ful streyte, lest they diden som folye" (722–23), for as a virginal maiden she is too valuable a commodity to risk and is therefore confined by the stone wall for her own good; former wives (widows) such as Cleopatra and Dido are presented as inevitably seeking subsequent husbands to reify their status as wives and hence their value as women. Not only do "maydenes and wyves" suffer as women, but, more specifically, women suffer as maidens and wives; sexual status governs the quality and degree of suffering, with the greater sense of shame accorded the maidens (frequently identified as daughters also) who dared enter the sexual arena in disobedience to their fathers. Elaine Hansen observes the "double bind in which the female in [the narrator's] culture is caught: victimized if she follows the rules of love and lives up to medieval ideals of the feminine; unworthy, unloved, and unsung if she does not."[5]

Within the text, women are gendered and sexualized constructs articulated in masculine terms in relation to masculine decorums. The *miseria* theme that connects the legends asserts the relative positioning of women: "That were trewe in lovynge al here lyves; / And telle of false men that hem betrayen" (G.475–76). One becomes a "goode" woman only if one is chosen, for within these parameters women require men for self-identity, even as such identification results in reduction and abuse. In fact, the reduction to topos is so emphatic that the women of the *Legend* are hardly recognizable as women, or as human beings for that matter; as Hansen notes, "Just as Cleopatra and Thisbe calmly and quietly commit suicide, their fellow heroines never get angry when they are raped, left behind, or stranded on desert islands with wild beasts; they are sad but not frenzied or vindictive, and at worst they weep and swoon."[6] Hence a contingency of gender and gender representation is effected; the feminine exists only in relation to the masculine, and only in a clearly gendered relationship of dominance and submission necessitating the forfeiture of self-identity and self-determination. And yet the text seems to tire of its own relentless accounting of *miseria*; indeed, the narrator's own expressions of boredom throughout[7] suggest that it is boredom that precludes his completion of the *Legend*. I make a distinction here between the poet-Chaucer and the narrator/character-Chaucer; it is the narrator of the *Legend* who appears bored by his telling of repetitious narratives, and certainly there is no need to presume the same of the author outside the text, who, I would argue, uses the narrator's boredom to underscore the tedium of the unwavering allegiance to generic form. Perhaps the legends cease because there is nowhere for the text to go other than through an interminable cycle of unremarkable thematic repetition; the contrived structure and diluted content doom the *Legend* even as the narrative begins.

But the *Legend of Good Women* is equally concerned with textual process and exhibits a typically Chaucerian concern with self-reflexive or metatextual constructions. The Prologue is overtly concerned with reading and writing, and it calls attention to textual construction as process, thereby elucidating the dynamics of its own articulation. As Jill Mann argues, "It is in [Chaucer's] consciousness of the intermediary role of literature in creating and nourishing these stereotyped interpretive patterns . . . that the real sophistication of the *Legend* lives."[8] For example, a connection between translating and making is articulated by Cupid, who asks, "Hast thow nat mad in Englysh ek the bok / How that Crisseyde Troylus forsok" (G.264–65), and by Alceste, who comments, "But for he useth bokes for the make, / And taketh non hed of what matere he take" (G.342–43). Alceste speaks too of the poet's "makynge" as she lists the works that "He hath maked" (G.403), and commanding that "he shal maken" (G.427) the legends, instructs, "[t]he moste partye of thy tyme spende / In makynge of a gloryous legende" (G.472–73). The Prologue is clearly concerned with the role of the poet as maker, as one who creates texts and who articulates in those very texts his awareness of himself as maker and of the texts as being made.

Given the foregrounding of both concerns, is there a connection between the manifestation of the *misera* motif and Chaucer's self-reflexive attention to his own role as "maker"? We might approach this question by way of Alceste's cataloging sequence:

> He hath in prose translated Boece,
> And Of the Wreched Engendrynge of Mankynde,
> As man may in Pope Innocent yfynde;
> And mad the lyf also of Seynt Cecile.   G.413–16

To "make" a text is to engender it; textual construction is a process of creating, and it may be understood in ambiguously gendered terms. To the extent that language is informed by cultural conceptions of gender, en/gendering evokes both creating and gendering. The title "Of the Wreched Engendrynge of Mankynde," perhaps a lost translation of Innocent III's *De miseria condicionis humane*,[9] is therefore particularly intriguing, for the "misery of the human condition" has become "wreched engendrynge," an engendered or begotten state of wretchedness. Innocent's invective against anything sexual repeatedly uses conception—engendering—as the locus of filth and misery:

> In carnali quippe commercio racionis sopitur intuitus, ut ignorancia seminetur; libidinis irritatur pruritus, ut iracundia propagetur; voluptatis saciatur affectus, ut concupiscencia contrahatur. Hic est

tyrannus carnis, lex menbrorum, fomes peccati, languor nature, pabulum mortis, sine quo nemo nascitur, sine quo nullus moritur.

[Certainly in fleshly intercourse the gazing of reason is lulled to sleep, so that ignorance is sown; the itch of lust is provoked, so that anger is propagated; the feeling of sensual pleasure is felt keenly, so that concupiscence is brought about. This is the tyrant of the flesh, the law of members, the tinder of sin, the languor of nature, the nourishment of death, without which no one is born, without which none dies.][10]

Chaucer's translation—or, more accurately, replacement—of Innocent's title demonstrates a concern with textual construction as an active, gendered, and deliberate event. The poet-maker, in the process of creating, engenders language and text. Moreover, humanity itself has become overtly, if ambiguously, gendered: "*Man*kynde." Though the genitive construction allows for the interpretation that the "wreched engendrynge" is imposed by, rather than upon, "mankynde"—that the reality of wretchedness is that it is engendered by masculine agency and inflicted on feminine objects—it is perhaps ironic that *miseria* should be associated with *man*kind in the prologue of a text obsessed with women's suffering.[11] The label seems at once both paradoxically self-reflexive and ironically ambiguous.

But "wreched engendrynge" is more than an ironic metatextual moment in the *Legend of Good Women;* the phrase describes a metapoetics of gendered textual construction incorporated throughout Chaucer's works, particularly the tales of *pitee* included in the *Canterbury Tales.*[12] My concern with the *miseria* motif, and its textual implications, is not necessarily to recuperate Chaucer's reputation by finding a significance in the depictions of suffering that somehow exonerates Chaucer of the misogyny informing such depictions; instead, I wish to analyze the operation of a gendered poetics signifying an en/gendering of narrative and text articulated in relation to two masculine constructions of quasi-valorized women—the virgin ("maydenes") and the wife ("wyves")—in order to develop a connection between masculine constructions of feminine representations and the dynamics of orthodoxy and subversion. I shall therefore consider Chaucer's representations of gendered suffering in four related *Canterbury Tales*—those of the Physician, the Second Nun, the Clerk, and the Man of Law. By doing so, I hope to determine the extent to which the *miseria* inhering in these representations articulates a feminine poetics through metaphors of en/gendering framed by an overt masculine hermeneutic. I hope to demonstrate that these texts use sexualized tropes of cruelty and pain subversively, as does the *Legend of Good Women,* to challenge narrative decorum even as they overtly assert cultural orthodoxy.

2

Chaucer's tales of *pitee* exploit the discrepancies between the two gender models of carnality and plurality. Observing the hierarchical definitions of gendered representation of his culture, Chaucer evokes a negative "carnal" feminine, the subject of textual manipulation and submissiveness; in addition, and, I would argue, more important, Chaucer uses feminine representations to signify poetic polysemy in conjunction with an erotics of reading and writing that is itself ambiguously and ambivalently gendered and sexualized—and punished. Representations of social/sexual status (virgin, wife) are used in conjunction with sexualized tropes of suffering to construct a reflexive poetics of "wreched engendrynge," of the misogyny problematized through gendered decorums and the Christian orthodoxy they both privilege and subvert. Hence the tales of *pitee* overtly privilege a Christian hermeneutic that is, on closer analysis, a masculine hermeneutic pitted against itself within the parameters of conflicting gendered epistemologies.

Resembling the structure and the relatively diluted content of the tales in the *Legend of Good Women,* the *Physician's Tale,* one of the least liked and most maligned of Chaucer's *Tales,* posits the misogynistic *sentence* that virginity is more important than the virgin herself.[13] Virginia represents to her father Virginius the ideally inaccessible and sexually unavailable maiden, and the fourteen-year-old girl's virginity is what marks her worth: "As wel in goost as body chast was she, / For which she floured in virginitee" (VI.43–44). Attached to the "virginitee" ideal are the traits of humility, abstinence, and patience, among others;[14] each represents a submissiveness, a willing acquiescence to patriarchal codes of gendered decorum. The glorification and valorization of these traits in the tale—what R. Howard Bloch has argued constitute "a poetics of praise" or "a rhetoric of excessive praise"[15]—displace the value and even the necessity of the woman who embodies these attributes and instead acknowledge only the attributes themselves.

Moreover, sexual chastity is linked here, as it is conventionally, to chaste speech; Virginia's words, like her body, represent a chaste ideal, subject to masculine control. The Physician's description of Virginia's body and language not only unite the two in an idealized embodiment of sexual chasteness but deliberately contradict other negative feminine stereotypes in order to set up a simplistic good/bad dichotomy: "Discreet she was in answeryng alway" (VI.48). The odd emphasis on shame in the Physician's description—"Shamefast she was in maydens shamefastnesse" (55)—speaks to a cultural unease with the female body; women, the Physician asserts, should be ashamed *as* women. Because their bodies are desired by men, women are expected to assume responsibility both for that desire and for the culture's own shame thereof. By denying her own sexuality, the virgin satisfies the patriarchal code; she is taught to fear the men who desire her, to blame herself for their desire, and to conform to their notion of "mayde" in order to earn their forgiveness for her female body.

This transfer of responsibility and shame is further exacerbated by the expectation of the virgin's silence: her silence legitimizes the cultures's denial of responsibility and perpetuates its misplaced obligations. Although Virginia is a pagan character inhabiting a pagan narrative, her characterization and circumstances echo obviously Christian doctrine; with regard to virginity, Virginia's story evinces a hagiographic motif of virtuous suffering. Indeed Virginia, as described by the Physician, embodies Jerome's virginal ideal, whereby fear and silence govern:

> Sexus femineus suo iungatur sexui: nesciat, imo timeat cum pueris ludere. Nullum inpudicum verbum noverit et si forte in tumultu familiae discurrentis aliquid turpe audiat, non intellegat.[16]
>
> [The female sex should associate with the same of sex; she should not know how, indeed she should fear to play with boys. By no means should she know an unchaste word and, if among the bustle of a household she should hear something unclean, she should not understand it.]

Hence the virginal ideal refutes the nonvirginal feminine stereotypes of duplicity, mutability, garrulousness, and immodesty in language. To be a virgin, the Physician insists, echoing Jerome, is to speak the language of virginity—that is, to reject the language of women and to speak the language of men appropriate for women: silence and obedience.[17]

R. Howard Bloch has made a cogent argument that Virginia is doomed because, according to Jerome's beliefs, she is seen by others as an object of desire; visual penetration, as it were, suffices to negate her virginal status, and hence her death is not unexpected. Death is inevitable in a tale that privileges virginity, for, as Bloch argues, "a certain inescapable logic of virginity, most evident in medieval hagiography, leads syllogistically to the conclusion that the only good virgin—that is, the only true virgin—is a dead virgin."[18] Jerome's fanatical writings on virginity point to such a likelihood, indicating that the virgin does not look forward to an easy or pleasurable life on earth: "ante lacrymas scitura, quam risum; prius fletum sensura, quam gaudium. Necdum introitus, jam exitus" [she is to know tears, before laughter; she will feel sorrow, sooner than joy. Hardly an entrance, now an exit].[19] As Peter Brown has demonstrated, virginity historically could serve as a sign of membership in a Christian community, one that "everyone could share, independent of their sex and of their levels of cultural and social status"; sexual renunciation was available to anyone, "made open to all."[20] But the *Physician's Tale* reveals what happens when such a tenet is practiced in isolation. No longer a sign of Christian community, or even of self-discipline, virginity is perverted into a private, personal source of masculine pride and domination—a medium of exchange within the parameters of a homosocial economy.[21]

Virginius therefore murders his daughter in order to preserve his own masculine determination of feminine value; she is worthless to her father should her sexuality escape the control of patriarchal valuation. The Physician's diatribe on parental authority underscores the text's presentation of Virginia as Virginius's *property*, as subject to her father's ironclad ownership and directed inculcation, describing the necessity of "governaunce" and "governynges" (VI.72–82). Again the Physician's narrative points to Jerome: "Matris nutum pro verbis ac monitis, et pro imperio habeat. Amet ut parentem, subjiciatur ut dominae, timeat ut magistram" [Her mother's nod for a word and advice, and for a command let her have this. She should love her as parent, obey her as mistress, fear her as teacher].[22] Both Jerome and the Physician assign the duties of virgin-rearing to women (mother, governess), while reserving authority for the father, though the Physician pays lip service to the silent mother: "Ye fadres and ye moodres eek also, / Though ye han children, be it oon or mo, / Youre is the charge of al hir surveiaunce" (93–95). Virginia is so closely aligned with her father's absolute authority that she is marked as his property, proper to him only, and is inscribed with the name of her master in which resides the label of her social and sexual identity.

More insidiously, Virginius's obsessive attention to the sexual status of his daughter's body hints at incestuous desire, which, not surprisingly, is transferred into an economic and political arena that deflects its sexual overtones. There is thus a marked emphasis throughout the Physician's brief narrative on the father's own possession of the daughter's virtue, that her virginity is an asset or piece of property that, belonging to him, is threatened by Appius's desires. Virginius's concern, then, is not that Virginia is herself threatened but rather that his own interests are at stake, and thus he is quite willing to sacrifice her in defiance of another man's superior political position: "'Doghter,' quod he, 'Virginia by thy name, / Ther been two weyes, outher deeth or shame, / That thou must suffre; allas, that *I* was bore!'" (VI.213–15; emphasis mine). The passage in which Virginius informs Virginia of his quandary is remarkably centered on Virginius; his lament articulates his own woe at the prospect of losing his "gemme of chastitee" (223): "O doghter, which that art *my* laste wo, / And in *my* lyf *my* last joye also" (221–22; emphasis mine). As her father's property, she is subject to his decision: "Take thou thy deeth, for this is my sentence" (224). And Virginia is clearly her father's daughter, not only in that she is dominated by him but also in that she speaks the virgin's language of submissiveness and self-denial: "Blissed be God that I shal dye a mayde! / Yif me my deeth, er that I have a shame; / Dooth with youre child youre wyl, a Goddes name!" (VI.248–50). Her expressed wish to preclude shame is betrayed by the Physician's earlier observation that Virginia embodies the obligatory degree of shame befitting a woman, and her words thus echo her father's fanatical obsession with his own sense of entitlement.

Virginia stands as a token of the power struggle between her father and his political superior—and therefore the token is easily sacrificed, Virginia erased, to secure the father's victory. The remarkable valorizing of virginity in this tale, then, speaks to the dehumanizing impact of a masculine ideal. In her recent discussion of the *Physician's Tale*, Linda Lomperis argues, "[T]he effort on the part of the Physician seems to be one of bridling, containing, or shall we say, policing the physical aspects of the maid through a set of rhetorical strategies designed to focus attention instead either on sexual abstention or on metaphysical virtues, that is, on matters that actively point away from bodily activities. . . . On the whole, however, the tale actually records the Physician's failure to contain and control the body, the sexual."[23] But while the tale retains the body in the figure of the "body politic of late fourteenth century England,"[24] the text's literal female body—Virginia—is severed, destroyed. Thus within the tale virginity functions as a sign of controlled feminine sexuality and hence of masculine dominance and feminine submissiveness, to the point where the feminine ceases to exist in the flesh, remaining only as a remembrance of the politics of patriarchal domination as inflicted on the body of Woman.

As noted above, the Christian concern with virginity is played out in this tale as a trope of masculine language. Virginity is a masculine concept of womanhood, an artificial and unwarrantedly praised notion of what a woman might be; the Christian impulse to valorize virginity ostensibly represents a praising of Woman but in actuality represents a troubling misogyny: "virginity" valorizes the feminine by denying what makes the feminine feminine: sexuality. The masculine decorum appropropriates the feminine and subverts it; the woman who embraces virginity in effect ceases to be a woman and instead impersonates a masculine ideal. Accordingly, a woman who is not a virgin represents the threatening possibility of a feminine sexuality not wholly subject to masculine control, and hence the virgin is a patriarchal fantasy constructed in opposition to a feminine reality.

The virginity trope of masculine domination is underscored by the commentary supplied by the Physician-narrator and by the response of a member of his immediate audience, the Host. The Physician devotes more of his tale's space to his own exhortation than to the narrative movement itself; only a few dozen lines of the tale are allocated to the brief conversation between father and daughter and the subsequent killing of Virginia by Virginius, despite the Physician's insistence that it is Virginia's story: "This mayde, of which I wol this tale expresse" (VI.105).[25] Indeed an analogy may be drawn between father and daughter, narrator and text; each pairing illustrates apoplectic domination, an appropriation that kills its own subject through the very act of asserting possession. Virginia is no more important as a mimetic representation of a living being to the teller of her story than she is to Virginius within the tale; she is but a token or symbol of a privileged masculine ideal for which responsibility is deferred. The Physician attributes to Nature his own description of Virginia, as if he were unwilling to accept responsibility for the praise:

> As though [Nature] wolde seyn, "Lo! I Nature,
> Thus kan I forme and peynte a creature,
> Whan that me list; who kan me countrefete?
> Pigmalion noght, though he ay forge and bete,
> Or grave, or peynte . . . ."
> Thus semeth me that Nature wolde seye.   VI.11–15, 29

Ironically, the Physician does in fact "countrefete" the perfect "creature," constructing in his narrative the masculine-feminine ideal of virgin and attributing to his own creature those characteristics he wishes her to embody. Hence the Physician's absurd *moralitas*—"Heer may men seen how synne hath his merite" (276)—seems disconnected from the events of the narrative that are supposed to have occasioned it.[26] The point of the tale seems to be a reaffirmation of masculine constraining of the female body, and thus the *moralitas* seems remote and inappropriate even within the gendered dynamics of this sexualized patriarchal decorum.

Likewise the Host's outrageous blame-the-victim interpretation demonstrates the insidious misogyny inhering even in patriarchal codes of pathos: "Algate this sely mayde is slayn, allas! / Allas, to deere boughte she beautee! / . . . / Hire beauty was hire deth, I dar wel sayn. / Allas, so pitously as she was slayn!" (VI.292–98). The Host's assertion that Virginia's death is the price she has paid to purchase beauty underscores the misogyny that informs patriarchal notions of feminine desirability and behavior. The Host, like the Physician, completely sets aside the issue of Virginius's crime. Although the foremost compendium of canon law, Gratian's *Concordia* or *Decretum*, permitted the suicide of virgins to avoid defilement, homicide is not sanctioned, and therefore Virginius's murdering of his daughter should hardly be excused by the Physician's pilgrim audience.[27] Yet it is Virginia's attractiveness—not Appius's lust, not Virginius's selfishness—that the tale posits as the root cause of her death. Blaming a woman for her being involuntarily the object of another's lust was sanctioned by Jerome and other patristic misogynists,[28] and it illustrates an astounding dismissal of women as having any personal identity or right of existence of their own. The Host's words call attention to the glaring misogyny of the tale and reiterate as well that the tale is flawed as an exemplum and is thus an inferior demonstration of didactic poetry.

But the aesthetic and artistic weaknesses of the *Physician's Tale* work in connection with the virginity theme to articulate a metatexual level of gendered poetics: the tale is itself a "virgin" text, representing wasted potential and artificial constraints. In this respect, the tale parallels its own poetics of virginity and limitation, for the tale demonstrates the impact of excessive limitation on its manipulative suppression of the feminine flesh and on the polysemy of language and text. In straining to impose patriarchal limitations, the Physician strips the text of its fecundity and depth. But the *Tale* succeeds because of this failure: Chaucer demonstrates through the Physician's narrative that adherence to rigid masculine codes results not in a valorizing of those codes but instead in a crippling of the text by its own limitations. Hence the masculine-feminine ideal of virginity is exposed as both a misogynistic denial of Woman and a reflexive poetics of self-limitation.

This masculine-"feminine" concept of virginity informs the *Second Nun's Tale* as well, and in part to a similar, though ambivalent, end. The *Second Nun's Tale*, Chaucer's version of a well-known hagiography, is itself an unremarkable and familiar "virgin" text;[29] it too trumpets the virtues of virginity in a formulaic presentation that reflexively underscores its limitations. Like the legends in the *Legend of Good Women*, the *Second Nun's Tale* lacks individuality; it is largely a replication of a masculine ideal, with a strong sense of (non)sexual valorization. But the *Second Nun's Tale* is more complicated owing to its teller's Prologue and to the ambivalence inhering in the narrative's articulation of appropriation dynamics; it has as well a dimension of wit difficult to locate in the more extreme hagiographic-mode stories such as that of Virginia.

As a text obsessed with virginity, the Second Nun's narrative is obviously informed by Jerome's copious writings on the subject. Indeed, an instance of self-identity in the Prologue, which many readers dismiss as a certain location of intended revision, alludes to one of Jerome's more unusual tenets in relation to gender identity: "And though that I, unworthy sone of Eve, / Be synful, yet accepte my bileve" (VIII.62–63).[30] Jerome's assertion that the ideal woman of Christ is rewarded by having her name changed from "woman" to "man" is demonstrated here in the Nun's invocation to the Virgin Mary;[31] she acknowledges her connection to Eve but refers to herself not as a daughter of Eve—that is to say a woman—but as a son. Her virginity entitles her to an honorific masculine identity; she remains "of Eve," and therefore liable for Eve's sin, but her sacrifice of her female body and its concomitant sexuality purchases the masculine name. Hence the Nun's elaborate pseudo-etymologizing of the name "Cecilie" with an emphasis on whiteness and purity: the symbolic interpretation of the name affords public appreciation of a private sacrifice. (Of course the Second Nun's praising of Mary, like that of most medieval Christians, overlooks the irony that Mary's hallowed status is owing to her being the virgin *mother*—her virginity is fetishized by her admirers, but it is her maternal accomplishment that secures her place in the Church.)

Within the *Tale*, the obsession with virginity demonstrated by Cecilia speaks as well to the text's own participation in a code of masculine decorum. Cecilia's desire to remain chaste is uncompromising: "She nevere cessed, as I writen fynde, / Of hir preyere and God to love and drede, / Bisekynge hym to kepe hir maydenhede" (VIII.124–26). Cecilia herself articulates the desire: "O Lord, my soule and eek my body gye / Unwemmed, lest that I confounded be" (136–37). The idea of virginity clearly governs Cecilia's masculine-"feminine" behavior, and indeed virginity is for Cecilia—as for Jerome, John Chrysostom, Ambrose, and others—fetishized. All aspects of Christian faith seem to converge in this patriarchal concept of the nonsexual—and hence valorized—woman eagerly embraced by Cecilia as her means of occupying as privileged a position that a Christian nonmale might attain.

There is a clear sense that Cecilia, like Paul, Jerome, and other patristic misogynists, rejects the female body, her own flesh, and punishes herself for being a woman. Indeed, on her wedding day, "Under hir robe of gold, that sat ful faire, / Hadde next hire flessh yclad hire in an haire" (132–33). This remarkable self-torment and rejection of the flesh underscores her desired participation in a patriarchal decorum: Cecilia serves God and patriarchy by denying her femininity through a fanatical devotion to virginity and a punishing of the female flesh. One could of course situate Cecilia's behavior in a context of Christian asceticism and its sometimes extreme rejection of the body and the flesh, perhaps most memorably articulated in Innocent's *De miseria:*

> Conceptus est enim homo de sanguine per ardorem libidinis putrefacto; cuius tandem cadaveri quasi funebres vermes assistent. Vivus, gignit pediculos et lubricos; mortuus, generabit vermes et muscas. Vivit, producit stercus et vomitem; mortuus, producit putredinem et fetorum.   3.1

> [For one is conceived of blood made putrid through the ardor of lust; in the end, like mourners, worms stand by one's body. Alive, one brings forth lice and internal worms; dead, one begets vermin and flies. Alive, one produces dung and vomit; dead, one produces putridness and fetidness.]

But Cecilia not only torments her physical body—she does so on her wedding day, an occasion that obviously foregrounds her sexual status as a woman. By denying her sexuality, Cecilia achieves Paul's desired androgynous state: "non est masculus neque femina" (Gal 3.28). The virgin Cecilia is, to an extent, neither masculine nor feminine, impersonating a masculine ideal by denying her sexual identity.[32] And the typed characters in the tale are shown to respond appropriately: the "good" valorize Cecilia's devotion and the "bad" reject her piety.

Appropriately, the tale is told by the Second Nun, a character as generic and nondescript as the topos she articulates. As Gail Berkeley Sherman observes, "The Second Nun and the Nun's Priest are the only pilgrim storytellers represented anonymously, facelessly, and as a function of another in the General Prologue; the nun is one of the few pilgrim narrators whose prologue represents no interaction with the pilgrim audience. She is in truth the 'Second Nonne,' the 'other no one,' the anonymous vehicle for, and creation of, the language attributed to her."[33] A virgin herself owing to professional occupation, the Nun would logically be concerned with virginity and its reception and would logically valorize its desexualizing impact on women seeking to participate in masculine decorum. Despite feminist readings of Cecilia and the Second Nun that find an empowerment in sexual renunciation—for instance, Luecke's argument that "[b]oth utilize virginity . . . as the only means available to them to effect freedom of action and both scorn as well as exploit the power of the establishment to make martyrs of them"[34]—generic hagiographical praise both inscribes and limits the virgin text. Asceticism may be a choice, but if chosen to suit patriarchal decorum, then the feminine is effectively erased, subsumed by a masculine code that insists on sexual renunciation as the requisite price of admission. In this respect, the tale's articulation of a poetics of "wreched engendrynge" corresponds to the powerfully masculine incorporation of doctrine in a narrative largely void of true feminine instrumentality.

3

The *Man of Law's Tale* and the *Clerk's Tale* are more sophisticated and more complex treatments of gendered poetics than the "virgin" texts of the Physician and Second Nun. Both use the other, more complicated masculine-"feminine" concept—the wife—to illustrate decorums of imposition and control. These narratives demonstrate not the excesses of virgin constraints but the more subtle workings of masculine dominance and feminine submission within the parameters of more typical social and sexual behavior. The Man of Law's Custance and the Clerk's Griselda embody a misogynistic ideal that is both ambiguous and ambivalent, ultimately privileging a masculine hermeneutic that nonetheless lays the groundwork for ideological challenge.

The *Clerk's Tale* of patient Griselda, probably the best-known medieval example of feminine submissiveness, supplies a curiously ambiguous depiction of the "good" wife.[35] Griselda, like Virginia, is valued for her womanly virtue with an emphasis on her feminine attributes: "vertuous beautee" (IV.211); "With everich obeisaunce and diligence" (230); "Commendynge in his herte hir wommanhede" (239). And yet she is, for most of the tale, not a virgin but a wife, though obviously constructed in terms of a masculine ideal. Griselda, like the effeminate Clerk who tells her story, is idealized as a passive, gentle, and seemingly unthreatening presence.[36] Griselda's presence, in fact, is so passive that she represents utter submissiveness: silence. For while Griselda is a wife, and therefore not overtly connected to the ideal of virgin silence, as a wife she is so contrived, so obviously constructed as a textual embodiment of masculine ideals—not unlike those espoused by adherents to similarly masculine codes of Mariolatry[37]—that she participates in a (non)sexual decorum of feminine closure. And unlike the more famous Wife of the *Canterbury Tales*, Griselda embodies a masculine marital ideal that includes motherhood. Griselda is depicted as practicing what Dame Alisoun only preaches, using her "instrument" not as a tool of emotional and financial manipulation but as the necessary means by which her conventional marital duties, including conception and childbirth, are to be fulfilled. And, as we shall see, Griselda's response to her requisite participation constitutes a subtext of misogamous rhetoric.

Certainly misogamous propaganda was widespread during Chaucer's day, serving two distinct purposes: to encourage women to eschew marriage and family in favor of devotional virginity and to provide men with a discourse that could help ensure the perpetuation of patriarchal social codes. Not content merely to valorize virginity for its own sake and to appeal to women through treatises on its merits, theologians sought compliance through scare tactics as well, using distorted, graphic descriptions of sexual obligations and pregnancy as rhetorical devices.[38] One of the better-known treatises, the anonymous thirteenth-century *Hali Meidenhad*, underscores the submissiveness demanded of wives in fulfilling these duties:

[H]eo schal his wil, muchel hire unwil, with muche weane ofte. alle his fulitohchipef & his unhende gomenes—ne beon ha neauer swa with fulthe bifunden, nomeliche i bedde—ha schal, wulle ha, nulle ha, tholien ham alle. Crist schilde euch meiden to freinin other to wilnin forte witen hwucche ha beon!³⁹

[She is obliged to his will, much against her own will, though she love him never so well, with much misery often. All his lasciviousness and his ungracious merriments—be they never so with filth found, especially in bed—she is obliged, willy nilly, to suffer them all. May Christ shield each maiden from inquiring or from wishing to know what they may be!]

Such descriptions were not unknown to Chaucer. Consider, for instance, the description of May and January's wedding night in the *Merchant's Tale*, which, despite its comical elements, is perhaps the most appalling and repulsive consummation scene in Middle English poetry; not only is May subjected to January's amorous behavior, but, as the Merchant tells us, "[t]hus laboureth he til that day gan dawe" (1842)—it is interminable. And afterward, as he sings, "The slakke skyn aboute his nekke shaketh" (1849), which perhaps underscores the depiction of desire in this episode as being wholly one-sided (though the Merchant coyly insists, "But God woot what that May thoughte in hir herte. . . . She preyseth nat his pleyyng worth a bene" [1851–54]). The *Meidenhad* author's text, like the *Merchant's Tale*, speaks to the powerlessness of the wife in complying with social and sexual expectations and obligations: unappealing as the husbands' demands might be, the wives are obliged to participate. Further, his description of pregnancy, specifically its effect on the woman's body, underscores the powerlessness of the pregnant woman with respect to her own body—it becomes the source of her torment:

Ga we nu forthre, & loki we hwuch wunne arifeth threfter i burtherne of bearne, hwen thet streon in the awakeneth & waxeth. & hu monie earmden anan awakeneth therwith, the wurched the wa inoh, fehted o thi seolue flesch, & weorrith with feole weanen o thin ahne cunde. thi rudie neb schal leanin, ant ase gres grenin. thine ehnen schule doskin, & underneothe wonnin; & of thi breines turnunge thin heaued aken sare. Inwith i thi wombe, swelin thi butte, the bereth the forth as a weaterbulge.⁴⁰

[Let us continue further. Look we at what joy arises afterward in the bearing of children when the seed in you awakens and grows. How many miseries anon awaken therewith that cause you woe enough, contend with your own flesh, and war with many tribulations on your own kind (kynde). Your radiant face shall grow lean and as grass is green. Your eyes will cloud and underneath darken, and of your brains turning your head will ache sorely; within your belly will swell the womb, that bulges out like a water bag.]

I interpose these passages here to contextualize my reading of the *Clerk's Tale*: the Clerk's narrative of Griselda's marital experience is as extreme, though more subtly and ironically so. Marriage and motherhood constitute a trope of powerlessness desired by both husband and wife: Walter subordinates Griselda, who willingly accedes to maintain her status as his wife, thoroughly. The text offers a critique of patriarchal codes of feminine behavior through its images of submission; suffering as a wife and as a mother is cast not in the graphic manner of *Hali Meidenhad* or the *Merchant's Tale* but more figuratively so, in connection with orthodox gender decorum and the responses it invites. Griselda is presented as an ideal that ultimately undermines its own valorized status.

We might additionally consider Julia Kristeva's theorizing of motherhood in relation to Griselda's role as mother. Arguing that Western culture has historically and oppressively reduced Woman to her role in reproduction, Kristeva suggests in *Stabat Mater* that new representations of maternity are needed to avoid the detrimental social impact of such reductivism.[41] She argues that the Christian maternal image of the Virgin fails to give meaning to motherhood because it elides those aspects of maternity that patriarchal culture finds unsettling.[42] Hence Mariolatry—the cult of the Virgin—valorizes the usurpation of Woman's contribution by a patriarchal hegemony; the Virgin's impregnation by the Word of the Father offers a certainty of paternity otherwise unavailable, and the virgin mother's body is wholly subjected to paternal control even after conception, gestation, and delivery have been successfully performed.

The *Clerk's Tale*'s incorporation of the motherhood trope suggests that only Griselda's tears mark her as a true mother. With regard to the Virgin's corporeal representation, including her tears, Kristeva further notes, "We are entitled only to the ear of the virginal body, the tears, and the breast. . . . And yet Marian pain is in no way connected with tragic outburst; joy and even a kind of triumph follow upon tears, as if the conviction that death does not exist were an irrational but unshakable maternal certainty, on which the principle of resurrection had to rest."[43] Griselda is described as acting "Ful lyk a mooder" (IV.1084) only when she sheds tears. These tears, like those of the *Mater dolorosa,* constitute the mother's responding to evidence of restoration based on a maternal loss. To be a mother, the narrative reiterates, is to suffer, for children beget tears.

Griselda is depicted as an ideal wife/mother. She bears the desired heirs for their father and willfully forfeits her rights and privileges germane to their upbringing: "And thus she seyde in hire benigne voys, / 'Fareweel my child! I shal thee nevere see'" (IV.554–56). Further, Griselda echoes the antimaternal and misogamous propaganda in her assertion that the children being taken away from her is welcome, insisting, like the *Hali Meidenhad* author, that pregnancy leads only to pain and obligation—the true "wo" of marriage: "I have noght had no part of children tweyne / But first siknesse, and after, wo and peyne" (645–51). Her relinquishing the children is problematic to many modern readers, who wonder at the absence of maternal commitment and the complete lack of remorse or blame.[44] Indeed, Griselda actually praises "benyngne"[45] Walter for not having the children killed and suggests that the children do likewise: "O tendre, o deere, o yonge children myne!...God of his mercy / And youre benyngne fader tendrely / Hath doon yow kept" (1093, 1906–8). In Griselda's largely dispassionate relinquishing of the children, we see a mother offering up her children in order that she might retain her own status as wife, a startlingly self-interested strategy depicted as a gesture of valorized submissiveness. So extensive is the narrative's insistence on her willingness to please Walter that the text reads almost as a parody of the "good wife" genre: how can Griselda be "good" when she serves so selfish and cruel a master? Griselda's obedience serves only Walter and, to the extent that she desires to please her husband/King, herself. (Thus the children are eliminated from the scene until the daughter is reintroduced as a rival for Walter's hand.)[46]

For all her quasi-valorized feminine attributes, however, Griselda is described foremost in relation to her inhuman patience, and as "stedfast," a decidedly unfeminine trait. Griselda is an ideal woman in part because she is an unwomanly woman—that is, she exemplifies a masculine ideal that contradicts misogynisic stereotypes of the mutable, "slydyng," and unstable feminine.[47] Her firm commitment to suffering and her unwavering patience finally convince Walter that she is a worthy woman; paradoxically, those traits typically valorized as masculine ultimately define her femininity. But Griselda displays other unwomanly/manly behaviors—her leadership abilities, her verbal efficacy when initially permitted to speak[48]—that problematize her qualifications as wife from Walter's perspective. Hence, as Elaine Hansen argues, "To prove her 'wommanhede,' Griselda must suffer and submit; the more obviously unsuitable part of her virtue—her allegedly inherent but nevertheless unnatural manliness and power—must be punished and contained."[49]

Griselda is indeed ill-treated by Walter, but she is a problematic victim. Not only does she invite domination by choosing to promise complete obedience—"And heere I swere that nevere willyngly, / In werk ne thoght, I nyl you disobeye" (IV.362–63)—but she is passively aggressive in her behavior; she is, as Robert Longsworth has remarked, relentlessly submissive.[50] As Harriet Hawkins has demonstrated, "Chaucer makes it glaringly evident that Griselda's suffering resulted from her having been born into social and sexual categories that made her vulnerable to tyranny, and from a tyrant's ruthless exploitation of her vulnerability."[51] However, Griselda is paradoxically proud of her behavior, as is suggested by Griselda's insistence that no new wife could withstand Walter's tortures as has she: "She koude nat adversitee endure / As koude a povre fostred creature" (IV.1042–43). Arguably Griselda exploits those same categories, albeit to a submissive end; she manipulates by acquiescing, thereby illustrating the antifeminist topos of the duplicitous woman even as she suggests an attempt at personal empowerment in the face of oppression.

And yet the tale posits her behavior as an unattainable ideal, not as an exemplum for wives to follow—which, as the Clerk notes, would be a futile effort—but as a reminder that every person should suffer steadfastly when confronted by *miseria:*

> This storie is seyd nat for that wyves sholde
> Folwen Griselde as in humylitee,
> For it were inportable, though they wolde,
> But for that every wight in his degree,
> Sholde be constant in adversitee
> As was Griselde.   IV.1142–47

If we set aside the allegorical presence here that has received much attention—that of the soul's submissiveness to God[52]—we might interpret instead the tale's adamant insistence that "every wight . . . be constant" to mean that everyone be masculine, that one uphold patriarchal codes of decorum. This would mean privileging the kind of patriarchal ideology demonstrated in the tales of the Physician and the Second Nun. Hence, in terms of poetic process, poetry would stop, constrained by excessive limitation, which in seeking to deny the feminine denies the plurality or polysemy of improper, figurative signification. But the text offers no definitive reading; it insists on debate and supplies ample evidence for many readings. In this respect, I would argue, the *Clerk's Tale* posits itself as an ambivalently feminine text: mutable, polysemous, and yet framed by a masculine hermeneutic. Inasmuch as the Clerk's narrative resists closure, it nonetheless participates in a well-defined gendered decorum of limitation.

The *Man of Law's Tale* similarly evinces the feminine characteristics of errancy and resistance to closure. The Man of Law's Custance is likewise depicted as relentless in her patient suffering (though apparently less selfish in her motives) and she is depicted, like Griselda, as virgin, then wife, then mother. Sheila Delany has noted, "For most readers Constance is among the least attractive of Chaucer's women, sharing with patient Griselda (*The Clerk's Tale*) the repulsive masochistic qualities of extreme humility and silent endurance," though in a less formulaic presentation that, while obviously contrived and indeed fantastic, more actively engages the fate of Woman in literary activity.[53] Indeed, when first directed to marry the Sultan, Custance articulates her situation in a generalized sense of what women are and can expect:

> But Crist, that starf for our redempcioun
> So yeve me grace his heestes to fulfille!
> I, wrecche womman, no fors though I spille!
> Wommen are born to thraldom and penance,
> And to been under mannes governance.   II.283–87

Hope Weissman argues, "Constance's grandiose appropriation of patriarchal cliches concerning the female nature . . . succeeds in reducing her saintly servitude to mere biological and social necessity," which "proves to be a literalization, and a *reductio ad absurdum,* of Trivet's hagiographical idealization of Christian patience."[54] But what does this "appropriation" signify? Custance articulates a patriarchal reality that, even if clichéd, governs the narrative; her identification is apt but in no way empowers her, nor does it become her own(ed).

Custance's lament constitutes a remarkably reflexive articulation of Chaucer's poetics of en/gendering because it accurately locates misery and relativity within the parameters of gendered decorum. Custance identifies herself as "wrecce woman," owing in part to her lack of decision-making power and in part to her appreciation of Woman's subordinate status apropos social institutions of gender and decorum (in the immediate context, marriage). Moreover, she asserts that women are born "to been under mannes governance," an elucidating articulation of binary relativity. Just as women are under "mannes governance," so, too, the feminine is limited by masculine parameters, by masculine codes of behavior and status. She recognizes that the feminine flesh is subject to masculine governance and that the story of woman's suffering is told through the thraldom of the body and the penance of the soul. Hence Custance's observations underscore the gendered poetics operating throughout the Man of Law's narrative: the feminine sense of language is bound both to and by the masculine, and gendered decorum overtly privileges a heterosexual orthodoxy of active masculine domination and passive feminine compliance.

But the Man of Law's narrative demonstrates as well that it is not without ambivalence and ambiguity that this gendered decorum obtains. Gendered ideologies seem to contradict themselves throughout, and the only truism in the text is that the feminine be subject to masculine manipulation or control;[55] indeed, Custance is a narrative construct of the masculine Man of Law, himself the narrative construct of a poet operating largely within the parameters of a patriarchal orthodoxy.[56] But Custance herself is a polysemous text, resisting closure and troubling any attempt to fix her within orthodox parameters; as Juliette Dor remarks, "Chaucer can present Constance as the traditional stock figure of the lives of saints without coming to the monological conclusion that that is all she is."[57] She initially represents the virtues of virginity, with that nonwoman, nonsexual status approved by patriarchal codes, and yet throughout the text she suggests a sexuality not only restricted but dangerous. The deaths that occur throughout—particularly those of the Sultan, the would-be shipboard rapist, and, indirectly, Alla—may be attributed to Custance's capacity to arouse, as perceived by others.[58]

Moreover, the contradictory parameters of patriarchal orthodoxy are manifest in Custance as she embodies the paradox of holy wives, who must set aside their status as "hooly thynges" in order to take up the sexual role insisted on by the same theology that, ironically enough, endorses such treatises as *Hali Meidenhad*:

They goon to bedde, as it was skile and right;
For thogh that wyves be ful hooly thynges,
They moste take in pacience at nyght
Swiche manere necessaries as been plesynges,

> To folk that han ywedded hem with rynges,
> And leye a lite hir hoolynesse aside,
> As for the tyme—it may no bet bitide.   II.708–14

If wives are holy women, then they are necessarily nonsexual. And yet wives are, by definition, sexually bound to their spouses. Thus, Carolyn Dinshaw notes in her analysis of Custance, "Wives must stop being wives, as it were, if they want to be wives. The paradox of this wedding night is left intact and reveals a crucial patriarchal formation of woman. 'Hoolynesse' cannot encompass female sexual behavior; what is revealed when wives lay their defining holiness aside is an effect of masculine desire."[59] Sexually and socially, Custance, like her Middle English sisters, is good because she suffers and suffers because she is good; within the generic code of hagiographic praise, goodness is rewarded with pious pain. Within the parameters of patriarchy, suggests the Man of Law, men simultaneously desire two conflicting ideals: the nonsexual holy woman, who is to be valorized and fetishized, and the object of masculine desire, who is to be desired with a cautious disdain. Hence, too, at the level of narrative and text, gendered decorums exhibit tension between relative positions of hermeneutic process, which, like their thematic counterparts, cannot easily be reconciled.

That Chaucer depicts feminine sexualized suffering does not mean of course that he endorses it, nor does it suggest that he necessarily evinces frustration regarding the status of women in society. What the treatment of women in Chaucer's work does suggest, however, is that Chaucer is fully aware of gender difference and that gender is theorized as part of Chaucer's own reflexive poetics. The process of textual "makyng," whatever the poet's motive, cannot help but situate itself in relation to the nuanced language of gender decorum and its polemical antecedents. Thus the illusion of solidarity between the poet and his women dissolves into a more complex and unstable set of uneasily coexisting ideological formulations. Chaucer's texts demonstrate an acute awareness of the subordination and asymmetricality inhering in gendered decorum, and through representations of female characters shown to participate in the structures of oppression and limitation Chaucer exposes the unresolved problematic of contingency; through the narrative operations of such characters as Virginia, Cecilia, Griselda, and Custance, we see the poet coming to terms with the anxious imbalance of gender and its implications for textual construction.

Each of these submissive women is praised for acquiescing to codes imposed by a society desiring to pursue the limits of control, and hence these texts say far more about masculine designs than about the motivation of women who suffer for their sex. Indeed, the *Legend of Good Women* and the *Canterbury Tales'* demonstrations of *pitee* constitute a sad commentary on institutionalized misogyny: the represented women are victims of their literary and cultural environments. Despite the illusion of a feminine presence and feminine voice in the various characterizations, these women speak not in their own voices but in—and, more important, of—the dominant voice of patriarchal culture. A reader concerned by the sexualized treatment of cruelty and suffering in these texts can hardly be moved by the "goode"-ness of these women but, rather, should be troubled by the glorification of feminine submissiveness and victimization and by the cultural and social implications inhering in constructions germane to "wreched engendrynge." The texts may assert an orthodoxy of affected valorization, but beneath a benignant surface of respect and adoration lies an abyss of requisite sorrow and pain.

※ *Chapter Four*

Marks of Womanhood in the Ballades

Women characters, we have seen, give the illusion of a feminine presence and voice. This is not to say, of course, that the texts they inhabit do not exhibit a feminine dimension but rather that the characters themselves are hardly the autonomous, self-determined originators of their own representation. In *Chaucer and the Fictions of Gender*, Elaine Tuttle Hansen observes that "Woman, in the form of the female character, is brought to represented life precisely in order to be killed off, silenced, displaced, ignored, again and again."[1] Female characters vivify cultural and epistemological conceptions of gender within the frame of the fiction and underscore various social and sexual implications of gender associations and their corresponding epistemological foundations. Accordingly, as we have seen, the Wife of Bath, Griselda, Cecilia, Criseyde, and other such female characterizations inhabiting Chaucer's major texts supply a productive basis for interpreting Chaucer's semantics of gender appropriation. But what happens, we might ask, when female characters are absent? Representations of gender are obviously not limited to character alone; Woman may be presented indirectly—addressed though unanswering, described but without voice, suggested by metaphoric allusions to gender-specific categories. Let us therefore consider as well those narrative moments that articulate gender categories in the absence of a fictive feminine presence, where marks of womanhood inscribe the text's gendered poetics as signifiers of an indirect presence, and where categories of gender operate as part of the narrator's—and ultimately the poet's—rhetorical line.

Chaucer's shorter poems are quite instructive in establishing and elucidating the poet's treatment of gender categories and representational strategies in relation to narrative reflexivity. The *balades* in particular provide insightful instances when feminine representations are addressed by a narrative voice that excludes women, even as it is through this voice that they are defined.[2] Individually, the ballades are brief observations or meditations, sometimes humorous, of a commonplace theme or topic, articulated by a narrator whose own persona constitutes the text's single fictive voice, the only "character," as it were. Each takes as its subject some cultural perception of gender construction and each sketches out a concern with the traditions or, less frequently, the countertraditions apropos of these decorums. Together, the ballades may be read as a critique of conventional gender hermeneutics and, consequently, as a commentary on Chaucer's own poetic enterprise. In this chapter I begin by surveying the individual ballades' evocations of Woman in conjunction with various topoi of gender construction and representation, in order to delineate the ballades' individual angles and recurring manifestations; I shall then consider the theoretical implications of these models and their complex interrelationships of gender and power, narrator and poet.

1

A brief look at current psychoanalytic lines of thought and their philosophical antecedents can frame our understanding of the association of feminine and absence germane to Chaucer's ballades. As psychoanalytic and deconstructionist theories have made evident, patriarchal culture operates in connection with what Derrida labels "phallogocentric" language, which combines the privileged "centrist" status of the phallus and the Logos.[3] The phallus—a symbol of masculine presence—dominates the power structures of gender and language, in contrast to the fear-inducing absence symbolized by feminine "lack" (as Luce Irigaray notes in her critique of Lacanian psychoanalytic theory, Western discourses of desire dictate that Woman's "sexual organ represents *the horror of nothing to see*")[4]. Derrida has critiqued and rejected binary logic because of its presupposition of closure, but his somewhat uncritical insistence on the duality of presence and absence in the "free play" of the signifier obviously and ironically points to the essence of *différance*.[5] Absence would therefore seem an omnipresent condition of language and textuality, and it is manifest in narrative articulations of fear and desire—the former corresponding to loss, and the latter, nostalgia.

If Lacan's principles of psychoanalytic theory are valid, then he has developed a useful model of the masculine psyche and a critical methodology with a utility and practicability valid to the extent that it is governed by its masculine identity (it is, however, utopian in its implicit bias toward white, bourgeois, two-parent households). But what of the feminine—is there a valid feminine model to be located in Lacan's own phallocentric discourse? For Freud and Lacan are but recent articulators of a concept with a tradition dating beyond the pre-Socratics: that of woman as a defective man, as lacking what makes a man. Aristotle's (in)famous dictum in the *De generatione anamalium*, for example, clearly locates feminine inferiority in lack: "Just as it sometimes happens that deformed offspring are produced by deformed parents, and sometimes not, so the offspring produced by a female are sometimes female, sometimes not, but male. The reason is that the female is as it were a deformed male. . . . [A]nd we should look upon the female state as being as it were a deformity, though one which occurs in the ordinary course of nature."[6] Similarly the influential Greek physician Galen associates the feminine with mutilation, a grotesque manifestation of lack that suggests castration, his *De usu partium*: "[S]o too the woman is less perfect than the man with respect to the generative parts. . . . for there needs must be a female. Indeed you ought not to think that our Creator would purposely make half the whole race imperfect and, as it were, mutilated, unless there was to be some great advantage in such a mutilation."[7] So Lacan reiterates in his *Seminaire III*, echoing Freud's unquestioned assumption of masculine superiority: "The feminine genitals have a character of absence, of emptiness, or of hole which causes them to be found less desirable than the masculine genitals in the latter's provocative aspect, and causes an essential dissymmetry to appear."[8] Hence the crucial significance of "castration" in both Freud's and Lacan's philosophies: castration represents the ultimate, yet originary, horror, that of the masculine forfeiting its phallic primacy and becoming what it most fears and detests, a nonman (woman).[9] Symbolically located in the language of patriarchy, castration anxiety reifies masculine primacy by underscoring phallic power and, more insidiously, feminine inferiority. Freud's obsession with castration anxiety and Lacan's restatement of the fear as metaphoric reality not only perpetuate the ancient equating of feminine and absence but also attempt to legitimize the masculine fear of loss that fuels phallocentric dominance.

What stands out in Freud's and Lacan's revisionist philosophies is their theorizing of feminine desire from this phallocentric perspective. Both

Freud and Lacan theorize feminine sexuality and feminine desire as part of their psychoanalytic methodologies, but problematically so, particularly as they endorse ways of countering the perceived deficiency of women (e.g., motherhood, baby-as-substitute). Even Lacan, in whom some feminists find an ally,[10] seems more to reinforce conventional stereotypes than to challenge them, dressing them up in the language of his new discourse. Both men purport to speak for women, to articulate women's experiences and desires, though from a position of superior authority, and both succeed in absenting women from discourses of the psyche. Thus, I would argue, Freud and Lacan's theories frequently come across either as patronizing in their pseudovalorization—such as in Lacan's challenge to locate *jouissance* "beyond the phallus"[11]—or as overtly misogynistic—as in Freud's insistence that women merely fantasized incestuous seductions when they were children and were never really abused.[12] Such contemporary positions, we shall see, are not unlike those occupied by the narrator of the ballades.

Gender figures prominently in the ballades, but the vehicle by which it operates is not presence but absence, an association conceived through epistemological binarity and reified in its cultural manifestations. Again the positive/negative valuation of binarism governs the association, and the psychosexual dimension of the associations, rooted metynonimically in the anatomy of sexual difference, provides a mechanism for articulating the implications and consequences of the "missing" women. Medieval theology accepts Paul's assertion that "scientes quoniam dum sumus in corpore, peregrinamur a Domino" [while we are in the body we are absent from the Lord],[13] and thus the status of corporeality—the flesh—that precludes spiritual achievement implicates Woman and motivates her being absented from the masculine text. The incomplete dialogue that constitutes each text—that is, the masculine monologue that creates an illusion of the absent and therefore wholly submissive and contingent "other"— foregrounds the conventional love/hate literary and cultural relationships of masculine and feminine: the narrator is the sole voice, and whether he overtly denigrates women through commonplace barbs and insults or praises them with insidiously antifeminist *fin' amors* clichés, he speaks the language of patriarchal literary activity.

The ballade known as *Against Women Unconstant*, or *Newefangelnesse*,[14] overtly draws off antifeminist commonplaces in the narrator's complaint against an unnamed woman. It is a personalized complaint, ostensibly directed toward a single woman—"Madame"—and yet not personal; it is a series of familiar, stereotypical complaints, commonplaces of antifeminist grumbling:

> Madame, for your newefangelnesse
> Many a servaunt have ye put out of grace.
> I take my leve of your unstedfastnesse,
> For wel I wot, whyl ye have lyves space,
> Ye can not love ful half yeer in a place,
> To newe thing your lust is ay so kene.
> In stede of blew, thus may ye were al grene.   1–7

The poem describes the woman with conventional metaphors of fickleness and instability; she is compared to a mirror's superficiality, a weathercock's fluctuating in the wind.[15] These topoi of medieval poetry articulate antifeminist perceptions of feminine instability and mutability; here they are presented as if to a specific individual, though the cultural context of the topoi attaches them to a decorum that, by extension, blames Woman for the world's uncertainties.

The poem is also striking for its overtly satiric reference to the insidious antifeminist strategy of quasivalorization (e.g., Mariolatry, *fin' amors*), which points to the insincerity of men who purport to valorize women with excessive or unwarranted praise. Just as the idealized Rosemounde is "of al beaute shryne," the disparaged "Madame" is to be enshrined for her "brotelnesse."[16] Distorted valorization preserves and perpetuates an antifeminist topos:

> Ye might be shryned for your brotelnesse
> Bet than Dalyda, Creseyde or Candace,
> For ever in chaunging stant your sikernesse;
> That tache may no wight fro your herte arace.
> If ye lese oon, ye can wel tweyn purchace;
> Al light for somer (ye woot wel what I mene),
> In stede of blew, thus may ye were al grene.   15–21

That the unnamed woman might be "shryned for [her] brotelnesse" more so than the notorious women named directly is delightfully ironic—how might this unnamed woman therefore be known? This local irony underscores that which governs the poem, that it is more about the narrator than his anonymous, absent subject. It is a poem about his own perception of Woman and his attempts to shape her identity, and through the narrator's reification of conventional associations he shows himself to be situated squarely within the confines of a patriarchal decorum.

Additionally, the narrator's use of the word "newefangelnesse" in his denigration of conventional feminine "brotelnesse" is itself an ironic, reflexive occasion of "newefangelnesse." Having been coined by Chaucer himself, the word and its subsequent uses are examples not only of novelty but of "unstedfastnesse," of the unpredictability and newness enabled by the creation of words hitherto unknown. The narrator is therefore implicated through a literary enactment of an ideological convention of his own making—he participates in a feminine epistemology even as his text ostensibly denigrates its gendered implications. The narrator, like the poet, in effect feminizes himself through reflexive articulation that exposes its own underpinnings; language is not static and, as the "newefangelnesse" coinage demonstrates, poetic meaning is problematized yet made possible by "brotelnesse." In short, the narrator foregrounds his own contribution to the very mutability against which he ostensibly rails.

Chaucer returns to the theme of feminine mutability and its narrative implications throughout the ballades in conjunction with various decorums of gender representation. Feminine mutability as the origin of human misery, for instance, is taken up in three of the so-called "Boethian lyrics," where Boethian themes are expressed in a tone of Christian misogyny.[17] In these poems the Christian attribution of Man's Fall to Woman coincides thematically with the Boethian treatment of the myth of the Golden Age (*prior aetas*),[18] and together the conflated representations produce a commonplace theme of antifeminist lamentation: Man laments the loss of his Edenish age and implicates Woman in the loss. This conflation, as illustrated throughout the *Former Age*,[19] for example, bears further examination:

A blisful lyf, a paisible and a swete,
Ledden the peples in the former age.
They helde hem payed of the fruites that they ete,
Which that the feldes yave hem by usage;
They ne were nat forpampred with outrage.   1–5

....

Allas, allas, now may men wepe and crye!
For in oure dayes nis but covetyse,
Doublenesse, and tresoun, and envye,
Poyson, manslawhtre, and mordre in sondry wyse.   60–63

The narrative's movement from unity to plurality—from "A blisful lyf," "a paisible," "*the* former age" to "oure dayes," "Doublenesse," "sondry wyse"—underscores its participation in the cultural misogyny that its imagery evokes. The complete and full dominance of unity that defines the former age gives way to the confusion and disorder of plurality; masculine stability is replaced—or at least compromised—by feminine instability. Further, images of life and growth give way to descriptions of death; spiritual bliss is compromised by flesh and death, and this fear of death, of the temporal flesh, manifests itself in a lament from which Woman is curiously absent: "[M]en wepe and crye" for the loss of their former age, and the nostalgic desire governing the poem therefore speaks of men's desire to recuperate Man's loss.

Perhaps the most striking lament in the poem, then, is the narrator's recurring nostalgia for an era in which Man's work is not necessary—fruits are provided "by usage"; corn grows "unsowe of mannes hond"; men need not acquaint themselves with "fyr" or "flint," "quern" or "mill"; cultivation is not necessary since the earth's bounty is supplied without human labor. Recalling the punishment set forth in Genesis—

> Quia audisti vocem uxoris tuae, et comedisti de ligno, ex quo praeceperam tibi ne comederes, maledicta terra in opere tuo: in laboribus comedes ex ea cunctis diebus vitae tuae.   Gn 3.17

> [Because you have listened to the voice of your wife, and have eaten of the tree from which I commanded that you not eat, cursed is the earth in your work: in labor you shall therefore eat all the days of your life.]

—we can trace the lament back to Eve's seducing of Adam, because of which (so the biblical account goes) Adam must work for a living. An underlying lament of the *Former Age,* then, is the forfeiture of Eden and the inception of labor as a consequence of Woman's temptation. Typical of antifeminist convention, Woman in the *Former Age* is held accountable for some undesirable reality and yet is absented from the text that articulates the blame.

The biblical origins of the *Former Age*'s lament further inform the text's treatment of gender in relation to epistemological associations. The first epistemological binarism known to humankind in the creation myth—good and evil—is overtly linked to sexual difference; woman succumbs to an anterior temptation, and Man to the temptation of Woman. Hence the immediate shame associated with the transgressions: "Et aperti sunt oculi amborum, cumque cognovissent se esse nudos, consuerunt folia ficus, et fecerunt sibi perizomata" (Gn 3.7) [And the eyes of both were opened, and when they perceived themselves to be naked they sewed fig leaves, and they made for themselves aprons]. The sexual body is immediately perceived as a source of shame, and the shame articulated as a consequence of knowing. To know good and evil, the story suggests, is to know male and female, masculine and feminine; to know sexuality is to know shame.[20]

Significantly, too, the lament calls attention to the implementation of power structures that mark the transition from paradise to this world. One specific example is manifest in the *Former Age*'s attention to hierarchy in relation to sustenance, implicated as a consequence of the fall. The poem depicts the desired food sources of paradise as plant-based, of the earth: "mast," "hawes," "corn," "fruites." Animals exist but are not included as part of the passive human inhabitant's food chain. The second of the two creation accounts in Genesis depicts a similar model of passive gathering as opposed to active hunting and killing: "Produxitque Dominus Deus de humo omne lignum pulchrum visu, et ad vescendum suave. . . . Parecepitque ei dicens: Ex omni ligno paradisi comede. De ligno autem scientiae boni et mali ne comedas" (Gn 2.9, 16) [And the Lord God brought forth of the ground all manner of trees, fair to behold, and pleasant to eat of. . . . And he commanded him saying: Of every tree of paradise you may eat: but the tree of knowledge of good and evil, you shall not eat]. But after the transgression of sexual knowing, flocks are raised, flesh eaten, the most prized animals sacrificed to ensure further abundance—"Abel quoque obtulit de primogenitis gregis sui, et de adipibus eorum" (Gn 4.4) [Abel also offered of the firstlings of his flock, and of their fat]. And the first garments sanctioned by God comprise the skins of lesser beasts: "Fecit quoque Dominus Deus Adae et uxori eius tunicas pelliceas, et induit eos" (Gn 3.21) [And Lord God made for Adam and his wife, garments of skins, and clothed them]; God replaces the fig-leaf aprons with the skins of animals.[21] Hence through the fall, human domination over other beasts is effected, as is Man's domination over Woman. The fall of the Edenish former age initiates a rule of strength: the stronger dominate the weak.[22] Although the first implementation of Man's power over creation takes a verbal form—the naming of animals—further implementations take on a far more brutal and hierarchical form.

While Eve is created to serve as Adam's "adiutor simile sibi"—a helper similar to himself, in the creation myth—and is therefore born into a status of inferiority, the disparity of power relationships attains a brutal, self-perpetuating dynamic after the expulsion from Eden. It is a commonplace of medieval theology that an awareness of sexual difference is a consequence of the fall; as noted, the first gesture of shame exhibited by humans is the covering up of genitals, a veiling of sexual difference and the troubling issues it seems to promote. Appropriately, too, the veil comprises animal hides, a trophy of human conquest. What seems inextricable from the awareness of sexual difference and gender distinction is inequality, the subordination of the feminine. Knowledge of sexual difference gives license to initiate and perpetuate systems of imbalance, which, we have seen, are rampant throughout medieval Christian culture.

Though the poem ends on a somewhat ambiguous note, complicated by the missing line preceding the final stanza,[23] figures of sexuality and desire are evoked to mark a distinction between the "former age" and "this world":

> Yit was not Jupiter the likerous,
> That first was fader of delicacye,
> Come in this world; ne Nembrot, desirous
> To regne, had nat maad his toures hye.   56–59

The "likerous" Jupiter, "fader of delicacye," overtly introduces sexual desire to the poem, suggesting that carnal desires are at least partly to blame for the decline of the Golden Age. Owing to the ubiquitous medieval correlation of the feminine and carnal/sexual interests, the implication, again, is that Woman is to blame. Unchecked sexual desire undermines the ordered society, the image implies, and because men desire women the consequences of this desire are said to be Woman's fault. Jupiter may be the literary "fader" of lust, but in "this world" the association of Woman and flesh irrevocably obtains.

More curious is the identification of "Nembrot" and "his toures hye," a likely evocation of the tower of Babel and its consequential garbling of speech. A. V. C. Schmidt has made a strong case for "Nembrot" and the "toures" representing "fortified structures of any and all periods, emblematic of man's domination of his fellows," and argues that "'Nembrot,' far from confusing the picture of the Golden Age evoked by Chaucer, is subtly integrated with the classical image as a cultural emblem of clearly definable value."[24] But while Nembrot is associated with "toures" (plural), in the poem, one tower in particular comes to mind, for a poet as concerned with language as Chaucer could not be unaware of the significant connotations of Nembrot/Nimrod in relation to Babel. The allusion references an episode in which an obviously phallic manifestation of *superbia* is punished with a form of feminized punishment—that is, the building of an enormous tower results in multiplicity, a confusing of speech. In effect Nimrod's distorted sense of his own masculinity is transformed into a spectacle of the feminine; *unity* is implicated in the desire to build the tower and hence *disunity* is the penalty:

> Ecce, unus est populus, et unum labium omnibus: coeperuntque hoc facere, nec desistent a cogitationibus suis, donec eas opere compleant. . . . Et idcirco vocatum est nomen eius Babel, quia ibi confusum est labium universae terrae: et inde dispersit eos Dominos super faciem cunctarum regionum.   Gn 11.9

> [Behold, it is one populace, and one lip/tongue for all: and they will have begun to do this, neither will they leave off of their intentions, until they have completed them in labor. . . . And on that account the name was called Babel, because there the lip/tongue of the whole earth was confused: and from there the Lord dispersed them abroad over the face of all the region.]

The biblical episode of Nimrod may therefore be read as a metaphor for the loss of the former age; both transformations entail a gendered dynamics whereby the strength and unity of the masculine are said to be undermined by or enmeshed with an obviously negative sense of the feminine.

Lak of Stedfastnesse likewise treats the theme of feminine mutability as the origin of contemporary misery, though the lamentation is couched more in the language of philosophical meditation than in situational detail. Like the *Former Age, Lak of Stedfastnesse* begins with the narrator's nostalgia for a time long past and hitherto unavailable—

> Somtyme the world was so stedfast and stable
> That mannes word was obligacioun,
> And now it is so fals and deceivable
> That word and deed, as in conclusioun,
> Ben nothing lyk, for turned up-so-doun
> Is al this world for mede and wilfulnesse,
> That al is lost for lak of stedfastnesse.   1–7

Language manifests the transformation, which the narrator regards with regret and contempt. The narrator points to the division of "word and deed" as a symptom of the world's decline—"mannes word," once "obligacioun," has become "fals and deceivable." The correlation of word and deed here echoes the *Boece*'s restatment of Plato: "sith thow hast lernyd by the sentence of Plato that nedes the wordis moot be cosynes to the thinges of which thei speken" (3.pr.12).[25] Division of word and deed— an overt disjuncture of *verbum* and *res*—foregrounds a frightening truth of human discourse, that language is tenuous, predicated on faith and consensus. There is no inherent, essential coincidence of the real world and the verbal signs that point to it, and the "proper" is always subject to the possibility of the "improper." Should the consensus be divided or abused, the possibility of deceit presents itself. What is therefore suggested further in the poem is that the truth and certainty of Man's literal word have been complicated by an agency that renders them deceptive, capable of multiple meanings that may be exploited and used to exploit. Language, the narrator laments, no longer exhibits "stedfastnesse"; word and deed are divided, no longer exhibiting the masculine traits of "stedfast and stable," and the divisive instrumentality effecting the slippage is gendered feminine owing to its epistemological associations.

In accordance with antifeminist tenets, the narrator seeks to assign blame and immediately lists conventionally feminine concepts as likely candidates:

> What maketh this world to be so variable
> But lust that folk have in dissensioun?
> For among us now a man is holde unable,
> But if he can by som collusioun
> Don his neighbour wrong or oppressioun.
> What causeth this but wilful wrecchednesse,
> That al is lost for lak of stedfastnesse?   8–14

Men are divided by the instability of their corrupted language, suggests the narrator. The abstractions used to articulate the origin of the world's culprit variability are effectively gendered feminine through the recurring "lak of stedfastnesse," a decidedly feminine flaw in medieval culture. Indeed, the causes of the world's miseries are reduced to a single movement, from masculine to feminine: "The world hath mad a permutacioun / Fro right to wrong, fro trouthe to fikelnesse, / That al is lost for lak of stedfastnesse" (19–21). Like the *Former Age*, *Lak of Stedfastnesse* presents a gendered dynamics of masculine-to-feminine effected by a feminine agency. Here the transition is made more overt—it is described specifically as "permutacioun"—and is more explicity gendered through the sequencing of right and wrong, truth and fickleness. The refrain line concludes the poem with a reiteration of agency and blame that speaks of loss without the potential for recuperation; the lamentation underscores a bitter belief that the damage inflicted by Woman defies restitution.

A similar reiteration characterizes a third Boethian ballade, *Fortune*, or *Balades de Visage sanz Peinture*. This triple ballade is presented as a *consolatio* dialogue, with the illusion of two speakers: the "pleintif" and the personified abstract with whom he engages in conversation.[26] Here Fortune is depicted as voicing a defense, though the characteristics attributed to Woman in the persona of Fortune are conventionally patriarchal:

> This wrecched worldes transmutacioun,
> As wele or wo, now povre and now honour,
> Withouten ordre or wys discrecioun
> Governed is by Fortunes errour.   1–4

The "pleintif" insists that Fortune is responsible for all the negative things associated with "errour" and that he will defy her. Fortune, however, makes an argument for the value of "errour":

> I have thee taught divisioun bitwene
> Frend of effect and frend of countenaunce;
> Thee nedeth nat the galle of noon hyene,
> That cureth eyen derked for penaunce;
> Now seestow cleer that were in ignoraunce.
> Yit halt thyn ancre and yit thou mayst arryve
> Ther bountee berth the keye of my substaunce,
> And eek thou hast thy beste frend alyve.   33–40

Fortune's insistence on the utility of "errour" evokes the medieval ontology (by way of Augustine: "Si enim fallor sum," If I err, therefore I am)[27] of error: that wandering is a necessary part of finding one's way, that one comes to knowledge only by erring, by making a journey or pilgrimage consisting as much of detour as design.[28] Hence learning is a consequence of error, and hence Fortune's value as an instructor is made clear, as is that of the other artificial women of the *consolatio* tradition.[29] Her discussion of friendship (presumably *amicitia*, the bonds between men)[30] aptly calls attention to the necessity of making distinctions ("divisioun"). Indeed, while the narrator insists that he knows friendship from his own reason, Fortune makes a strong case for an epistemology deriving from error.

But despite the wisdom attributed to the character's articulation, her words are provided by the same narrator who gives voice to the plaintiff; the dialogue reveals Fortune not as a woman's voice given audience but as a mouthpiece for a univocal or monologic discourse. Fortune is neither self-determined nor a speaking voice per se. Hence she is shown to advocate the same antifeminist topoi as are depicted in the other ballades:

> Thou pinchest at my mutabilitee
> For I thee lente a drope of my richesse,
> And now me lyketh to withdrawe me.
> Why sholdestow my realtee oppresse?
> The see may ebbe and flowen more or lesse;
> The welkne hath might to syne, reyne, or hayle;
> Right so mot I kythen by brotelnesse.
> In general, this reule may nat fayle.   57–64

Her characterization and voice are merely products of narrative illusion, and the narrative is devoted more to traditional antifeminist commonplaces than to any countertraditional challenges. Fortune is shown to defend her position in the patriarchal order, for while the inclusion of a female characterization purports to equivocality, the character speaks the narrator's language (and the poet's—a point to which I shall return).

Indeed, the description attributed to her reifies a condition of Man's fallen order similar to that depicted in the *Former Age*—"This world hath ever resteles travayle" (70)—and speaks to its ironic steadfastness, its certain instability: "In general, this reule may nat fayle" (64). The rule of phallic primacy is dominant, though the possibility of subversion is hinted at ("In general"), leaving room for deviation, however unwelcomed and remote. The description of the sun and rain likewise speaks of the world's unpredictability, evoking the Sermon on the Mount's explanation of the arbitrariness of life: "ut sitis filii Patris vestri, qui in caelis est: qui solem suum oriri facit super bonos et malos: et pluit super iustos et iniustos" (Mt 5.45) [that you may be the children of your Father, who is in heaven: who makes his sun to rise over the good and the bad, and it rains over the just and the unjust]. Fortune's discourse on mutability, then, underscores a constrast between earthly, feminine instability and spiritual, patriarchal Truth. Earthly life is subject to "Fortunes errour," but spiritual life is governed by the Father.

Hence Fortune is shown to insist on the ultimate patriarchal ideal of a heaven void of Woman's influence:

> The hevene hath propretee of sikernesse,
> This world hath ever resteles travayle;
> Thy laste day is ende of myn intresse.
> In general, this reule may nat fayle.   69–72

These lines reiterate a key passage of Boethius's *Consolation*, that Fortune's influence is limited to earth, that she herself is subject to the Divine, and that, therefore, men may anticipate release from disorder and instability in heaven—

> An tu in hanc uitae scenam nunc primum subitus hospesque uenisti? Vllamne humanis rebus inesse constantiam reris, cum ipsum saepe hominem uelox hora dissoluat? Nam etsi rara est fortuitis manendi fides, ultimus tamen uitae dies mors quaedam fortunae est etiam manentis.   2.pr.3

—which Chaucer translates and interprets in the *Boece:*

> Artow now comen first, a sodeyn gest, into the schadowe or tabernacle of this lif? Or trowestow that any stedfastnesse be in mannes thynges, whan ofte a swyft hour dissolveth the same man (that is to seyn, whan the soule departeth fro the body)? For although that zelde is ther any feith that fortunous thynges wollen dwellen, yet natheles the laste day of a mannes life is a maner deth to Fortune, and also to thilke that hath dwelt.   2.pr.3

Heaven and earth are contrasted as well by their agencies of mediation; Fortune, like Boethius's Philosophy, is a feminine representation of the human condition: Woman is the bearer of unwelcome secular truths, while the Son of Man is the bearer of his Father's good news. The heaven of patriarchal discourse serves as a kind of masculine utopia, which, despite the contradiction surrounding its interpretation in the works of the Church Fathers, articulates a desire to eliminate women.

Despite the cultural hegemony of patriarchy and the privileged position of men within it, the ballades narrator of course finds his secular world wanting, and evinces a recurring nostalgia for an age long past. Two further such expressions are provided by the ballades *Gentilesse*, which sketches out a patriarchal ideal of the quintessential man (where Woman is present only as the vessel of "heyres"), and *Truth*, which valorizes men's self-discipline (and from which Woman is similarly absent). *Gentilesse* overtly genders the subject of its praise:

> The firste stok, fader of gentilesse—
> What man that desireth gentil for to be
> Must folowe his trace, and alle his wittes dresse
> Vertu to love and vyces for to flee.   1–4

The "fader of gentilesse" is credited as the locus of this desirable masculine attribute, which for women apparently remains elusive—hence its tremendous value in a patriarchal society, for as long as a valorized characteristic is held unavailable to women within social parameters, both masculine privilege and feminine inferiority will be maintained. As Luce Irigaray argues in her recent critique of contemporary culture—but which nonetheless seems fitting here—masculine values dominate: "*The decline of sexual culture goes hand in hand* with the establishment of different values which are supposedly universal but turn out to entail *one part of humanity having a hold over the other*, here the world of men over that of women."[31] Indeed the masculine narrator of *Gentilesse* speaks to men and of men; women do not figure in this indulgent expression of masculine nostalgia. Whether the poem asserts that "gentilesse" is contingent upon character rather than birth, or that a man of noble birth must show himself worthy, "gentilesse" is desired by men and praised by those who wish for the days of the "firste stok."[32] In contrast to the ballades that use topoi to fault women and lament their perceived instrumentality, *Gentilesse* excludes women altogether, praising a masculine topos and glibly encouraging other men to follow its example.

Truth, or *Ballade de Bon Conseyl*, likewise offers encouragement to men who wish to observe its exclusive ideals:

> Flee fro the prees and dwelle with sothfastnesse;
> Suffyce unto thy thing, though it be smal,
> For hord hath hate, and climbing tikelnesse,
> Prees hath envye, and wele blent overal.
> Savour no more than thee bihove shal,
> Reule wel thyself that other folk canst rede,
> And trouthe thee shal delivere, it is no drede.   1–7

Like *Gentilesse*, *Truth* is a collection of commonplaces informed by philosophical themes that offers advice to men in a sociopolitical context; both celebrate self-discipline, order, and other such traditionally gendered-masculine ideals. Both are highly conventional and, despite their skillful form, aesthetic achievement, and overwhelming popularity, they are largely unremarkable restatements of cultural orthodoxy.[33]

But they are useful as points of contrast. Two other ballades, each overtly devoted primarily to a single gender category, help mark the sharp contrast between masculine/feminine gendered ideals by sketching Woman through conventional, idealized portraits. *To Rosemounde*, a somewhat satiric depiction of both the woman and the would-be lover, adheres to conventions of desirability in its articulation of *fin' amors* conventions of idealized womanhood. Like *Newefangelnesse*, *To Rosemounde* is addressed to an individual—here named—who is not herself a participant in the narrative. The poem consists of a series of *fin' amors* commonplaces representing a romantic masculine notion of a feminine ideal, cast as a voyeuristic fantasy:

> Madame, ye ben of al beaute shryne
> As fer cercled is the mapamounde,
> For as the cristal glorious ye shyne,
> And lyke ruby ben your chekes rounde.
> Therwith ye ben so mery and so jocounde
> That at a revel whan that I see you daunce,
> It is an oynement unto my wounde,
> Thogh ye to me ne do no daliaunce.   1–8

The narrator objectifies the woman's body and articulates his desire as a product of vision. From the vantage point of the narrator's gaze, the desired woman is said to be both the instigator of the narrator's desire and, more important, its creation: the narrator's text constitutes the desired body of the absent woman, whose fictive presence, as it were, is merely a fantasy that elides her absence. The narrator's inclusion of odd, ludicrous images—for instance, "Nas never pyk walwed in galauntyne / As I in love am walwed and ywounde" (17–18)—marks the poem as satiric; he pokes fun at himself and at the ludicrous literary conventions of *fin' amors* ("ful ofte I of myself devyne / That I am trewe Tristam the secounde" [19–20]).[34] But the poem wittily indicts the topoi of romance, even if its incorporation of the parodied images perpetuates antifeminist ideology.

The narrator of *Womanly Noblesse*, more serious in tone, purports to praise a woman as he fondly recalls her youth and beauty:

> So wel me liketh your womanly contenaunce,
> Your fresshe fetures and your comlynesse,
> That whiles I live myn hert to his maystresse
> You hath ful chose in trewe perseveraunce
> Never to chaunge, for no maner distresse.   5–9

The narrator's praises mark his own indulgence; these are the longings of nostalgia, the articulation of memories that constitute a memoir of an absent other vivified textually only within the select recollections of the desiring voice.

Curiously a masculine ideal is given the most extensive praise. "Stidefast governaunce," the opposite of the fickleness usually attributed to women by men who love/hate them, is used to mark the woman's perfection. The feminine object of desire in this ballade is, like the Clerk's Griselda, praised for exhibiting unfeminine behavior that is paradoxically praised as her greatest womanly achievement. In the guise of praise, however, the poem reveals that what the narrator desires is unavailable, that it is a past status no longer recuperable. Indeed, the *Lenvoye* overtly states that it is the former image, a memory or "remembraunce," of the woman that matters to the narrator:

> Auctour of norture, lady of plesaunce,
> Soveraigne of beautee, floure of wommanhede,
> Take ye non hede unto myn ignoraunce,
> But this receyveth of your goodlihede,
> Thynkyng that I have caught in remembraunce,
> Your beaute hole, your stidefast governaunce.   27–30

It is her memory, the idealized portrait etched in the narrator's mind, that will endure. The praise therefore speaks to an underlying irony—and a cruel one at that—that feminine youth and beauty are not "stidefast"; transitory and temporary, they will disappear and, presumably, the woman's own value and the narrator's articulated praises with them. In the guise of praise for stability, Woman's mutability is once again foregrounded and implicitly deemed undesirable.

The ballades, then, articulate commonplaces of antifeminist cultural conventions—some less subtly than others, some mediated by irony or deflected by humor—that operate in connection with a cultural decorum that perpetuates classical and Christian misogyny. Indeed it is difficult to imagine how any reader of the ballades could walk away with the impression that Chaucer is "wemenis frend," that his portraits of women are in any way sympathetic or empowering (other than that they participate in a history of patriarchal subordination that has given rise to contemporary resistance).[35] Literary decorum is indeed a product of cultural context, and texts that privilege and reify decorum thereby perpetuate the characteristics and values of that context.

Historically and ideologically the ballades are situated squarely within the parameters of misogynistic convention. The texts emphasize interpreting, rather than representing, sexual and gendered bodies. The cultural realities inhering in each poem attend the text's literary uses of gender rather than any deliberate mimetic associations apropos sociohistorical reality, and the interpretive function of gendered structures contributes to the articulation of gender as theoretically inscribed. Despite the dearth of women characters and voices, Woman is held accountable for sin, evil, hardship, and the like. The poems use the topoi in specific, even idiosyncratic, ways, but there is little novelty to be gleaned from the antifeminist platitudes and reification of patriarchal primacy. Indeed read together the poems become somewhat tiresome in their largely unremarkable repetition, much like the narratives constituting the *Legend of Good Women*. This is not to say of course that they are undeserving of critical attention—in fact, like the *Legend* these poems have much to tell us about the gendered operations of representational systems, particularly as the narrator appropriates the feminine and absents her to facilitate his own designs.

2

This reading of the ballades obviously demands a reckoning with Chaucer's own degree of participation or implication. A constant thread running through the ballades is the narrator's determination of how Woman might be defined and represented, for as the narrator controls and shapes his text(s), so he controls and shapes how Woman will be represented. More than a collection of antifeminist commonplaces, the ballades speak of their own agency, their own status as representation. The ballades may reify rather than dismantle cultural stereotypes, but they offer us the opportunity to interpret these relationships—to gain an appreciation of how and why the narrative's incorporation of gender categories operates and to what possible ends. It is therefore to the role of the narrator and the relationship of poet and narrator that we should turn.

The consistency in the critical position occupied by the narrative voice throughout the ballades warrants a treatment of "the narrator" as a recurring figure, in whose voice the collection of ballades is recited. The narrator's most overtly frequent complaint is feminine mutability, the capacity for limitlessness, change, and disorder conventionally gendered feminine and attributed to Woman: "fickleness," "lak of stedfastnesse," "newefangelnesse," and like terms appear in a context of lament, for the narrator reiterates a sense of anger and grief directed at Woman's role in Man's Fall. While this position is the stuff of medieval commonplaces—and indeed the ballades articulate this perspective by means of topoi—the relentless emphasis supplied by the ballades speaks collectively to the narrative obsession with subordination and relativity inscribed by gender.

On the level of narrative operation and texual transmission, mutability calls attention to the power struggle that operates within any narrative event—the challenge of the narrator to control his text. It is the feminine aspect of language and textuality that seems to cause problems for the masculine narrator; the chaotic potential of feminine limitlessness fuels an anxiety on the part of the narrator that can be resolved only through an assertion of his own certainty, his own ability to constrain or to impose limits. The desire for certainty, closure, and stability is pervasive in medieval discourses: theology, philosophy, grammar, rhetoric, politics.[36] The ballades' gendered textuality mirrors cultural constructions of gender in connection with a positive/negative binary; the feminine is assigned the role of the negative, inferior component, while the self-determined masculine representation assumes the privileged postion. And yet overt masculine valorization—such as *Truth, Gentilesse*—betrays its feminine contingency, and overt misogyny betrays an interconnectedness that destabilizes patriarchal operations, for while the feminine is treated with disdain and subjugated to an inferior position, it is neither eliminated nor fixed. Thus in conjunction with cultural orthodoxy and its psychosexual underpinnings, the narrator would appear to resent his medium, in particular its potential to escape or resist his control.

As a character voice in his own text, the narrator's function is to articulate the telling in which his own choices and concerns play a part. Caught in the double bind of fear and desire, the narrator's disdain for the feminine—manifest in his insistence on the text's incorporation of antifeminist ideological commonplaces—underscores his anxiety that the text might transcend his own control, that in effect his own masculinity might be undermined as his perceived weakness is exposed. For the narrator, weakness is a sign of femininity, and to be perceived as ineffectual is to be reduced to a woman's status of absence and marginality. But the narrator's fear of his own inefficacy underscores its self-realization; his apparent determination to control the construction of Woman is undermined by the very absence upon which his texts are predicated. Such absence promotes a sense of empowerment; the pervasiveness of epistemological binarism makes impossible any complete negation through language. The presence of any item necessarily evokes its counterpart within the ubiquitous governance of epistemological binarity, on which the ballades' treatment is predicated, and invites consideration of both the duality and the underlying motivations for disproportionate representation. In other words, the overt absence of Woman in the ballades perhaps piques our interest to determine not only the extent to which these texts actually do exhibit marks of womanhood but also why we must glean the traces, why overt representation has been declined in favor of absence in the process of textual construction.

Controlling the narrator in this respect is the poet, whose relationship to his narrator is not unlike that of narrator and text; the privilege and propriety of authority and obedience are called into question as the narrator participates in a hermeneutics articulated through gender. Because the text may be interpreted as a feminine medium shaped by the masculine narrator and, by extension, the poet, gendered relationships operate at the levels of both bodily metaphor and gendered reflexivity. How the masculine shapes or inscribes the feminine text defines the text's parameters and constitution. The masculine gesture toward stability, closure, and totality is a gesture toward the literal, and yet, as we have seen, a contradiction informs the text, for the literal is feminine owing to its metaphoric association with the carnal, even as it is simultaneously polysemous owing to gendered epistemologies of plurality. Hence the paradox of misogyny: contradictory associations become targets of disdain and anxiety, and there is no out, no reconciliation. Indeed, that very notion of contradiction—contingent on plurality and ambiguity—insists on a feminine presence within the conflicting medieval hermeneutics. The narrator's angry decrial of instability speaks to his desire to reify the dominance of the masculine through a vehement insistence on feminine subordination, even as his doing so inscribes a feminine dimension to his texts.

The drama of gender is played out in the sequence of ballades to an ambiguous end. In reading the ballades, we see conventional patriarchal codes at work, but their relentless foregrounding demands scrutiny. Chaucer, then, while no "feminist" himself, exposes his texts' relationship to the cultural, ideological orthodoxy out of which they arise. His own position seems to resist the extremism of, say, Jerome or Walter Map, but his orthodoxy often operates covertly, leading readers to proclaim him a protofeminist even as he exhibits compliant participation in a misogynistic literary culture. And while some of his works speak to a concern with relativity and subordination, he likewise refuses to take up a position of overt resistance. One might therefore determine from the ballades that Chaucer's concern with gender inhabits his lightweight lyrics and generic philosophical meditations in much the same way as its presence is manifested in his major works. Chaucer sees the critical connectedness of gender to all other human pursuits, even as its textual applications remain problematic and unresolved.

The foci of the ballades surface throughout Chaucer's oeuvre as the poet returns to and reassesses these and related issues. Many of the ballades articulate complaints that transcend *fin' amors* confections and instead address larger, more dire problems faced by humanity through the ages, including those associated with human relationships and their underlying issues of gender. Chaucer of course is not so naive as to think that these problems will be ameliorated by verse. He knows that Art does not feed the hungry, cure the ill, or convince men to stop waging war, and he concedes that brutality and suffering are perpetual, that they are to endure in a way that his own words perhaps cannot. Paradoxically, however, it is this very knowledge that would seem to compel him to write, for to abandon poetry is to embrace the spiritual nihilism that he so laments—painful as it may be, the poet must write. Chaucer's excursion into the language of convention and genre in connection with the ballades speaks to his awareness of his role as poetic maker, to his acceptance of the values and limitations of his enterprise, and to the ultimate implication of the poet in the patriarchal literary orthodoxy of his culture and his world.

※ *Chapter Five*

The Jangler's "Bourde"

Having considered the critical utility of absence in texts that endorse Woman's marginality, I shall now turn to an instance in the *Canterbury Tales* where an attempt is made to recuperate an absent other but where the gesture is troubled by the gender considerations of narrative appropriation. The ballades-narrator's strategy of integrating pseudovalorization and anifeminist commonplaces is itself a medieval commonplace; time and again we find narrators who, unable or unwilling to maintain a consistent position, favor instead an uneasy vacillation between the two manifestations of misogyny, the subtle and the overt. Such conventions as *fin' amors*, Mariolatry, and hagiography offer a pervasive and redundant litany of Woman in her glory, couched in terms of patriarchal acceptance; while disguised in the language of praise, the misogynistic underpinnings of such strategies betray themselves upon scrutiny, no less so than the more blatant articulations that mask anxiety, resentment, and fear. The *Manciple's Tale* obviously draws off these and related conventions but is complicated by the intimate relationships suggested by the teller and his tale, particularly that of mother and son.

※ 1

Readers have long noted the irony of the Manciple's digression on silence: as the Manciple praises his mother's words of caution against prolixity, he imposes forty-four lines of recitation on his captive audience, running a full, tedious circle from "My sone, thenk on the crowe, a Goddes name! / My sone, keep wel thy tonge" (IX.318–19) to "Kepe wel thy tonge and thenk upon the crowe" (362).[1] Further, while betraying the point of the lesson, the Manciple continually portrays himself as a mouthpiece for his mother's platitudes,[2] stressing his submissive attachment to her with the eleven occasions of "My sone."[3] Even so, I will argue that the Manciple's digression represents much more than the irony of a simple-minded son rehearsing the platitudes of his equally simple "dame," for in its reproduction of the sayings of a distinctly feminine speaker, the digression compels us to consider the role of gendered speech in Chaucer's work. On their most literal level, the words—though not necessarily the timbre, intonation, or posture—belong to a woman, the Manciple's mother. Her "voice" provides the maxims even as the Manciple performs them. Yet as the Manciple effects the illusion of the dame speaking, we sense that she is an incomplete presence, a turgid voice made known through nothing more than the Manciple's selective appropriation, which, while overtly lauding the wisdom of the mother, nonetheless holds her up to ridicule. In effect, we see that the Manciple is capable of saying one thing but meaning quite another. Consequently, this cross-gendered performance prompts numerous questions about text, voice, and context, which, in turn, can inform our understanding of the *Manciple's Tale*'s critical proximity to the *Parson's Tale* and, more important, to the *Retractions*.

Readers have commented that the *Tale* proper is divided into two parts, one on the nature of women's lust and one on the nature of speech. The two parts, I believe, treat the same topic, owing to antifeminist tenets linking feminine flesh and feminine speech. The Manciple's version of the crow fable underscores the conflation through his narrative asides that, while somewhat contrived or disjointed on occasion, effectively sustain a link between the two manifestations of the language theme. The Manciple's repetition of his mother's words corroborates the various related anifeminist tenets articulated throughout his tale. The Manciple's depiction of his mother, moreover, both reifies and destabilizes the materiality of language evinced by the *mater*. Isidore of Seville's widely known etymology of "*mater*" foregrounds this connection:

> Genitores autem a gignendo; et parentes quasi parientes. Idem et creatores. Crementum enim est semen masculi, unde animalium et hominum corpora concipiuntur. Hinc creatores parentes dicuntur. Mater dicitur, quod exinde efficiatur aliquid. Mater enim quasi materia; nam causa pater est.[4]

> [Those who beget moreover (are named) from begetting; and parents because they bring forth. The same also for creators. Growth for

instance is the seed of the male, whence the bodies of animals and humans are conceived. Hence parents are called creators. A mother is so called for from there something is produced. Indeed a mother is as it were matter/material; for the cause is the father.]

With obvious echoes of Aristotle's equating of woman and matter,[5] Isidore gives materiality a more focused particularity through the specificity of *mater*, distinct from *femina*:

Vir nuncupatus, quia maior in eo vis est quam in feminis: unde et virtus nomen accepit; sive quod vi agat feminam. Mulier vero a mollitie, tamquam mollier, detracta littera vel mutata, appellata est mulier. Vtrique enim fortitudine et inbecillitate corporum separantur.[6]

[Man is named, because greater power is in him than in women; hence also the name strength is taken; or because he forcefully drives women. Yet woman from softness, or softer, with a letter withdrawn or changed, has woman been named. For both are distinguished by the strength and weakness of bodies.]

Both *femina* and *mater*—expressions of softness, mutability, and materiality—represent the feminine that may be manipulated by the masculine, be it bodies or texts.

In hindsight we know of the tale's having been told to the Manciple by his mother—"My sone, thenk on the crowe" (IX.362)—despite his earlier generic attribution ("As olde bookes maken mencioun"), and yet so much of the Manciple's version is devoted to personal asides and thematic digressions that we might therefore conclude that the personal additions are the Manciple's own and that they constitute the speaker's own perceptions and beliefs (and, by extension, the Manciple, as Chaucer's own narrative construct, reveals the poet's own attitudes, though ambiguously—a point to which I shall return). The Manciple's unwarranted insistence on women's virtue, for example—"Alle thise ensamples speke I by thise men / That ben untrewe, and nothyng by wommen" (IX.187–88)—is disjointed from his narrative depiction of a conventional cuckolding episode, here exacerbated by the low social status of the nameless and voiceless woman's "lemman." The Manciple's assertion that men are untrustworthy and "likerous" is betrayed by the story that ostensibly occasions it, and a quite different assessment is endorsed instead. Woman, as represented by the wife, is shown to be deceitful and adulterous; it is she, according to the Manciple's implicit argument, who embraces the "Flessh . . . so newfangel" (193), she who, prone to temptation, is deserving of mistrust. The Manciple's digression on men's desires, then, like his digression on silence, damns women with hypocritical praise and absolves men through disjointed exemplification masquerading in the guise of respect.

Indeed the Manciple's narrative is so obviously part of a misogynistic tradition that his digression on women corroborates, rather than challenges, its context and history. The wife in the story is reduced wholly to her sexual utility: first as she is Phebus's wife, then as she is "swyved" by her "lemman," then as she is reclaimed by Phebus in a gesture of authority and ownership. Her minimal characterization posits her within the tale as an object, Everywoman as adultress, Woman as deceit. The unnamed wife contrasts with the unnamed mother appended to the narrative, for while both are anonymous female figures identified only by social/sexual functions, the mother is given no overt sexual dimension other than her status as mother; she is masculine in her authority and the Manciple feminine in his purported acquiesence. The depictions of the wife and the mother thus point to the insidious hypocrisy inhering in the Manciple's contrived attempts at observing decorum. (In this sense the Manciple is perhaps not unlike the Wife of Bath, for he too is shown to articulate a quasi-feminist discourse that speaks more to an advocacy of hegemonic patriarchy than to any real interest in challenging its strictures.)

The insincerity of the Manciple's language is underscored by his exaggerated attention to proper speech. The Manciple's famous lines on the relationship of word and meaning are used to promote a false sense of compassion:

> And so bifel, whan Phebus was absent,
> His wyf anon hath for hir lemman sent.
> Hir lemman? Certes, this is a knavyssh speche!
> Foryeveth it me, and that I yow biseche.
>   The wise Plato seith, as ye may rede,
> The word moot nede accorde with the dede.
> If men shal tell proprely a thyng,
> The word moot cosyn be to the werkyng.   IX.203–10

His affected recoil constitutes a superficial adherence to social decorum in language that is obviously betrayed by the context in which it is spoken; the Manciple's tale and his interpolated digressions do indeed impugn women. "Words" may in fact be "cosyn" to the "dede," but the Manciple's explication points to the need to question not the "word" but the "dede"— for it is motive and connotation that infuse the text with its inconsistency and misogyny, not the use of supposedly degrading words. And the Manciple's insistence that he is bound by the rules of language to use the word most literally suiting what it represents certainly rings false embedded as it is within a fictional narrative.

The excessiveness of the disclaimer becomes more pronounced if one considers that the tale's supposed vulgarity ("lemman," "swyve," "dighte")[7] comprises words already spoken by tellers of prior tales and is, therefore, hardly in need of apology. The Miller, Reeve, and Wife have used the terms, as has the Monk.[8] On the one hand, then, one could read the disclaimer as an attempt by the Manciple to include himself in the company of narrators already having spoken words of vulgarity; the ubiquitous use of the words renders the disclaimer unnecessary, though it is, ironically, the disclaimer that brings this reality to the attention of the audience. But the Manciple's strategy in issuing the disclaimer could just as well be to enhance his narrative's facade of equivocality. The glaring misogyny of the tale and the more subtle misogyny of the digressions cannot be eliminated by the Manciple's disclaimer but may be tempered enough to seem more palatable, thereby alleviating the speaker's complicity in perpetuating misogynistic commonplaces. In this sense the disclaimer functions as a kind of inchoate retraction, appended to words that have already entered the public realm in order to give the audience an illusion of the speaker's private intentions (which, in Bakhtinian terms, points to the the vacillation of language between the public and private realms).[9]

Additionally, the Platonic "cosyn" and "dede" evocation underscores the intimacy of language and of the teller of this tale. "Cosyn" denotes kin, flesh and blood relatives.[10] As has been noted, flesh corresponds—within the context of the ubiquitous Pauline/Augustinian semiotics—to carnality, and carnality to the literal. It is fitting, therefore, that a literal word should be "cosyn" to what it represents, that it should operate on the most basic, literal, carnal level. Accordingly the Manciple's allusion to Plato operates as an endorsement of literal, certain language.[11] And yet "cosyn" is used metaphorically to suggest this literalism. Words do not comprise flesh and blood relationships, obviously, even if in limited instances the "dede" to which they point does so in their stead. But language offers a set of figurative connotations, connections, and relationships that transcends literal certainty to offer a multitude of more abstract and potentially more significant possibilities, though not without producing a sense of uncertainty, doubt, and possible confusion.[12] And thus the complications further presented by the gendered histories of literal/figurative demarcations within conflicting epistemologies infuse the Manciple's overtly simple endorsement with a polysemous dimension of complexity and ambiguity. That the Manciple uses a figurative phrase to endorse literal language reiterates the inconsistencies in his attitude toward "tidyngs" and helps the text achieve its ambivalent outlook on the role of poetry and the poet.

Chaucer exploits the conventions associated with these antifeminist ideologies to sustain a marked alliance between teller and tale. Just as the Manciple rehearses his mother's advice with little evidence of sincerity or conviction,[13] so Phebus is shown to participate in trite conventions of romance and tragedy that conveniently set aside the horrid events occurring within the frame of the narrative. For instance, Phebus's praise of his dead wife, while superficially laudatory, seems to convey a subtle sense of condescension and disdain:

> O deere wyf! O gemme of lustiheed!
> That were to me so sad and eek so trewe,
> Now listow deed, with face pale of hewe,
> Ful giltelees, that dorst I swere, ywys!   IX.274–77

Alive and with her adultery exposed, the wife is first shown, understandably, to provoke Phebus's jealousy and anger. Rashly, he kills her to end his own pain and humiliation (hence the crow, as witness to his shame, must also be eliminated, though the fate of the third witness—the "lemman"—is unreported). Yet once dead and therefore no longer a witness to Phebus's shame, the wife is reclaimed by Phebus as his prize property, restored to her former status as his "gemme." In the Manciple's reworking of the Ovidian myth, the wife is of greater value to Phebus dead than alive, for Phebus can then rewrite her history to suit his own desires without fear of having his reconfiguration exposed or betrayed.[14] She becomes, in retrospect, the perfect "deere wyf." And despite his gallant professions of self-blame—"Where was thy wit and thy discrecion? / O every man, be war of rakelnesse!" (282–83)—Phebus neglects to punish himself; he has been dominated by "rakelnesse," he claims, casting himself in the role of victim. Accordingly, Phebus speaks the language of conventional antifeminist discourse and thus, despite his claiming "For sorwe I wol myselven slee!" (291) and questioning "Why nere I deed?"

(273), he remains very much alive and in control. Hence the episode may be interpreted as a literary enactment of an ideological gesture of dismissal.

The tattle-tale crow reifies codes of loyalty and order—culturally marked as masculine—that operate at the expense of the subordinated feminine. Rather than speak to the wife to warn her of his observation—"The white crowe, that heeng ay in the cage, / Biheeld hire werk, and seyde never a word" (IX. 240–41)—the crow eagerly informs Phebus instead, after much flattery: "'Phebus,' quod he, 'for al thy worthynesse'" (IX.249). The crow's overt loyalty to Phebus is manifest in his decision to reaffirm the masculine bonds of their relationship. As a representative of the submissive component of that order—as Neville Coghill, V. J. Scattergood, Louise O. Fradenburg and others have demonstrated[15]—the crow's tattling must first enhance the image of Phebus's mightiness so that the jarring lowliness of his wife's behavior might be perceived as all the more egregiously disrespectful and disobedient. And indeed the crow phrases the tattling in the most blunt, literal terms: "For on thy bed thy wyf I saugh hym swyve."

But the crow's participation goes awry as he exaggerates his role to his and the wife's detriment. It is apparently not enough for the crow to inform; he chooses to be emphatic and loquacious in his conveying of the episode to Phebus:

> What wol ye moore? The crowe anon hym tolde,
> By sadde tokenes and by wordes bolde,
> How that his wyf had doon hire lecherye,
> Hym to greet shame and to greet vileynye,
> And tolde hym ofte he saugh it with his yen.   IX.257–61

The crow, then, is not unlike the Manciple's mother in his feminine prolixity, and he is made to suffer for this feminine behavior. Significantly, Phebus revokes the gift of speech that he has bestowed upon the crow, displeased by the crow's use of it: "Ne nevere in al thy lif ne shaltou speke" (297), "And [Phebus] refte hym al his song, / And eek his speche, and out at dore hym slong" (305–6).

An analogy may therefore be drawn between the crow's transgressive speech and the text's association of gender and language. "In muchel speche synne wanteth naught" (IX.338)—feminine speech, represented conventionally by prolixity, is the subject of the Manciple's narrative; how the feminine is potentially dangerous and how its danger might be contained constitute a metaphoric subtext of the Manciple's digression on silence and of the silencing of Woman as played out in the tale's violent acts of retribution instigated by language. This feminine-language subtext makes a marked contribution to the tale's governing theme of "false" language. As I have argued throughout this study, Chaucer's poetry assimilates a medieval gendered poetics whereby the feminine represents a chaotic, threatening, and limitless reaching out toward infinity—that which transcends order and certainty—while the masculine suggests a desire to order and harmonize, to construct certainty and to schematize meaning. Gendered epistemological categories are contradictory—for instance, Woman is equated with both silence (submissiveness, marginality) and loquaciousness (immodesty, ostentatiousness)—and thus their treatment in the text promotes a sense of ambivalence. Poetry and fiction, though, clearly embody the feminine aspects of language; textuality operates on both literal and figurative, unisemous and polysemous, levels, and textual representation underscores feminine language's capacity to promote ambiguity, and hence to deceive. The medium of poetry is "countrefete[d] speche," and the poet's task is to articulate "tidynges" simultaneously "false" and "trewe" (IX.360).[16]

The Manciple's treatment of the crow's jangling asserts that prolixity is more than an unwelcome annoyance—such excesses of speech are shown to be deadly. The false speech of janglers promotes betrayal and deception (as William Langland similarly comments in his own treatment of speech in *Piers Plowman*, "Ac japeres and jangeleres, Judas children, / Feynen hem fantasies, and fooles hem maketh" [B.Prol.35–36]). Hence the Manciple's own concern with flattery, the "glossing" of one individual by another, for one who routinely lies in order to deceive others knows to be wary of what he hears. The Manciple knows firsthand the slippery efficacy of flattery[17] and that, as the crow demonstrates, like any implementation of self-serving guile, it can be thwarted and turned back on its origin.

It is not surprising then that the Manciple exhibits an obvious fear of language in his stated desire to maintain complete control over what is said to whom and in what context. As the Manciple duplicates his mother's words and her voice to articulate a masculine tenet, he demonstrates a desire to control or to contain both the feminine and the maternal—the *mater* of flesh and text must, from his perspective, be contained. His use of the mother's voice gives an illusion of essential experience that purports to validate the maxims, but his appropriation constitutes an ideological gesture of usurpative suppression. Certainly the Manciple's overt concern with controlling speech reflects a masculine order and a reiteration of hierarchical gender epistemologies manifest in language. Indeed, throughout the tale the Manciple calls attention to his professed desire for (masculine) control even as his (feminine) narrative resists: "What nedeth it his fetures to discryve?" (IX.121), he asks before lapsing into an eight-line description; "But now to purpos" (155), he insists shortly before launching another digression; "What wol ye moore?" (257), "ther is namoore to sayn" (266), he comments in the more than fifty lines devoted to Phebus's reaction to the crow's "sadde tokenes" and "wordes bolde" (258).

Thus the Manciple, in appropriating the voice of his mother, speaks in a woman's voice to warn against feminine speech in a *moralitas* ironically connected to the Manciple's own telling of a fable. Certainly the apparent falseness of poetic language concerned the theologians. Augustine's *Contra mendacium*, for example, provides an extensive defense of figurative language and makes critical distinctions between metaphoric language and lying; these comments are well known in *sentence*, but their centrality to medieval poetics warrants their citation here:

> Quae si mendacia dixerimus, omnes etiam parabolae ac figurae significandarum quarumcumque rerum, quae non ad proprietatem accipiendae sunt, sed in eis aliud ex alio est intelligendum, dicentur esse mendacia: quod absit omnino.[18]

> [If we call these lies, then all parables and figures which signify anything whatsoever, which are not to be accepted in their proper sense, but in them one thing from another is understood, will be said to be lies: which idea must be abandoned wholly.]

Augustine's commentary delves beyond abstract theorizing and specifically considers fables and other such uses of improper language:

> In quo genere fingendi humana etiam facta vel dicta irrationalibus animantibus et rebus sunsu carentibus homines addiderunt, ut eiusmodi fictis narrationibus, sed veracibus significationibus, quod vellent commendatius intimarent.... Quod utique totum fingitur, ut ad rem quae intenditur, ficta quidem narratione, non mendacii tamen, sed veraci significatione veniatur.[19]

> [In this kind of feigning, humans have attributed deeds or sayings to irrational animals and in animate objects, in order that by narratives

of this sort which are fictitious, but have true signification, they could communicate in a manner agreeable. . . . Which certainly is feigned in total, that one may reach what is intended, by a narrative that is fictitious, but not mendacious, since it has truthful signification.]

Hence the Manciple's digressions germane to propriety and decorum: the Manciple's motive for telling the tale would seem to be fueled by a desire to replicate his mother's didacticism, which ultimately insists on "proper" rather than "improper" speech. The Manciple's fear of polysemous language seems not to include his own; his excessive admonition against "tidyngs," after all, is obviously betrayed by its placement at the conclusion of a fable. Yet both Manciple and mother advocate silence as the only sure preventative for misdirected or mistaken speech, and both illustrate the futility of such an improbable directive; both are garrulous and both recite the fable of the crow as an *exemplum* of why one should refrain from speech in general and fables in particular. Through such contradiction the text points to its own ambivalence and, by extension, the poet's.

Mother and son evidence a fear of language that motivates the reduction of thought to platitudes. Platitudes are offered by both as safe (masculine) speech, universally acknowledged as having some truth and merit; they are offered as a safe substitute for the potentially subversive or provocative consequences of original ideas and expression. The Manciple's canting elucidates his narrative to the extent that it invites interpretation through ironic juxtaposition, but the performance is largely uninspired and uninspiring in itself. Excessive yet insufficient, the turgid series of platitudes is merely redundant rather than elucidating. The literalism advocated by the maxims produces a semblance of certainty, but it paralyzes language and thought; to limit speech is to forfeit its utility and instrumentality, to kill it in effect by preserving it. It is fitting then that the crow's primary offense is his use of blunt, literal language. He speaks in "sadde tokenes" and "wordes bolde," rather than a more subtle and hence more forgiving "countrefete[d] speche." While literal truth might preclude misinterpretation, it does so only at tremendous cost, and the Manciple's obedient words therefore speak ultimately of their own silence.

🜨 2

The Prologue episode of the Cook, Host, and Manciple aptly frames the *Tale*'s theoretical engagement with appropriation and decorum by situating language in relation to structures of power and their oppressive silencing of submissive—feminized—voices.[20] The Manciple is shown, in an ironic foregrounding of his later performance, to be eager to tell his tale of the value of non-telling:

> "Wel," quod the Maunciple, "if it may doon ese
> To thee, sire Cook, and to no wight displese,
> Which that heere rideth in this compaignye,
> And that oure Hoost wole, of his curteisye,
> I wol as now excuse thee of thy tale." IX.25–29

Veiled by the submissive language of acquiescence, the Manciple not only usurps the Cook's audience but demonstrates a self-serving prolixity as well: he uses twenty-one lines to say, in effect, "let me go next instead." Here the Manciple demonstrates the insincerity of conventional language and the rationalized necessity for deceptive speech should social circumstances warrant a veiling of the true self. The adherence to decorum illustrated here is echoed throughout the *Tale*'s many digressions, whereby the Manciple makes a show of his attention to linguistic decorum—"Her lemman? Certes, this is a knavyssh speche!" for example. In these instances an appearance of propriety is privileged for purposes of audience manipulation.

More tellingly, the Manciple further silences the displaced Cook as he abandons his words of insincere etiquette in favor of humiliating insults that attack the Cook's unspoken words:

> And, wel I woot, thy breeth ful soure stynketh:
> That sheweth wel thou art nat wel disposed.
> Of me, certeyn, thou shalt nat been yglosed.
> ....
> Hoold cloos thy mouth, man, by thy fader kyn!
> The devel of helle sette his foot therin!
> Thy cursed breeth infecte wole us alle. IX.32–39

The Manciple attacks the Cook not for what the Cook has said but for what he *might* say; the Cook is silenced on the basis of presupposed intention. The Manciple's presupposition apropos the Cook's tendency toward vulgarity is connected to a medieval commonplace: drunkenness as the instigator of vulgar speech. This passage perhaps echoes as well a further trope, best known through its presentation in Innocent's *De miseria*: the association of a drunken man's fetid breath and vulgar speech.[21] In the context of this metaphor, the Manciple's fierce condemnation of the Cook's breath would seem to underscore the Manciple's initial complaint, that the Cook should not be permitted to speak. Thus the Manciple insults both the Cook's physical presence—his alleged halitosis—and his potential tale. Whether the Manciple has heard the Cook's earlier coarse narrative— "[He] hadde a wyf that heeld for contenance / A shoppe, and swyved for hir sustenance" (I.4421–22)—or is presumptively attributing foul language to a drunken man, the Manciple is successful in censoring the Cook and in appropriating the Cook's alleged proclivities toward vulgar speech, with the Host's approval.[22] The inebriated and therefore weakened Cook forfeits speech entirely, replacing it with gesture: "And on the Manciple he gan nodde faste / For lakke of speche, and doun the hors hym caste" (IX.47–48). The Manciple silences the Cook, just as the Manciple's Phebus will be shown to silence the crow. The trope of censorship played out in this episode—the closing of another's mouth, the silencing of his tongue—ties language to an ideological hierarchy manifest in social discourses, and, significantly, the trope is reiterated in the tale of the crow and in the Manciple's mother's teaching.

Here in the Prologue, as in the *Tale* and its peroration, the overtly censorious Manciple is exposed as ineffectually self-censoring. Confronted by the Host with the possibility of the Cook's later vengeance, the Manciple quickly attempts to revoke the truth of his earlier utterance: "That that I spak, I seyde it in my bourde" (IX.81). The loquacious—and therefore feminized—Manciple uses unrestrained speech, then seeks to erase its impact. Such an attempt at revocation exposes the Manciple's desire to restore masculine dominance and control; having shown himself to be weak and loquacious the Manciple seeks recourse through an ideologically charged imposition of control. The episode thus foregrounds not only the Manciple's tendency toward feminine speech but his concomitant insistence on foregrounding his own masculinity. His jangling against jangling betrays his gesture of closure, and this gesture is repeated thematically in the tale of the crow and textually in his attachment of the peroration to the tale. He speaks of the consequences of suppression as he himself is shown simultaneously to desire suppression and to undermine the illusion of desire through the obvious inefficacy of his attempted renunciation.

Another assertion apropos revocation forms the basis of Chaucer's notoriously perplexing *Retractions*. Both assertions represent a desire to maintain an (masculine) illusion of control over (feminine) words, and both demonstrate an ironic attempt to remove the speaker from his own discourse, to leave it for others to decide. Just as the Manciple insists that his inflammatory utterances be revoked and reconstrued as an utterance of jest, "in [his] bourde" (though the spoken words remain the same), so too the *Retractions*-narrator expresses a desire to revoke his secular words in order that they might be reframed by words of piety and devotion. But words recanted are still known, and these self-renunciating janglers can therefore speak only in jest. The Manciple cannot fully revoke the words that have been said, even as he hopes to alter their context and hence the audience's perception; similarly, the poet cannot cancel what has already been read or heard, though he might attempt to supply a new interpretive frame. (As Lacan and Derrida have argued, words canceled or under erasure do not cease to exist; words shunted to the margins take up a new position, and their influence cannot long be ignored.)[23] Both instances of retraction show that an utterance can only be said to be "retracted," that subsequent alterations may complicate the original but do not negate its having taken place (though an audience may conspire to pretend otherwise, as in the case of a marriage annulment, for example, or a jury being instructed to ignore a witness's remark).

This is not to say, however, that Chaucer, in the *Retractions,* is merely a self-renunciating jangler speaking only in jest. Such a generalization would overlook profound differences in the voices and texts of the Manciple, Parson, and, ultimately, the poet. But it is significant to note the parallels of the Manciple's and Chaucer's interest in renunciation as a narrative and rhetorical technique. For it is doubtful that Chaucer embraces a theological heavy-handedness such as is advocated in the *Retractions,* despite the obvious parallel of its penitential rhetoric to the Parson's treatise.[24] Instead, I would argue, Chaucer feigns regret of his life's secular works in order to make a keen point: we are to imagine a kind of world where codes of silence, like those posited in the *Manciple's Tale,* the *Parson's Tale,* and the *Retractions,* have been successfully implemented, a culture void of "translaciouns and enditynges of worldly vanitees" (X.1085), where joylessness and rigidity are celebrated as part of God's grace and where the sole purpose of existence is to pray grimly for salvation. Such a bleak and barren world—the dream of many literalists but the bane of those who wish to acknowledge their full humanity—is anathema to Chaucer's life's work. How we read the *Retractions* determines and is determined by how we attempt to understand Chaucer's complex and ambivalent relationship to his culture. The Manciple and his tale illustrate the political necessity of careful speech; so too the poet's *Retractions* speaks to the cultural and political necessities of feigned acquiescence, an etiquette for negotiating the delicate relationships of religion, politics, and art. The *Retractions*, like the *Manciple's Tale*, advocates silence in order to speak out against it.

The poet's treatment of retraction is amplified by the Manciple's narrative's ambivalent demonstration of hypocrisy. We should recall the pilgrim-Chaucer's paradoxical praising of the Manciple's guile in the *General Prologue*: "Now is nat that of God a ful fair grace" (I.573), and the similar irony in the Manciple's mother's lesson, also attached to God and a presumably Christian morality. The Manciple and his mother advocate silence except "To speke of God, in honour and preyere" (IX.331), insisting that speaking to and of God is the only valid utterance even as they themselves violate the directives. It is therefore quite fitting that, like the Pardoner though less overtly, the Manciple is depicted as professing to recite a moral text even as his behavior is said to be otherwise. (Though a crucial distinction between the two is that the Manciple does not claim dishonesty for himself but rather is identified as such by the narrator of the *General Prologue*.) The *General Prologue* portrait indicates, somewhat cryptically, that the Manciple has indeed learned to use language effectively in his professional capacity:

Now is nat that of God a ful fair grace
That swich a lewed mannes wit shal pace
The wisdom of an heep of lerned men?   I.573–75

If we are to believe the pilgrim-narrator of the *General Prologue*, then clearly the cynical Manciple has been selective in his adherence to moral advice, and clearly he has no qualms about pontificating hypocritically. But his self-serving appropriation of language aptly corresponds to his mother's instruction, which is after all given to facilitate the Manciple's own social and professional interactions; the mother advises the Manciple to hold his tongue not as an act of benevolence to others but in order to protect himself from the consequences of damaged relationships. The goal of the silent tongue is to avoid divisiveness, to circumvent the threat of multiplicity and doubt: "for to muche speche / Hath many a man been split" (IX.325–26), "Right as a swerd forkutteth and forkerveth / An arm a-two, my deere sone, right so / A tonge kutteth freendshipe al a-two" (340–42); significantly, the vocative address "my deere sone," which reiterates the connection between mother and son, reflexively bisects the Manciple's articulation of the maxim of divisiveness. The *Manciple's Tale*, then, advocates a disjointed code of speech and silence marked by an ironic contradiction of self-serving morality and a facade of etiquette that shields fearful truths. Janglers may be "to God abhomynable" (IX.343), but in the discourses of human interaction their instrumentality effectively resides.

The Manciple's contradictory notions regarding Christianity seem to be reiterated in the *Retractions*, where the narrator professes to desire salvation and seems willing to forfeit his human speech in order to achieve it. Silencing thought and speech in order to avoid circulating potentially subversive—that is, non-Christian—ideas about humanity suggests that the potential consequences of any hermeneutics of doubt can be silenced only by fear; the only certainty, the only "truth," is fear. Thus the Manciple overtly privileges artificial, ritualized, and unquestioning speech, the language of prayer and the language of platitudes, both masculine structures of controlled speech. The Parson's treatise, with its tiresome and prolix rendering of rigidly codified commonplace patriarchal directives, likewise conflates language and the feminine and insists that both be subject to patriarchal structures of control, ultimately privileging silence. The second part of Penitence, for example, rehearses the tired yet ubiquitous Eve-as-flesh and flesh-as-temptation motifs, reiterating that Woman is to blame for Man's Fall: Eve's speech is deemed responsible for Adam's choosing to consent, and concupiscence manifests itself in the negativeness of feminine flesh (X.330–50). The Parson's section on Ire emphatically denounces flattery, jangling, and japing as abuses of the tongue, "fals signyficaunce of word" (607), "the synne of double tonge" (643), "vileyns wordes and knakkes of japeris" (652). In context these types of slippery—polysemous— language ab/uses are gendered feminine, thereby incorporating feminine polysemy and feminine negativeness. This is not to say that the Parson should be considered a representative misogynist but rather that his text articulates misogynistic Christian commonplaces that point to Woman's silence (of tongue and flesh) as a patriarchal ideal. The Parson's directives, like the Manciple's censorious maxims, then, betray their purpose by revealing the stark, apoplectic instrumentality of attempted certainty and closure. But silence is truly the death of the spirit, and Chaucer's purported devotion to theological orthodoxy underscores not the necessity and efficacy of containment but rather the triumph of his own resistance. Hence the *Parson's Tale* and the *Retractions*, while as platitudinously conventional as the aesthetically maligned *Manciple's Tale* that motivates them, appropriate convention in order to expose its ideological underpinnings;

feigned acquiescence operates as the vehicle by which gaps between speakers and texts are exposed.

Together the disjointed yet unified contents of fragments IX and X posit an argument about the nature of language and truth-telling that forcefully evokes the poet's ambivalence. Chaucer is a deeply spiritual poet, acutely aware of the ultimate insufficiency of the very language that he must champion. That he values human speech and what it represents does not necessarily compromise the spiritual positions taken up by the poet throughout his texts. It does, however, underscore both the degree to which the poet and his narrators are necessarily divided and the paradoxical intersections of "false" and "trewe" in the poet's own "tidynges." A product of a theologically and politically Christian culture, the poet is aware that language, though fallible and imperfect and therefore subject to abuse, can be powerful and effective, essential to human existence. Neither cynical nor naive, Chaucer does not pretend to offer certainty or "truth," even as he dismantles codes of rigidity and silence, unwilling to settle into complaceny with a didacticism that seeks to speak in a single voice. A fittingly resistant and indeterminate conclusion to the *Canterbury Tales*, the *Retractions* points to the ambivalence of a poet who sees the inadequacy of his poetry in the larger context of the ineffable and yet knows that he can do no more.

Chapter Six

The Summoner's Subversive Erotics

> Written on the body is a secret code only visible in certain lights; the accumulations of a lifetime gather there. In places the palimpsest is so heavily worked that the letters feel like braille.
> —Jeanette Winterson, *Written on the Body*[1]

In book XI of his *Etymologiae,* Isidore of Seville provides a descriptive etymology of Man (*vir*) and Woman (*mulier*) that recapitulates the Aristotelian physiological and epistemological foundations of cultural gender construction:

> Vtrique enim fortitudine et inbecillitate corporum separantur. Sed ideo virtus maxima viri, mulieris minor, ut patiens viri esset; scilicet, ne feminis repugnantibus libido cogeret viros aliud appetere aut in alium sexum proruere. Dicitur igitur mulier secundum femineum sexum, non secundum corruptionem integritatis: et hoc ex lingua sacrae Scripturae.[2]

> [For both sexes are distinguished by the strength and weakness of their bodies. Thus the greater strength is man's, the smaller woman's, so that she might be forbearing of man; to be sure, if men were repelled by women, sexual desire might compel men to seek another or to rush forth to another (i.e., their own) sex. Therefore she is called woman according to the feminine sex, not according to the corruption of condition: and this from the tongue of sacred Scripture.]

What is particularly intriguing about Isidore's description is not his conventional rationale for endorsing feminine subordination, which obviously by the seventh century had become fully institutionalized and socially prolific, but rather a remarkable assumption underlying the rationale: that men desire sexually other men. Indeed, suggests Isidore, women are the object of men's lust only because they are so easily dominated; if men and women were of equal physical strength, Isidore assumes, women would deny men sex altogether, and men would not bother trying. Thus, Isidore reasons, it is a good thing that women have such physical weakness in order to avoid rampant homosexual activity among men.

The Archbishop's matter-of-fact acknowledgment of homoerotic attraction coupled with his endorsement of feminine subordination indicates a profound ambivalence on Isidore's part in relation to gender construction, sexual behaviors, and social identity. Such ambivalence points to the complex and difficult position of homosexuality in relation to the dominant Christian orthodoxy of the Middle Ages. In his groundbreaking study, John Boswell has demonstrated that attitudes toward and perceptions of homosexual acts and those who practiced them vary significantly and erratically throughout the medieval period, becoming more intolerant as the church fathers simultaneously clamp down on usury.[3] While vitriolic diatribes are to be found in any era, theologically informed social attitudes are marked by an underlying ambivalence and vary unpredictably from the relative tolerance of the eleventh and twelfth centuries (during which time, Boswell argues, an urban gay subculture thrived),[4] to the fierce condemnation of Albertus Magnus's *Summa theologiae*, which describes "sodomy" as a grave sin, and to the sensationalist, inflammatory rhetoric of his pupil Thomas Aquinas's own influential *Summa theologiae*.[5] Chaucer, we might recall, began to write in a socially volatile period, during which Geoffrey le Baker's well-known *Chronicon*—a graphic account of Edward II's emblematic homicide and Hugh de Despenser's mutilation slaying[6]—circulated widely. However embellished this popular account and however much the homicides were motivated by political and economic resentments, homosexuality clearly factors in narratives of Edward's demise, indicating homosexuality to be an issue capable of evoking intense social, political, and theological reactions. As Michel Foucault observes of "that utterly confused category" of sodomy, "the nearly universal reticence in talking about it [overtly and specifically] made possible a twofold operation: on the one hand, there was an extreme severity . . . and on the other hand, a tolerance that must have been widespread."[7]

In such a hostile, or at best ambivalent, climate, homosexual practices were common but covert, homosexual discourses ambivalent. That the social and sexual reality of human behavior in the Middle Ages was often at odds with the medieval Church is a literary commonplace, largely polarized as pedantic or humorous; one need only consider, for instance, the didacticism of the Parson or the humor of the fabliaux, which targets the relatively safe foibles of heterosexual relationships. But nonorthodox sexualities have an important place in literature also, bringing to the text a more complex set of cultural interrelationships encompassing not only theological concerns relative to the proscriptions of Christian orthodoxy but also the social and political dynamics of the dominant heterosexual order's desire both to perpetuate and vilify sodomy's subversive constructions.

1

Representations of nonorthodox sexuality, gender construction, and sexual difference in Chaucer's work have received some productive treatment in recent years, particularly in relation to the sexually ambiguous character of the Pardoner in the *Canterbury Tales*.[8] Chaucer's Pardoner epitomizes sexual ambiguity and ambivalence owing to the narrator's notorious observation, "I trowe he were a geldyng or a mare" (I.691), underscored by the verbal exchange of Pardoner and Host (who, the narrator notes, "of manhod hym lakkede right naught" [I.756]), in which the Host threatens the emasculation—"I wolde I hadde thy coillons in myn hond" (VI.952)—of one whose own "manhod" has already been questioned. The narrator-Chaucer's use of the labels "geldyng" and "mare" is atypical and, despite much critical attention, remains largely ambiguous;[9] the implications of "geldyng" suggest some kind of sexual impairment, and, in conjunction with the Pardoner's "smal" voice and lack of a beard, effeminacy or perhaps eunuchry.[10] As Monica McAlpine has demonstrated, "mare" is the more ambiguous of the two labels, but it is equally necessary to promote a sense of effeminacy and uncertainty;[11] together, the labels "geldyng" and "mare," in conjunction with the narrator-Chaucer's own uncertainty, suggest an ambiguously homosexual Pardoner.[12]

The Summoner, I shall argue, is likewise a figure of sexual ambiguity and ambivalence, though less overtly, and, further, the text that he narrates itself articulates a reflexive gendered poetics, a subversive erotics. The Pardoner and Summoner are further aligned by their obvious placement in the *General Prologue*—

> With [the summoner] rood a gentil Pardoner
> Of Rouncivale, his freend and his compeer,
> That streight was comen fro the court of Rome.
> Ful loude he soong "Com hider, love, to me!"
> This Somonour bar to hym a stif burdoun;
> Was nevere trompe of half so greet a soun.   I.669–74

—and the fairly obvious double entendres of their association: the two ride together, and the Pardoner sings of (or, more likely, *to*) his "love," a label that seems to apply in context to the Summoner himself, who supplies the Pardoner with a "stif burdoun."[13] And the curious insistence that the "gentil" Pardoner is both "freend" and "compeer" of the Summoner—underscored by the repetition of the possessive pronoun—perhaps invites further interpretation of the connection between the "gentil," passive Pardoner and the coarse, aggressive Summoner.

Pardoner and Summoner are linked also by the conspicuous ambiguity of their represented sexual orientation in relation to normative presuppositions. Both are given ambiguous—and unflattering—portraits that hint at homosexual behavior while providing details that would support, for the conventionally inclined, a reading of heterosexual interests, though the Pardoner's sexuality is manifest, paradoxically, in absence, and the Summoner's in an ambiguous positivism that destabilizes its own pretense of orthodoxy. The Pardoner's sexual identity is overtly problematized, for example, by the narrator's gelding/mare labels and goat's voice description, and yet he is later depicted as professing, in conversation with the Wife of Bath, to be in want of a wife, though dissuaded at the moment: "I was aboute to wedde a wyf; allas! / What sholde I bye it on my flessh so deere?" (III.166–67). The Pardoner could be claiming an interest in marriage as an evasive tactic, to avoid the pilgrims' scrutiny of his sexual inadequacies; he may even be interested in a sham marriage to provide himself a social cover. The text cannot support any single reading definitively, however, and to make any assumptions would be to presume more history and motive than that for which the text provides evidence. The physical description of the Summoner's facial features in the *General Prologue* may be associated with syphilis or other sexually transmitted disease,¹⁴ and it will be useful to recall in context that such diseases may be transmitted from man to man as well as from woman to man. Thus while the Summoner's malady does not necessarily indicate homosexual behaviors, it does not preclude the possibility. The mawkish and apparently syphilitic Summoner is described in terms of churlish *heterosexual* behavior—"lecherous as a sparwe" (I.626), "a gentil harlot" (647), "Ful prively a fynch eek koude he pulle" (652), "In daunger hadde he at his owene gise / The yonge girles of the diocise / And knew hir conseil, and was al hir reed" (663–65)—that may correspond as well to churlish *homosexual* behavior, for the "fynch" subjected to his private, lecherous "pulle[ing]" could be a male or female,¹⁵ and the identification of "girles" that he has "hadde" could correspond to youths in general, including young men, and not specifically young females.¹⁶ The Summoner, like the Pardoner, is characterized by a sexual ambiguity that leans toward homosexuality.

The Summoner's implied sexuality parallels his implied performance as a summoner; just as homosexuality would be perceived by an orthodox Christian audience as an aberration or perversion, so too the Summoner's exploitative execution of his sanctioned duties might be understood as corrupt or perverse behavior. He is depicted as a predator, both sexual and financial. The Summoner, like the Pardoner, has his sexuality problematized and subtly affronted by the narrator-Chaucer in connection with indications of corrupt and sanctimonious official behavior; neither pilgrim is what he seems to be personally or professionally. The Summoner's *General Prologue* portrait informs the narrative voice of his Prologue and *Tale*; we need not glean the Prologue and *Tale* for further evidence of the Summoner's sexual history or inclinations (though it will be useful to consider the Summoner as both character and narrative construct), but the information supplied in the *General Prologue* can better help us to appreciate the nuances of textual erotics and the implications of sexual(ized) difference in the Summoner's narrative performance.

My interest in the Summoner and his text concerns not the question of whether the Summoner and Pardoner might share a relationship beyond that overtly described in the text or whether the Summoner might be critically labeled in sexual terms as has been the Pardoner but rather how the Summoner's own sexual ambiguity and sexualized ambivalence inform his contribution to the *Canterbury Tales*. In short, I am concerned with the Summoner's own articulation of a narrative erotics, specifically how that language provides a perspective of sexual(ized) subversion on reading Chaucer's text. I would like first to consider the *Summoner's Tale* in relation to its depictions of "groping" in order to demonstrate the workings of a reflexive trope of hermeneutic gesture predicated on Christian orthodoxy. Then, by situating the gesture in relation to gendered epistemologies, I hope to demonstrate that even as the text ostensibly insists on the propriety of a heterosexual orthodoxy, it simultaneously destabilizes its own illusory privileging of a monolithic decorum of gender.

2

The *Summoner's Tale* centers on an image of "groping," which may be read as a trope of gendered hermeneutic representation. To "grope," according to the *MED*, is to feel with one's hands, often in search of something specific; to "examine, probe, or investigate someone or something."[17] The term invites obvious sexual connotations as well, for to "grope" someone (in the *OED*'s "indecent sense")[18] is to feel or fondle him or her for purposes of titillation. To "grope," then, is to participate actively in a process of discovery, imposition, manipulation, and perhaps exploitation, and there is an implication of masculine aggression owing to the forcefulness of the indicated action, whether the object of the groping be male or female. "Grope" is a word used infrequently by Chaucer,[19] but, as it is often the case in the *Canterbury Tales* that language introduced in a *General Prologue* portrait resurfaces in the voice of the corresponding pilgrim, one of the few occasions of "grope" is provided by the portrait of the Summoner, described as having been groped by those wishing to test the legitimacy of his pretentious Latin nattering: "But whoso koude in oother thyng hym grope, / Thanne hadde he spent al his philosophie" (I.644–45). Here, the process of groping exposes the Summoner's intellectual and theological pretentiousness: in his tale, "grope" will be foregrounded and problematized as a physical and hermeneutic gesture.

The crux of this reading of the Summoner's narrative is the groping of Thomas by the predatory Friar John, performed at Thomas's request. In its immediate context, "grope" is used in its most denotative sense—of feeling or probing—as part of Thomas's command to John,[20] with sexual and scatological connotations:

"Now thanne, put in thyn hand doun by my bak,"
Seyde this man, "and grope wel bihynde.
Bynethe my buttok there shaltow fynde
A thyng that I have hyd in pryvetee."   III.2140–43

Thomas's invitation, adhering to the fabliau convention of comeuppance and its preparation, is contingent on the greedy Friar's quest for gold. Thomas makes the offer knowing that the Friar is predisposed to comply, that his desire for personal gain negates any hesitation about the obviously scatological and sexual implications of the act to be performed.[21] Within the narrative frame Thomas assumes a feminized, submissive role and issues the invitation ("Com, hider, love to me"). True, many readers associate the Summoner with Thomas in order to perpetuate the "quiting" structure as a critical frame for Fragment III, whereby the Summoner, in quiting the Friar's unflattering depiction of a summoner in the *Friar's Tale*, shows Thomas quiting a churlish friar. However, if the specifics of the *General Prologue* portraits are considered, then a clear analogy can be made both between the pilgrim-Summoner and Friar John, and also between the pilgrim-Pardoner and Thomas. Echoing the Pardoner's occupational gesture as well, Thomas will offer the Friar a false "relic" of sorts, the "yifte" of the fart.

To this extent the Friar within the *Tale* is analogous to the Summoner without: the Friar gropes enthusiastically and the Summoner describes the adventure with equal relish:

> "A!" thoghte this frere, "That shal go with me!"
> And doun his hand he launcheth to the clifte
> In hope for to fynde there a yifte.
> And whan this sike man felte this frere
> Aboute his tuwel grope there and heere,
> Amydde his hand he leet the frere a fart.   III.2144–49

The Friar's behavior, then, is invited. While groping may be understood as imposition, it is effected without coercion, and in this context groping is not to be equated with rape or other acts of unwelcomed or ineluctable sexual violation. The Friar assumes an aggressive role and eagerly gropes the "tuwel" of his "compeer" in search of the unnamed "thyng," located "in pryvetee," that is, inhabiting the zone of secret, private, and sexual territories.[22] The Friar's groping describes a physical process of discovery effected by imposition. So too it may be read as a hermeneutic gesture likewise concerned with discovery, for a moral lesson concerning gluttony inheres in the fabliau's attention to satire, the effective "fruyt" of a successful "grope." Just as Moses receives, in the Friar's earlier anecdote, "the lawe that was writen / With Goddes fynger" (III.1889–90),[23] so Thomas receives Friar John's finger but responds, as it were, with his own text.

This is not to suggest that some hidden Truth is to be revealed by dint of hermeneutic process; the hermeneutic trope suggested by this twofold physical/discursive gesture insists that meaning does not reside in some hidden location, waiting to be revealed, but rather that the process informs as much as it uncovers. Indeed, the "thyng" found by the Friar is much like his own prolix chatter.[24]

Western culture has long derived great mirth from literary representations of flatulence. Such literary occasions may be understood as manifestations of what Bakhtin refers to as "carnival," a rubric under which "all that is sacred and exalted is rethought on the level of the material bodily stratum or else combined and mixed with its images."[25] Chaucer's most famous literary fart, for instance, that of Nicholas in the *Miller's Tale*, remains one of the most popular moments for readers of the *Canterbury Tales*. Such representations obviously bring to the text more than provocative humor; we may find additionally in these representations of vulgarly construed bodily processes an instructive parallel of flatus and speech. Readers of the *Summoner's Tale*, for instance, have long noted that Friar John's garrulousness may be likened to the fart that he later receives in a humorous manifestation of *contrapasso*, for Friar John's rambling, self-centered digressions are intrusive expirations, full of hypocritical *apologiae* and venomous complaint; his excessive speech, in effect, pollutes the environment shared by his audience within the text. And it therefore seems fitting that the text's overt *moralitas* is founded on Friar John being the recipient of the foul wind of another. (In the *Miller's Tale*, the connection of speech and fart is made overt: "'Spek, sweete bryd, I noot nat where thou art.' / This Nicholas anon leet fle a fart" [I.3805–6].) Thus literary farts are more than humorous occasions of vulgar representation; they are, to paraphrase Dante, "strange signals," reflexive, polysemous indicators of the inextricable coincidence of flesh and text.[26] The fart may inspire chuckles from readers, but it points as well to a far more complex role in the narrative's hermeneutics.

The parallel of belch and fart in the *Summoner's Tale* underscores the metaphor of fart-as-speech. Both signify foul, broken wind, and, projected from opposite ends of the alimentary canal, both share a common origin of the flesh in its most repugnant sense. In this respect, the conflation of belch and fart in Innocent's *De miseria* perhaps informs Chaucer's poem: "Turpiter egerit quod turpiter ingerit, superius et inferius horribilem flatum exprimens, et abhominabilem sonum emittens"[27] [What foully goes in foully comes out, expelling above and below a horrible wind, and emitting an abominable sound]. Bakhtin's description of textual forms of "the material bodily lower stratum" considers such conflations and addresses the figurative significance of expulsionary dynamics in relation to bodily images: "Down, inside out, vice versa, upside down, such is the direction of all these movements. All of them thrust down, turn over, push headfirst, transfer top to bottom, and bottom to top, both in the literal sense of space, and in the metaphorical meaning of the image."[28] A coincidence of *horribilis flatus* and speech is adduced in Friar John's discussion of Jovinian, in which he plays on the polysemy of *erucatavit* [has uttered, ejected, or belched] in the biblical verse, and which is punctuated by the sound of a belch:

"Lo, 'buf!' they seye, '*cor meum eructavit!*'[29]
Who folweth Cristes gospel and his foore,
But we that humble been, and chaast, and poore,
Werkeris of Goddes word, nat auditours?"   III.1934-37

From Friar John's perspective, "*cor meum eructavit*" [my heart has uttered] suggests as well that the heart, the origin of utterances, figuratively belches ("buf!") and, with respect to Innocent's conflation, farts as well. Belching and farting are expulsions from the body that, when made in the presence of others, constitute an imposition as well; the Friar's words are as foul and as intrusive as is his humorously sacriligious belch. Such is, in part at least, the message that Thomas's recompensatory fart wittily makes known. That the Friar actively seeks out the "thyng" by groping between the cleft of Thomas's buttocks underscores the irony—and supplies the humor—of the *contrapasso*.[30]

The link between eros and language, manifest in theological and poetic theory via Augustine's understanding of the interconnectedness of the two and its ubiquitous application in medieval poetics, constitutes what may indeed be described as an erotics of textual process. The connection is manifest in the *Summoner's Tale*, for example, in the commonplace of an obviously sexualized emphasis on the Friar's writing utensils and other official apparatus: "With scrippe and tipped staf, ytukked hye, / In every hous he gan to poure and prye" (III.1737-38); "His felawe hadde a staf tipped with horn, / A peyre of tables al of yvory, / And a poyntel polysshed fetisly" (1740-42). (An erotics of language is further suggested by the text's attention to "glossing," a point to which I shall return.)

But this language model invites a twofold concern with regard to potential distortion: the threat of unisemy should imposition become too personal or private, and the threat of meaninglessness should polysemy run unchecked. The latter concern finds relief (for those who wish it) through orthodox Christianity's insistence on the Word as an ultimate limit.[31] By anchoring meaning to a transcendental signified, medieval Christianity ensured that signification's potential multiplicity could be given appropriate parameters and that therefore the dominance of the Word underlying all discourse would obtain. Roy Peter Clark has made a cogent argument for the presence of a "Doubting Thomas" motif in the *Summoner's Tale,* which, I believe, underscores this relationship of language and orthodoxy.[32] Clark's analogy, however, likens the Summoner's *Thomas* to the gospel Thomas (and avoids aligning the Friar himself). On the other hand, if the Friar is cast in the gospel role, the analogy effectively illustrates the relationship of Word and gesture: just as the gospel Thomas literally gropes the flesh of the incarnate Word in search of certainty and the security of unequivocal knowing, so too Friar John gropes the man's "tuwel" in a gesture of inquiry and exploration. In this context, the Friar's groping may be read as a parody of the scriptural groping-of-the-Word episode that through a paradoxically conventional yet subversive representation reinforces orthodoxy.

The concern that unisemy might be effected by abusive or excessive personalizing of language is less easily remedied, however, for in practice the parameters of medieval Christian orthodoxy were themselves abused, supporting a hegemony of privatization. The Summoner's Friar articulates such a hegemonic usurpation:

> And therfore may ye se that oure preyeres—
> I speke of us, we mendynantz, we freres—
> Been to the hye God moore acceptable
> Than youres.   III.1911–14

Hence, for instance, the Lollards' argument that the restrictive, oppressive signifying practices of patriarchal authorities be rejected, that patriarchal claims of interpretive privilege and closure be challenged, calls into question the legitimacy of such an appropriation as is illustrated by the Summoner's Friar.[33] In this sense, too, the Friar is indeed his author's construct, for, just as the Summoner appropriates Latin phrases toward a self-serving end, the Friar relishes exclusivity and manipulation and likewise abuses ecclesiastical authority in the process. Indeed, the Friar is shown—and the Summoner is implied—to manipulate both texts and "tuwel[s]."

The concern with exclusivity and privatization is played out in the *Summoner's Tale* through the text's attention to "glosynge," for Friar John's interest in and abuse of glossing contribute to the text's overt condemnation of self-glorification manifest in its treatment of textual erotics. The Friar's glossing is shown to be a personalized and arrogant appropriation of signification:

> I have to day been at youre chirche at messe,
> And seyd a sermon after my symple wit—
> Nat al after the text of hooly writ,
> For it is hard to yow, as I suppose,
> And therfore wol I teche yow al the glose.
> Glosynge is a glorious thyng, certeyn,
> For lettre sleeth, so as we clerkes seyn.   III.1788–94

Much has been written on the Friar's abuse of glossing, particularly as the character is shown to abuse language effectively as a predator and as a hypocrite. As Mary Carruthers has demonstrated, the Friar clearly misrepresents the Pauline insistence that "littera enim occidit, Spiritus autem vivificat" ("the letter kills, but the spirit quickens," 2 Cor 3.6). Rather than use the Pauline directive to ensure that figurative or spiritual meaning obtain beyond the literal or carnal level, the Friar ironically interprets the Pauline directive literally and thus wholly displaces the letter of scripture in his own sermonizing.[34] And, as Edmund Reiss has noted, the Friar lifts this and other exegetical directives out of context, deliberately misrepresenting both the letter and spirit of the full text.[35] Hence the Friar exploits the slipperiness of glossing to the extent that the literal text is absent: "I ne have no text of it, as I suppose, / But I shal fynde it in a maner glose" (1919–20). There is no literal text against which to measure the validity of the gloss, and thus the authority of the gloss derives solely from the speaker's own insistence on its legitimacy.

But if the text foregrounds its treatment of hermeneutic representation in connection with a depiction of an ambiguously sexual act, what are we to make of the erotic implications of this narrative performance, particularly as the text participates in a conventional concern with privatization? If we choose to locate the autoerotic or homoerotic connotations of the Friar's groping within an orthodox decorum, the groping gesture would seem to be predicated upon a fairly conventional trope, whereby sodomy is associated with idolatry, including idolatry of both letter and self. Within the parameters of this Christian orthodoxy, the Friar's self-serving appropriation of scriptural glossing represents a personalized and ultimately problematic usurpation that may be interpreted as self-desire, a turning toward the self through the perverted instrumentality of exclusive appropriation. In this context, given the Friar's personalized glossing it is no surprise that his treatment of Thomas's "tuwel," like his treatment of language, entails rigorous manipulation designed to glorify himself. In usurping the practices of glossing and groping to an end of personalized, privatized abuse, the Friar betrays his self-interest, his desire for self-promotion: the Friar is depicted as shameless in his self-serving groping of not only the "tuwel" but texts as well, and the Friar's interest in groping, like his interest in glossing, seems to be largely motivated by self-desire.

Further, the text's articulation of the sodomy trope is underscored by the character of the Friar, who, like the Summoner-narrator whose voice articulates the character's existence, is a predator, conning and duping those naive enough to accept his sanctimonious posturing. The Friar is depicted throughout the narrative as using the faithful as pawns in his self-serving game and, indeed, the Friar is as gluttonous for admiration as he is for luxury,[36] and, as demonstrated in his privatizing of prayer and appropriating of God's acceptance (III.1911–14), he is stunningly proud. The Friar's groping gesture therefore evokes a conventional satiric association of friars and sodomites, described by writers as diverse as Walther Maps and William Langland.[37] The privatized glossing and male-to-male groping depicted in the *Summoner's Tale* suggest on a fairly basic level the sort of sodomy that pertains to sexual acts deemed "unnatural" owing to their nonprocreative purpose, including onanism and oral and anal substitutes for intercourse considered more legitimate.[38] Within the parameters of this heterosexual orthodoxy, the *Tale* seems to reiterate conventional arguments against homosexual coupling by depicting the foul "fruyt" thereby produced, for homoerotic groping is shown to yield the "fruyt" of the "tuwel" rather than the fertile fruit of the womb, of heterosexual conception and childbearing.[39] Although the church fathers could never quite agree on what is or is not "natural" in relation to sexual behaviors, most antihomosexual writings argue that male-to-male coupling is "unnatural" because no conception is possible, that it defies the natural order of creation and is therefore an affront to God. The fart is, in effect, shown to be the bastard fruit of unnatural coupling.

But more important, the sin of sodomy, ambiguous at best in practical definitions, corresponds spiritually to a sin of *pride* rather than to any specific sexual behaviors. The scriptural grounds for this interpretation are found in the Genesis episode where the Sodomites are punished for an unspecified sin (*"scelere"* [pollutedness, profaneness])—and hence for their pride in nonconformity to God's wishes—and are elucidated in Sophonias: "Hoc eis eveniet pro superbia sua, Quia blasphemaverunt" [This to them shall happen for their pride, because they have blasphemed] (Gn 19.15 and Sph 2.10, respectively). The pride of the Sodomites is manifest as well in the form of their inhospitableness, for their foremost transgression appears to be their rudeness to the visiting angels, though this rudeness is expressed ambiguously—"educ illos huc, ut cognoscamus eos" [Bring the men out that we may know them] (Gn 19.5)—fueling later interpretations that homosexual rape is the actual threat, especially given that Lot offers up his virgin daughters to the mob in an appalling gesture of appeasement: "et abutimini eis sicut vobis placuerit, dummodo viris istis nihil mali faciatis" [abuse them as it shall please you, so that to these men you do no evil] (19.8).[40] The pride inhering in sins of inhospitableness is considered serious enough, we might recall, to warrant placement in the Ninth Circle of Dante's *Inferno*.[41] Pride (*superbia*) and its utterance, blasphemy, characterize the sins of Sodom, and they characterize as well the rude, hypocritical, and sanctimonious behavior of Friar John in relation to Christian orthodoxy.

The Summoner's narrative clearly operates within the parameters of an unflattering convention, designed not so much to implicate participants in specific sexual behaviors but rather to impugn sins of pride, such as the Friar's abusing of ecclesiastical privilege to a self-serving end. By extension, then, the sodomy motif connects the Friar's groping gesture with the orthodox condemnation of self-glorification through language. This in turn leads us to Dante's treatment of Brunetto Latini in *Inferno*, perhaps the best-known example of the medieval correlation of sodomy, self-desire, and pride.[42] In the encounter between Dante and Brunetto—the latter apparently punished for the unnamed sin of sodomy—Dante thanks Brunetto for teaching him the art of self-preservation through textuality: "m'insegnavate come l'uom s'etterna: / e quant' io 'l'abbia in grado, mentr' io vivo / convien che ne la mia lingua si scerna" ["you taught me how man makes himself eternal: / and while I live, my gratitude for that / must always be apparent in my words"] (15.85–87). At the end of their conversation, Brunetto reiterates his desire for preservation or glorification, which Dante obliges by recording the request in his account: "Sieti raccomandato il mio *Tesoro*, / nel qual io vivo ancora, e più non cheggio" ["Let my *Tesoro*, in which I still live, / be precious to you; and I ask no more"] (15.119–20). Eugene Vance, noting that "[t]he equation between idolatry, including idolatry of the letter, and sexual perversion became a subtle force in medieval poetics," explicates the analogy between sodomy and idolatry articulated in this canto and suggests that Brunetto's desire for eternal glorification is to be equated with the idolatry associated with those acts included under the rubric of sodomy.[43] The Friar's privatized appropriation of language—his glossing—within this convention is connected to his groping as an autoerotic or homoerotic gesture of self-glorification. Textuality, not sexuality per se, mediates desire, and Chaucer's text, like Dante's, uses the available convention to hint at nonnormative sexual expression's signifying of spiritual perversion.

The analogy as reiterated in the *Summoner's Tale* is prepared for by the Prologue's remarkable image of the "develes ers" and the friars housed therein,[44] an obviously distorted and exaggerated representation shown to a corrupt friar in a dream-vision parody:

> Right so as bees out swarmen from an hyve,
> Out of the develes ers ther gonne dryve
> Twenty thousand freres on a route,
> And thurghout helle swarmed al aboute,
> And comen agayn as faste as they may gon,
> And in his ers they crepten everychon.
> He clapte his tayl agayn and lay ful stille.   III.1693–99

Like a flatus or excrement, the swarm is expelled;[45] but, more significantly, the friars then return to this dwelling place in a grotesque gesture of penetration. Here, the text offers a grotesque presentation of the friar-as-sodomite motif, the friars inhabiting the "ers" of Satan (presumably the origin of such behaviors) in retribution for their idolatrous perversions. The sodomite friars—twenty thousand strong—inhabit the figurative site of their spiritual transgressions, much as Friar John is shown to inhabit manually the site corresponding to his own obsessive pride, where he finds in the climax of the encounter not the satisfaction of the desired "yifte" but the humiliation—in the form of a fart—of having himself been deceived.

Hence the quandary of how to divide the fart: the intangible fart lacks the substance necessary for literal division and displacment, and thus the Friar is confounded by his task: "To parte that wol nat departed be / To every man yliche, with meschaunce!" (III.2214–15). The fart can only signify improperly, as it is appropriated; it has no "proper" position within the Friar's limited economy of theological misreading; it is ineffable yet distinct, unownable yet a gift, vulgar yet profoundly significant. Indeed, the "man of greet honour" (2163) and his wife are, like the Friar, confounded by Thomas's cunning deed. The Friar is greatly vexed by the problem of how to fulfill his earlier promise to divide among his fellow friars whatever spoils he might obtain from Thomas. Of course, since the fart is a stand-in for the Friar's offensive utterances, and therefore a manifestation of *contrapasso* justice, the Friar could satisfy the oath simply by recounting the lesson—that is, by telling his brethren of his experience, as he does for an audience of lord, lady, and clerk. But the literal-minded Friar instead overlooks the obvious figurative significance of the flatus and concentrates wholly on the comparatively irrelevant issue of how to divide it.

Hence the literalist epistemology privileged by the Friar is challenged within the narrative by the Friar's perception of his task. The Friar's valorization of masculine unity is predicated on a rejection of division. He has argued, for instance, "What is a ferthyng worth parted in twelve? / Lo, ech thyng that is oned in himselve / Is moore strong than whan it is toscatered" (III.1967–69) and has demonstrated his commitment to this philosophy literally, by participating, through groping, in a gesture of male-to-male, two-in-one fusing with Thomas. Confronted with a task beyond his ability or willingness to perform, he must turn to another's "ars-metrike" and submit to Jankyn's bizarre, but literally appropriate, solution (which is imposed on not only the named culprit Friar John but his metaphorically equally sodomitic brethren as well). Accordingly, one could construe from the Summoner's Prologue and *Tale* a *moralitas* or *sentence* apropos of idolatrous sin and the punishments thereof, articulated hypocritically by a pilgrim whose own behavior violates these assertions. In this respect, one could argue, the *Tale* privileges a compulsory heterosexual decorum of gender, language, and morality.

※ 3

But it would be too easy to dismiss the treatments of glossing and groping in the *Summoner's Tale* as wholly limited to didactic or pedantic exempla on the propriety of Christian orthodoxy or as an antifraternal indictment evinced by way of generic satire.[46] The arguably homoerotic exchange is easy to read via orthodox heterosexual Christian decorum, but the text also brings a polysexual perspective to that ambiguous gesture, a complex interplay between erotics and hermeneutics that subverts orthodoxy.

A return to the erotic connotations of glossing and groping, to clarify their interconnectedness in terms of sexual and textual performance, might help us to consider how, together, glossing and groping expose the text's betrayal of orthodox propriety. To gloss a word, phrase, or passage is to supply a more readily accessible interpretation or annotation for purposes of clarification or explanation, and, owing to the word's etymology (*glossa*, "tongue"), enhanced by the medieval appreciation of the connectedness of eros and language, "gloss" connotes an erotic sense as well.[47] As we have seen, Chaucer exploits this connection most explicitly in the Wife of Bath's Prologue—"Men may devyne and glosen, up and doun" (III.26); "so wel koude he me glose / Whan that he wolde han my *bele chose*" (III.509–10)— where "gloss" operates as a destabilizing erotic metaphor and a discursive feature of narrative errancy, demonstrating that glossing may be performed both textually and sexually and that the tongue (*glossa*) is in effect bisexual, belonging to and representative of both the masculine and the feminine.[48] Further, the Wife is shown to connect glossing and groping in her declaration of heterosexual domination: she boasts that her submissive husband has given to her "of his tonge, and of his hond also" (III.815). Through the Wife's narrative, Chaucer links textual performance, orally and manually, to sexual manipulation.

The *Summoner's Tale* likewise articulates an erotics of glossing, though less explicitly, elucidated by its more extensive and (homo)sexually foregrounded treatment of groping imagery—the Friar in the *Tale* is depicted as glossing texts and groping men, evoking an erotics of textual/ hermeneutic manipulation that subverts orthodox gender identification. The relationship of letter and gloss is conventionally gendered by Pauline theology's association of the literal-carnal-feminine; as the Friar rejects the letter in order to privatize the gloss, so too he rejects the feminine in order to favor his own masculinity. His glossing embraces the masculine as it displaces the feminine: by denying the existence and import of the letter the Friar is likewise denying the feminine that corresponds to the carnal or literal, a gesture represented by the male-to-male groping. Although medieval theologians were eager to denigrate the feminine owing to its association with the carnal—and hence with sexuality—the duality of masculine and feminine with regard to language is contingent on both: the letter represents the carnal origin on which further meaning might be conceived, predicated as this model is on a heterosexual orthodoxy.

The Friar's rejection of the feminine is given further weight by the antifeminist diatribe that precedes the groping episode. Prefaced by a hint that Thomas has been acting in a manner unmasculine—"Youre inconstance is youre confusion" (III.1958)—the Friar's lengthy speech, ostensibly on anger, reiterates various antifeminist commonplaces. The Friar initially defends Thomas's wife, in a curious (and of course ironic, given the Friar's rude behavior)[49] reiteration of household decorum, that one behave in a hospitable manner toward others in the household: "And therfore, Thomas, trowe me if thee leste, / Ne stryve nat with thy wyf, as for thy beste" (III.1985–86). But this purported defense is quickly followed by a conventional retelling of the Eve motif, with a typical endorsement of the blame-the-woman directive:

> Ther nys, ywys, no serpent so cruel,
> Whan man tret on his tayl, ne half so fel,
> As womman is, whan she hath caught an ire;
> Vengeance is thanne al that they desire.   III.2001–4

Although the *Summoner's Tale* is largely void of the pervasive misogyny characterizing many other medieval texts—Chaucer's included—the presence here of antifeminist commonplaces contributes to the "groping" theme by providing the text with a feminine component that serves as both a contrast and a foregrounding.

Prior to the narrating of his tale, the Summoner is himself shown to reject the feminine in favor of an ambivalent masculine dispensation. The inchoate laughter and sportive threats of the pilgrim-Friar and pilgrim-Summoner, which mark the transition from the Wife of Bath's Prologue to her *Tale*, complicate and deflectively mask a curious interruption. For while the Friar merely laughs and comments that the Wife's lengthy preamble has been entertaining—"The Frere lough, whan he hadde herd al this; / 'Now dame,' quod he, 'so have I joye or blis, / This is a long preamble of a tale!'" (III.829–31)—the Summoner, however, ignores the Wife and her discourse entirely, usurping her audience to make his hostility toward the Friar overt:

> "Lo," quod the Somonour, "Goddes armes two!
> A frere wol entremette hym everemo.
> Lo, goode men, a flye and eek a frere
> Wol falle in every dyssh and eek mateere.
> What spekestow of preambulacioun?
> What! amble, or trotte, or pees, or go sit doun!
> Thou lettest oure disport in this manere."   III.833–39

In chastizing the Friar for what is actually a relevant and responsive interjection, the Summoner is far more intrusive, and his championing "disport" ironic, given the mirthlessness of his scolding. Saved by the Host in an overtly gendered defense ("Lat the womman telle hire tale" [851]), the Wife proceeds—but not before the Summoner's interruption achieves, albeit temporarily, two things: he forestalls the Wife's continuation of her discourse ostensibly valorizing sexual relationships between men and women, and he foregrounds his ability and desire to dominate, aggressively and arrogantly, another man, in an oddly symbiotic relationship of interdependency (further played out in their complementary narratives: the Summoner's interruption of the Friar [III.1332–35] balanced by the Friar's of the Summoner [1761–64]). The Summoner's behavior invites speculation regarding motive, and while any definitive explanation is impossible, the questions raised about the Summoner's interests and intent point to the complexity of the Summoner as both character and narrator, particularly in relation to gender, power, and language.

If we momentarily set aside the *Tale*'s obvious connections to orthodox paradigms of moral and sexual behaviors, we can choose to see how the narrative instead occupies a position of reflexive ambivalence. The *Summoner's Tale* then is a text that effectively betrays itself, insisting as it does that the problematic of gender construction apropos of public/private space[50] be foregrounded in relation to the text's own ars(e)-metrike/ *ars metrica*,[51] its own articulation of narrative gestures of sexual and hermeneutic ambivalence. Indeed the sequential rehearsings of the groping episode within the *Tale*—"And he anon hym tolde, / As ye han herd biforn— ye woot wel what" (2198–99), "and herde word by word / Of alle thynges which I have yow sayd" (2244–45)—serve to underscore the text's repetition of its own subtext of resistance. The repetition of the groping episode within the *Tale*, not once but twice, underscores the significance of the episode's subversive erotics—the rehearsals, said to be verbatim though absent in the literal narrative, insist that an otherwise marginalized perspective be foregrounded and that the *Summoner's Tale* itself be groped for method as well as effect, for a reflexive poetics of its own making.

The gendered nuances of language—epistemology, hermeneutics, poetics—are crucial to the performance of the Summoner's text. In this regard, the subversive erotics of the *Summoner's Tale* exposes the limitations of the orthodox model. The correlation of gender and language is itself an imposition *ad placitum*; it is a usurpation that seems almost arbitrary in its conventional identifications. We can determine that the Pauline model of the feminine literal and masculine spiritual, for instance, is contradicted by the Aristotelian/Pythagorean model, and yet for both the Christian and classical models an interplay of consciously gendered components is crucial to the workings of verbal signification. The text's deliberate constructions of gender definition, if permitted, would seem to point toward an alignment of gender and monolithic heterosexuality. But how might Chaucer himself be manipulating or destablizing decorum?

Friar John's rejection of the feminine letter problematizes his glossing only to the extent that the erotic performance of glossing is transformed. In this sense glossing, like groping, becomes a masculine act performed on a masculine body. And if glossing and groping are sexual/textual acts performed by and imposed on gendered bodies, they do not necessarily observe orthodox dictates: the masculine may gloss and grope the masculine and the feminine, and the feminine may likewise engage the feminine and the masculine. If orthodox imposition is rejected, then glossing and groping, *impositio ad placitum*, connote an erotics of polysemous textual practice, plural rather than monolithic, running a spectrum rather than occupying nonnegotiable poles of fixed location. Hence masculine and feminine, male and female, coexist and may be said to coincide, retaining individual identities even as superficial boundaries might temporarily be collapsed. In this sense, Chaucer, I would argue, rejects the essentialism of sexual identity as a contingency of gender construction, thereby turning the arbitrariness of gendered decorum against itself.

In destabilizing gendered decorum, Chaucer rejects as well the Pauline fantasy of androgyny ("non est masculus, neque femina" [there is no masculine nor feminine]), which seeks to deny sexualities by denying gender difference.[52] "Difference" is for Chaucer, as for other medieval thinkers and writers, crucial for epistemological distinction. At one level, we can see the reflexive operation of binary structures. But the components are themselves both arbitrary and contingent: contingent in that they are defined in terms of each other, arbitrary in that epistemological structures are themselves imposed, constructed. Indeed, while "male" and "female" identify biologically based sexual beings, "masculine" and "feminine," as gender identifications, are flexible constructs of cultural inscription. Given that gender construction is contingent upon a cultural privileging of binarism, the masculine/feminine couple persists even as gender identifications accommodate a spectrum of sexualities in practice;

how texts negotiate the gendered space between the poles of the binarism constitutes a destabilizing erotics that dismantles the narrative structures of a viable yet illusory orthodoxy. Thus while binarism may be essentially motivated, its applications transcend such constraints. By complicating gender decorum and foregrounding hermeneutic models, the subversive erotics of Chaucer's text dismantles the myth of the monolithic without apology and without contempt.

Notes

Introduction: Gender and the Craft of Making

1. All citations of Chaucer's work are from the *Riverside Chaucer;* fragment (or book) and line numbers are supplied in text throughout.
2. On Chaucer's "reflexive imagination," see Aers, *Creative Imagination*, 81–82.
3. See lines I.3855–63.
4. A succinct statement of the poetry-polysemy link is provided in the *Epistle X* to Can Grande, attributed to Dante; poetic language is described as *"polysemos,* hoc est plurium sensuum" [polysemous, that is, of plural/many senses]—*Dantis Alagherii Epistolae*, 10.7. I use "polysemous" not only to denote the plural senses of a single word or phrase but also to call attention to the many senses of language and indeed of a text itself.
5. See the insightful explication of this text in Dinshaw's *Chaucer's Sexual Poetics*, 1–10.
6. On the implications of this passage with regard to the *Troilus*'s overt concern with language and textuality, see Garbaty, "*Troilus* V, 1786–92 and V, 1807–27," 299–305; and see Chapter 2.
7. Marshall Leicester argues that the *Canterbury Tales* "is a set of texts that are about the subjectivity of their speakers in the technical sense and that Chaucer's subject is the subject, not, or only incidentally, the self" (*Disenchanted Self*, 14).
8. Olson, in "Making and Poetry in the Age of Chaucer," notes, "Chaucer employs 'makere' and 'makyng' to describe himself, his contemporaries, and their activity, and 'poete' and 'poetire' to designate the ancients, the most revered moderns, and their work" (274–75). On Chaucer as "maker," see also Kiser, *Telling Classical Tales*, esp. chapter 5, "'Poesey,' 'Makyng,' and 'Translacioun,'" 132–54; Schmidt, *The Clerkly Maker*, esp. 144–46, "Poet, Maker, Translator, Versifier"; Ebin, *Illuminator, Makar, Vates*, esp. 193–200. (Spiers, *Chaucer the Maker*, despite its intriguing title, is a thematic overview of Chaucer's poetry with little attention to its critical dimension.)
9. Tatlock, "The Epilog of Chaucer's *Troilus*," 631–32.
10. Kiser, *Telling Classical Tales*, 136–41.

11. See, for instance, lines 264–72; 340–352; 399–420; 426–31; 471–79; 538–41.

12. See lines 37, 99, 133–34, 225–26 of *Pearl*, in *The Poems of the Pearl Manuscript*, ed. Malcolm Andrew and Ronald Waldron, 53–110; *Sir Gawain and the Green Knight*, in the same volume, 207–300; and lines 3ff. of *Cleanness*, 111–84; Prol. 210–11, 1.1.2, 12.21–22 of William Langland, *The Vision of Piers Plowman*.

13. On Henryson's *Testament* in relation to "making" and gender, see my recent article "Froward Language and Wanton Play."

14. According to the *MED*, the verb "make" corresponds to activities of creating (*maken* < OE *macien*); see "maken" (1) 5a.

15. The *MED* notes that the noun "make" refers to one of a pair (*mak[e]* < OE *macche, gemaca*), akin to the modern "match" or "mate." See "make" (1) 2a.

16. See also Derrida, "The Law of Genre," trans. Avital Ronell, 55–81, and related commentary in Benstock, *Textualizing the Feminine*; and Baron, *Grammar and Gender*, 90–111.

17. Sedgwick, *Epistemology of the Closet*, 27–28. See also Finke, *Feminist Theory, Women's Writing*, on "gender as a relational system" (xii); and Dinshaw, *Chaucer's Sexual Poetics*, which is "concerned with masculine and feminine as roles, positions, functions that can be taken up, occupied, or performed by either sex, male or female" (9), a position that informs my own. (I would argue, however, that in her argument apropos of "reading like a man" (or like a woman), Dinshaw actually describes *gendered* rather than *sexual* reading and poetics—namely, reading in a masculine or feminine mode.) See also Hansen, *Fictions of Gender*, 12–15; and Crane's recent *Gender and Romance*, 3–15, which considers the interconnectedness of "gender" and "genre" in relation to romance traditions.

18. Sedgwick, *Epistemology of the Closet*, 28–29. See also the insightful discussion of gender and sexual difference in Dollimore, *Sexual Dissidence*, 249–75.

19. However, Butler, in *Gender Trouble*, questions gender categories' relationship to sex (esp. 16–17). Laqueur, in *Making Sex: Body and Gender*, likewise challenges the sex/gender presupposition (11). But, as Laqueur implies, sexual discourses speak of the presence of gender. Bennett, "Gender as Performance," argues that "saying that we belong to the category 'women' does not mean that we have trapped ourselves inside a term or inside of previous cultural understandings of what that term signifies" (106).

20. See, for instance, de Lauretis, "The Violence of Rhetoric," 245.

21. See Biddick, "Genders, Bodies, Borders," 393. Biddick acknowledges an indebtedness to Judith Butler for her line of thinking here. See Butler, *Bodies That Matter*, esp. 27–55. On cultural contexts and new historicist approaches of literary analysis, see the overview by Patterson in his *Negotiating the Past*, 3–39.

22. Bibia sacra iuxta vulgatam Clementinam, 1 Tim 2.11–15. Translations here and elsewhere, except where noted otherwise, are my own. Paul's statement on Eve is similar to that of Philo of Alexandria, *Questions and Answers on Genesis*, 1.43.

On Philo and gender, see the insightful analysis by Baer, *Philo's Use of the Categories Male and Female*.

23. Augustine, *De civitate Dei*, 22.24; cf. 12.26. Both passages elaborate on 1 Cor 3.7: "Itaque neque qui plantat est aliquid, neque qui rigat: sed qui incrementum dat, Deus" [Therefore neither he that plants is anything nor he that waters: but he that gives the increase, God].

24. See James Turner, *One Flesh*, who notes, "In sexual relations Paul recommends a reciprocity of power and surrender entirely at odds with the subordination he calls for elsewhere" (26). Some recent feminist readings of biblical sexuality underscore the contradictions and ambiguities of interpretation in their diverse findings; see, for example, Pardes, *Countertraditions in the Bible*, who finds that "If Paul can use the story of Eve's creation to validate his resolution that woman should not be allowed to teach, nor 'to usurp authority over man,' it is precisely because the Bible has accumulated tremendous social force over the many centuries in which it has been read and reread" (37); see also Bal's chapter "Sexuality, Sin, and Sorrow: The Emergence of the Female Character," in her *Lethal Love*, 104–30. I shall take up the Pauline contradictions of marriage and sexuality further in Chapter 1.

25. Karma Lochrie has made a cogent argument for a distinction between flesh and body in *Translations of the Flesh*, 13–53; however, one could additionally argue that body metaphors call attention to the flesh and, by extension, to the feminine. A notable challenge to the patristic anticarnal admonitions are the bodily images described by the mystics; see Riehle, *The Middle English Mystics*, esp. 24–103. See also the overview by Gallacher, "Chaucer and the Rhetoric of the Body," 216–316, which sketches out some of these issues in relation to Chaucer.

26. Augustine, *De doctrina christiana*, 3.5.9. See also commentary in Minnis and Scott with Wallace, ed., *Medieval Literary Theory and Criticism*, 65–71; Smalley, *Study of the Bible in the Middle Ages*, 1–26. On the "carnal" as feminine flesh, see Dinshaw, *Chaucer's Sexual Poetics*, 19–25; Lochrie, *Translations of the Flesh*, 13–55; Culianu, "A Corpus for the Body," 61–80.

27. See also Rich, "Compulsory Heterosexuality and Lesbian Existence," on the threat of men "being left on the periphery of the matrix" (643). On perceptions of men, maleness, and masculinity in the Middle Ages, see the collection of essays *Medieval Masculinities*, especially Bullough, "On Being a Male in the Middle Ages."

28. Consider the further descriptions of Prv 7.10–11, 25, and 27, respectively: "Garrula et vaga, / Quietis impatiens, Nec valens in domo consistere pedibus suis" [garrulous and wandering, / Not bearing to be quiet, nor to remain at home by her feet]; "Irretivit eum multis sermonibus, Et blanditiis labiorum protraxit illum" [She entangled him with many words, And drew him with the flattery of her lips]; "Viae inferi domus eius, Penetrantes in interiora mortis" [The way to hell is her residence, Penetrating to the interior chambers of death]. On the temptress motif in

relation to language, see Jager, *The Tempter's Voice*, esp. 191–240, and, on categories of women, McLeod, *Virtue and Venom*.

29. For example, Alanus de Insulis (Alan of Lille), *De planctu naturae*, Metr 1.15–20. Useful commentary on sterility and grammar in relation to Alan's *De planctu* is provided in Boswell, *Christianity, Social Tolerance, and Homosexuality*, 310–11; see also Ziolkowski, *Alan of Lille's Grammar of Sex*, 13–49; Alford, "The Grammatical Metaphor." In his chapter "The Hermaphrodite: Alan of Lille's *De planctu Naturae*," in *Barbarolexis*, Leupin demonstrates the presence of "hermaphroditic writing" (75).

30. Aristotle, *Metaphysics*, in *The Complete Works of Aristotle*, I(A).5.986a1. Pythagoras, or the Pythagorean school at least, is usually credited as the origin of the Opposites, which the Middle Ages would know primarily by way of Aristotle's works in translation. A useful overview of Aristotelian texts and their circulation in the Middle Ages is provided by Lohr's series in *Traditio*. An insightful and informed discussion of the Opposites from Pythagoras to Aristotle is Stokes, *One and Many in Presocratic Philosophy*. See also, O'Meara, *Pythagoras Revived*, esp. 128–38; and Hopper, *Medieval Number Symbolism*, 33–49. See also commentary by Lloyd, *The Man of Reason*, 2–9; Allen, *The Concept of Woman*; Maclean, *The Renaissance Notion of Woman*, esp. 2–3; Delany, "Anatomy of a Resisting Reader," 7–34.

31. Bloch, *Medieval Misogyny*, 26. See also DuBois, *Sowing the Body*, 181–85; Parker, *Literary Fat Ladies*, 184–88.

32. Bloch, *Medieval Misogyny*, 21.

33. Cixous, "Sorties," in *The Newly Born Woman*, 63; and Moi, *Sexual/Textual Politics*, 104.

34. Bynum, *Fragmentation and Redemption*, 151.

35. Lochrie, *Translations of the Flesh*, 25. I shall address the poetics and politics of virginity at length in Chapters 1 and 3. On women's bodies and silence in the *fabliaux*, see Burns, "This Prick Which Is Not One," in *Feminist Approaches to the Body*, 188–212, esp. 199–201, and *Bodytalk*, where she gives the subject extended treatment.

36. I do not intend here to reduce Jerome wholly to the position of misogynist, for certainly his copious writings offer humane and well-intended positions; for instance, in a discussion of Jerome's troubled translations of biblical passages involving women, Jane Barr finds "a great warmth and sensitivity" and a "more sympathetic and affectionate nature" than other readers ("The Vulgate Genesis," in *Equally in God's Image*, 122). But this does not negate the powerfully misogynistic quality of much of his writings. Jerome's personal relationships with women—namely, his close friendships with Paula and Marcella, his commune-like domocile with young women of their circles—are complex, often appearing paradoxical or even hypocritical. See Elizabeth Clark, "Friendship Between the Sexes," in her *Jerome, Chrysostom, and Friends*, 35–106.

37. Jerome, *Commentariorum in epistolam ad Ephesios* 3.28, PL 26.467–590, at 567.

Cf. similar statements by Philo of Alexandria, *Questions and Answers* 4.15; and Ambrose, *Expositio in evangelii secundum Lucam* 10.161.

38. Bloch, *Medieval Misogyny*, 27.

39. Consider, for instance, Augustine's attempt to reconcile sex, flesh, and resurrection in *De civitate Dei:* "Non est autem uitium sexus femineus, sed natura, quae tunc quidem et a concubitu et a partu immunis erit" [Now the female sex however is not a defect, but natural. And at that time of the resurrection it will even be free of copulation and childbirth] (22.17).

40. Anapoulous, "Writing the Mystic Body," 204n.12, commenting on Irigaray's "When Our Lips Speak Together."

41. Irigaray, *This Sex Which Is Not One*, 30, 23.

42. Benstock, *Textualizing the Feminine*, xvi.

43. While some feminists argue for a definition of the feminine that is not contingent on its postion in binarism, we should recall that medieval epistemology is very much articulated in terms of opposition and duality. Jean de Meun's famous explication in *Le Roman de la rose* (21543-52), for example, emphasizes the crucial role of difference—obtained by comparing opposites—in glossing or assigning definition, suggesting that one may "know" as personal experience both masculine and feminine genders, but obviously the same case cannot be made for male and female as sex.

44. See also Michie, *The Flesh Made Word*, 149. Spelman, *Inessential Woman*, traces the "essentialist" tendency from Plato's *Republic* to the present and argues that essentialism "obscures the heterogeneity of women and cuts off examination of the significance of such heterogeneity for feminist theory and political activity" (ix). See also the critiques by Schor, "This Essentialism Which Is Not One"; Fuss, "Reading Like a Femininst"; and Probyn, "This Body Which Is Not One." The attractiveness of Irigaray's title in English, *This Sex Which Is Not One*, as a source of titular parody and mimicry speaks to the inability of feminism to move away from "essentialism." See also the recent arguments set forth by Grosz (*Volatile Bodies*, 1994), and the recent collection *The Essential Difference*, ed. Naomi Schor and Elizabeth Weed, which includes essays from the feminist journal *differences*.

45. The category of feminist thought associated with contemporary French psychoanalytic theories differs from Anglo-American in its privileging of essential difference, for the French theorists maximize and insist on difference, whereas the Anglo-Americans de-emphasize or minimize difference in a gesture toward equalizing gender; the French school traces its project through an intellectual heritage that includes classical and Christian epistemological foundations.

46. The conflation and integration of the Aristotelian and Christian epistemological models are paralleled by a similar conflation of various physiological conceptualizations as well, including the Aristotelian equating of the feminine with matter. See, for instance, Jacquart and Thomasset, *Sexuality and Medicine in the Middle Ages;* Gottfried, *Doctors and Medicine in Medieval England*, esp. 192–99; Siraisi,

Medieval and Early Renaissance Medicine, 78–114; and Tuana, *The Less Noble Sex*, esp. 18–50.

47. See Frese, *An Ars Legendi for Chaucer's Canterbury Tales*, 251, on the "prizing of punctilious grammar."

48. Augustine, *Contra mendacium ad Consentium*, PL 40.517–48, at 533. See commentary in Shoaf, *Currency of the Word*, 33–34.

49. See Chenu, *Nature, Man, and Society*, 120ff., on *translatio verborum*, the transference of words. On "translatio" and related terms, see also Nims, "*Translatio*: 'Difficult Statement'"; Vance, *Mervelous Signals*, 312–25, 336–37; Nicholls, *Romanesque Signs*, 20–21; Colish, *The Mirror of Language*, 42–47.

50. Augustine, *Contra mendacium* 10.24; Isidorus Hispalensis (Isidore of Seville), *Etymologiarum sive Originum Libri XX*, 1.37.2; Quintilian, *Institutio oratoria* 9.1.4; Geoffrey of Vinsauf, *Poetria nova* 4.1.763ff.

51. See Freccero, "Medusa: The Letter and the Spirit," esp. 130, on the medieval insistence on the link between eros and language. The ubiquitous philosophical and grammatical term *impositio ad placitum*, imposed according to the pleasure of the reader, reiterates the link between the two. See also Augustine's *De doctrina christiana* 2.6.8, where Augustine speaks of the pleasure ("multo gratius") of textual discovery; Geoffrey of Vinsauf's *Poetria nova* 7.763–68, "placeat novitate sua" [let it please by its novelty]; Dante's *De vulgari eloquentia* 3.3 "videtur ad placitum" [it is seen/it seems (to signify) *ad placitum*]. Although, as Lee Patterson points out in "Ambiguity and Interpretation," "To imply that Augustine prefigures Barthes [*Le Plaisir du texte*] is a mischievousness that most medievalists will doubtless be unwilling to tolerate" (328), Augustine's thinking and its application in medieval poetics constitute what may be described as an erotics of reading.

52. Margherita, "Originary Fantasies," 116. See also Fradenburg, "'Voice Memorial,'" which considers connections between narrative, mourning, and gender from a psychoanalytic perspective.

53. Derrida, "The Art of Memoires," in *Memoires for Paul de Man*, 66.

54. I do not go so far as to embrace a separate language of the female body, or *l'ecriture feminine*, which has been proposed by French feminists. See Cixous, "The Laugh of the Medusa"; Irigaray, *This Sex Which Is Not One*, esp. 28–32 and 132–41; Kristeva, "Women's Time"; and Kristeva, "From One Identity to an Other," in her *Desire in Language*, 124–47. A pithy overview is provided in Moi, *Sexual/Textual Politics*. Other commentary is vast; see, for instance, Dallery, "The Politics of Writing (The) Body"; and Probyn, "This Body Which Is Not One."

55. See also lines I.733–42. See Leicester, *Disenchanted Self*, 13, on the "voice of the text." Such a reading seems to respect the subjectivity of the *General Prologue* narrator but must set aside the layered narrative structure of rehearsing.

56. Bakhtin, "Discourse in the Novel," in his *Dialogic Imagination*, 314. The poet/persona split has long been recognized in Chaucer studies; see, for instance,

Donaldson, *Speaking of Chaucer*; Lawton, *Chaucer's Narrators*; Barbara Nolan's insightful critique, "A Poet Ther Was."

57. Kundera, *The Unbearable Lightness of Being*, 39.

58. Derrida, "Mnemosyne," in *Memoires for Paul de Man*, 10–11.

59. Augustine, in *Confessions*, interprets analogically the links between life and death, history and language (4.10); an earlier expression of a similar sentiment is set forth in Heraclitus's Fragment B.10, which interprets "unity" and the "unlimited" as points along a continuum (for text see *Heracliti Ephesii Reliquiae*, similarly articulated in Parmenides' Fragment 8, esp. 35–41 and 50–61 [*Parmenides of Elea: Fragments*]). See also commentary in Stokes, *One and Many*, 86–108, esp. 100–102.

60. Vance, *Mervelous Signals*, xi.

Chapter One: Promiscuous Glossing and Virgin Words

1. Hansen, *Fictions of Gender*, 26.

2. Leicester, *Disenchanted Self*, 138.

3. See, for instance, Carruthers, "The Wife of Bath and the Painting of Lions," who reads Alisoun's argument as "triumphant"; Malvern, "'Who peyntede the leon,'" also reads the Wife as "triumphant" satire; Fries, "'Slydyng of Corage,'" comments in the conclusion to her analysis of Criseyde that Chaucer, through his depiction of the Wife, is a "truly practicing feminist" (59); Straus, "Subversive Discourse," contrasts her own analysis with the conventionally "hostile" or "dismissive" readings of Donaldson, Robertson, Donald Sands, and Beryl Rowland.

4. Hansen provides an extensive overview of *Wife* criticism in relation to feminist perspectives, *Fictions of Gender*, 26–57; see also Lindley's overview, "'Vanysshed Was This Daunce.'"

5. "Glose" derives from the Greek *glossa* (tongue). According to the *MED*, the word denotes commentary, interpretation, and explanation; further, the term is used to suggest blandishment, flattery, and cajolery. The word's origin, "tongue," is not lost on the Wife, however, and this underlying erotic sense informs her carefully constructed double entendres. See also Hanning, "'Maner Glose'"; Besserman, "Glosynge is a Glorious Thyng"; Peggy Knapp, "Wandrynge by the Weye."

6. My analysis is based on Mosse, *A Handbook of Middle English*, and Davis et al., *Chaucer Glossary*; see also Fyler, "Man, Men, and Women in Chaucer's Poetry," and Nyquist, "Ever (wo)Man's Friend."

7. See Dinshaw, *Chaucer's Sexual Poetics*, 193n.14. I agree with Dinshaw's assertion that "Chaucer has a deep and acute sense of the differences between the genders in Western patriarchal culture," and I use "bisexual" to include both, not to blur the crucial distinctions—differences—between them even as they may likewise participate within identical textual parameters. (See also Leicester, *Disenchanted Self*, 414–17.) Cixous, in "Laugh of the Medusa" defines "bisexuality" as

"the presence . . . of both sexes, nonexclusion either of the difference or of one sex, and, from this 'self-permission,' multiplication of the effects of the inscription of desire" (288).

8. Other Chaucerian disclaimers include the pilgrim-Chaucer's (I.727–44), the Miller's (I.3136–40), and the pilgrim-Chaucer's subsequent disclaimer of the Miller's disclaimer (3185–86). Straus, "Subversive Discourse," argues that the Wife's disclaimer "could be read as the Wife's acknowledgment of 'woman's place'—traditionally restricted to privacy, domesticity, and silence. . . . Under the guise of knowing her place, however, the Wife proceeds to transgress it" (529), but I read the Wife's disclaimer as mimicking the masculine disclaimers rather than as challenging them.

9. The connection between eros and language is ubiquitous in medieval poetics, and recent commentary is vast, as noted in the Introduction.

10. Dante's *Inferno* 5.137–38 supplies a textual model: "Galeotto fu 'l libro e chi lo scrisse: quel giorno piu non vi leggemmo avante" ["A Gallehault indeed, that book and he / who wrote it, too; that day we read no more"] (ed. and trans. Allen Mandelbaum); all further *Inferno* citations refer to this edition, with canto and line numbers supplied. See related commentary by Shoaf, *Currency of the Word*, 261n.6; Mazzotta, *Poet of the Desert*, 165–70; Karla Taylor, *Chaucer Reads*, 59–63; Gellrich, *Idea of the Book*, 149–54.

11. Chaucer's alignment of "tongue" and "hand" is, a possible play on the Latin sexual pun of tongue and hand (*glossae tradere*). On "*glossae tradere*" and "*cunnum lingere*" in the Latin tradition, see Ziolkowski, *Grammar of Sex*, 55–56, and J. N. Adams, *The Latin Sexual Vocabulary*, 134–36. Cf. the Wife's words to her third husband: "For if I wolde selle my *bele chose*, / I koude walke as fressh as is a rose; / But I wol kepe it for youre owene tooth" (III.447–49), and more tellingly, her description of how she punished her fourth: "Nat of my body in no foul manere" (III.485).

12. Vance, "The Differing Seed," in his *Mervelous Signals*, 232.

13. On such "moralizing" readings, see commentary in the articles by Lindley; Straus; and Hansen, cited earlier.

14. "Wyf," according to the *OED*, means not only "woman" in a general sense but "especially one engaged in the sale of some commodity," "the mate of a male animal," and "a woman joined to a man by marriage." The Wife evokes all four senses when she describes herself as "wyf," though she focuses on "wyf" in terms of marital status. See also Davis et al., *Glossary*, 171. The Wife's use of marriage as a means of economic gain is matched by Jankyn (see III.627–33).

15. The correlation of pleasure and text is suggested by the ubiquitous medieval theory used by St. Augustine, Dante, and others, *impositio ad placitum* (see n.54 of the Introduction); Shoaf notes in *Currency of the Word*, 175: "For [the Wife], '*le plaisir du texte*' is '*le texte du plaisir*'—and that is her '*ecriture*.'" See also Chenu, *Nature, Man, and Society*, 99–145. In contemporary theory this relationship is perhaps best

articulated by Barthes, *Pleasure of the Text*. In Kristeva's words, "our only chance to avoid being neither master nor slave of meaning lies in our ability to insure our mastery of it (through technique or knowledge) as well as our passage through it (through play or practice). In a word, *jouissance*" (Preface to *Desire in Language*, x).

16. Doane, *Desire to Desire*.

17. Feminist film theory analyzes "spectacle" in relation to women and desire; see, for instance, Mulvey's "Visual Pleasure and Narrative Cinema." "Spectacle" analyses derive from applications of the Lacanian "gaze"; see Lacan, "Of the Gaze as *Object petit a*," in *Four Fundamental Concepts*, 65–119. Sarah Stanbury has used feminist film theory effectively in medieval "gaze studies"; see, for instance, "The Virgin's Gaze."

18. The *MED* notes that "assemble" suggests, in addition to "come together, gather; join, blend," "[t]o have intercourse." On the use of "assemble" in conjunction with "fyr," see Leicester, "Of a Fire in the Dark," esp. 170–71.

19. Jerome, *Adversus Jovinianum* 1.28.

20. Fradenburg, "The Wife of Bath's Passing Fancy," 44.

21. Derrida, *Of Grammatology*, 144–45.

22. Bynum, in *Holy Feast and Holy Fast*, comments on the "wide range of positive resonances for both physicality and food" among religious women of the period (300). Gluttony, or excess, was harshly regarded; Dante, for example, places the gluttons in the Third Circle, "per la dannosa colpa de la gola" ["for the damning sin of gluttony"], *Inferno* 6.53. Langland, too, speaks harshly of gluttony, and links it to the mouth and tongue in *Piers Plowman* 5.367–69.

23. Ross, "Taboo-Words in Fifteenth-Century England," 150; see also Baum, "Chaucer's Puns," 240; Neuss, "*Double-Entendre*," 325–39.

24. Burns, "Knowing Women." Luce Irigaray suggests an extended analogy between oral and genital "lips" in "This Sex Which is Not One" and "When Our Lips Speak Together," both reprinted in *This Sex Which is Not One*, 23–33 and 205–18, respectively. See also Grosz, "The Body of Signification," 88. On medieval texts, see Vitz, *Medieval Narrative*, esp. 86–87, and Lemay, "Obstetrics and Gynecology"; Lemay's essay is particularly useful for its bibliography.

25. Caroline Bynum comments on medieval concepts of "erotic" in *Fragmentation and Redemption*, 79–117, esp. 86–87, suggesting that medieval perspectives on the body—and genitals in particular—as represented in art were not as sexually focused as are modern interpretations. Along these lines, see also Lochrie, "The Language of Transgression," esp. 119. Nichols, "Female Nudity and Sexuality in Medieval Art," however, argues that there is an underlying eroticism that focuses negatively on women, a "medieval concept that the female nude is an unnatural and immoral state for a woman" (176). See also Elizabeth Robertson, "Medieval Views of Spirituality," in her *Early English Devotional Prose*, 32–43.

26. In the epistle *Ad Eustochium*, Jerome denounces flattery: "Nulla est enim in hoc libello adulatio. Adulator quippe blandus inimicus est" [No flattery (is) in

these pages. A flatterer is indeed an enticing enemy] (PL 22.394–425, at 395). Dante too, for instance, comments on the flatterer's "sufficiency of tongue" in *Inferno* 18.109–36. See also related commentary in Radcliff-Umstead, "Erotic Sin in the *Divine Comedy*," esp. 64–67.

27. Dinshaw, "'Glose/bele chose': The Wife of Bath and Her Glossators," in her *Chaucer's Sexual Poetics*, 125.

28. Though secular rather than spiritual, the Wife's discourse is not unlike that of the mystics, who articulate spiritual experiences in vividly erotic language. On the mystics' erotic language, see Riehle, *The Middle English Mystics*, 24–103. Along these lines the Wife's erotica is "feminine," that is, aural rather than visual. On visual—masculine—religious pornography, see Miles, *Carnal Knowing*, 117–68. (See also the review article by Milhaven, "A Medieval Lesson on Bodily Knowing.")

29. On autoeroticism as positive, see Irigaray, "This Sex Which is Not One" and "When Our Lips Speak Together," in *This Sex Which Is Not One*, 22–33 and 205–18.

30. Not only does the Wife's narrative illustrate her desire for audience, but also within the narrative she speaks of her conversations with her female friend: "With my gossib, dwellynge in oure toun; / God have hir soule! Hir name was Alisoun. / She knew myn herte, and eek my privetee, / Bet than oure parisshe preest, so moot I thee! / To hire biwreyed I my conseil al" (III.529–33). The private relationship between the two women as the Wife describes it suggests a truer intimacy ("privetee") than any of the Wife's economically motivated sexual encounters with men.

31. Here the Wife evokes a medieval commonplace of fertility imagery based on seed and sowing used by Alan of Lille, Jean de Meun, Dante, and others, to suggest fertility, regeneration, and fruition. "Seed" in this sense corresponds to the "seed" of conception—with biblical origins—and, by extension, to "seed" as "word," informed in part by the Pauline sowing metaphor. See Bynum, *The Resurrection of the Body*, 1–18; for Pauline "virginity" directives, see 1 Cor 7.25–40. On "virginity" as a cultural and literary aesthetic informed by theological dicta, see Bloch, *Medieval Mysogyny*, esp. 93–112.

32. For an overview of medieval ideas regarding "seed" and conception, see Atkinson, *The Oldest Vocation*, esp. 46–52; Atkinson notes, "in the early Middle Ages the notion of 'two seeds' generally prevailed over strict Aristotelian theories of conception" (49). See also Brundage, *Law, Sex, and Christian Society*, 450–51, on physiological connotations of "seed" with regard to conception.

33. Jerome, *Ad Furiam, Epistola LIV* in PL 22.550–60, at 551.

34. Jerome, *Adversus Jovinianum* 1.36 (PL 271); see also Elizabeth Clark, "'Adam's Only Companion,'" esp. 18; and Kooper, "Loving the Unequal Equal," 44–56; and Kraemer, *Her Share of the Blessings*, 128–56.

35. Wilson and Makowski, *Wykked Wyves and the Woes of Marriage*, 161.

36. In *Adversus Jovinianum*, Jerome acknowledges that behavior norms change over time and that what is appropriate in one context may lose its priority in

another: "Obsecro te, lector, et id ipsum saepe commoneo, ut scias me, quae loquor, necessiatate dicere: nec detrahere his qui in lege praecesserint, sed servisse eos temporibus et consitionibus suis, et illam Domini implesse sententiam: *Crescite, et multiplicamini, et replete terram*" (1.24) [I implore you, reader, and this again I remind you, that you may know from me, that what I say is necessary to speak: not to disparage those who preceeded under the law but served them in their time and circumstance, and implemented the command of the Lord: *increase and multiply, and replenish the earth*].

37. Elizabeth Clark, "Christian Debate," 19; see also Ferster, *Chaucer on Interpretation*, 124–25, on the relationship between Jerome and St. Paul with regard to permitted behaviors. See also Peter Brown, *The Body and Society*, 410.

38. Moi, *Sexual/Textual Politics*, 104, commenting on Helene Cixous's "Sorties."

39. An insightful and informed discussion of the Gn 1.28 "Be fertile" directive to which the Wife alludes is provided by Cohen, *Be Fertile and Increase*, 271–305. John Mahoney attempts to locate the Wife's glossing of the "gentil text" in heretical movements such as the Free Spirit, "Alice of Bath."

40. On examples of medieval misogyny and their patristic origins, see Bloch, *Medieval Misogyny*, esp. 65–91. See also Patterson, "'For the Wyves love of Bath,'" which assesses the Wife's rhetoric in terms of these traditions.

41. The Wife embodies the ambivalence of the "carnal" in terms of the body. On the one hand, the carnal, as grotesque and vulgar as it may be, *is* the human state, yet the carnal is simultaneously condemned in theological discourse. Mark C. Taylor comments in *Erring: A Postmodern A/theology* (Ithaca: Cornell University Press, 1985), "The body as grotesque is the body that eats, drinks, shits, pisses, and fucks. The boundary between bodies is a permeable membrane; it has gaps and holes to let the inside out and the outside in. . . . When inside is only inside and outside is only outside, when eating, drinking, pissing, shitting, and fucking stop or are stopped, vital current no longer flows and the body truly dies" (172). This necessary carnality is acknowledged within medieval theology; see Kristeva's comments on St. Bernard in her *Tales of Love,* 150–69; Bynum's influential *Jesus as Mother*, 110–69; Damrosch, "*Non Alia.*" Cf. the validity of "carnal" as a starting point of interpretation as suggested by Langland throughout *Piers Plowman B*, for example, particularly Passus 1; see my "Langland's Christian Narcissus." Robertsonianism has insightfully—if excessively—explored "carnality"; see D. W. Robertson, Jr., *Preface to Chaucer*, 318–36.

42. Dinshaw, *Chaucer's Sexual Poetics*, 120.

43. Bakhtin argues that these dimensions are not necessarily dichotomized, that they need not be mutually exclusive. See "Discourse in the Novel," in his *Dialogic Imagination*, 342ff.

44. Vance, "Augustine's *Confessions* and the Poetics of the Law," in his *Mervelous Signals*, 9.

45. Outside the epistemology, valuation necessarily obtains; Mark C. Taylor

notes, "Invariably one term is privileged through the divestment of its relative. The resultant economy of privilege sustains an asymmetrical hierarchy" (*Erring*, 9). There is then an epistemologically contingent value relationship articulated by the dual, without necessarily a coincidence of internal and external valuation.

46. See Leicester, *Disenchanted Self*, on the Wife's "private" constructions that "do not produce a single, 'true' private self revealed behind the facade of the public performance" (99).

47. See Peggy Knapp, "Wandrynge," on Lollardy and visibility; and Blamires, "The Wife of Bath and Lollardy," who argues that "Chaucer is perforce using a defensive strategy, addressing Wycliffite controversies through a source [*Adversus Jovinianum*] safeguarded by its ancient pedigree" (233).

48. Bloch, *Etymologies and Genealogies*, 136. Apparently, forbidden (sterile) sexual activities involving women together were considered far less sinful and had far less dire consequences than did sexual sins involving men, though female "solitary vice" was considered equivalent to a woman's "vice with a woman." Medieval penitential handbooks identify the penitential obligations incurred by specific acts and thus provide some basis for comparison. For example, *The Penitential of Theodore*, in *Medieval Handbooks of Penance*, indicates that a man who "defiles himself" does penance for forty days (1.9), while a woman does three years (1.13). Men who commit sodomy together do at least seven years ("this is the worst of evils," 1.15), but a woman who "practices vice with a woman" does three years, the same penalty for "solitary vice" (1.12–13). See also Brundage, *Law, Sex, and Christian Society*, 398–400, 472–74, and Brooten, "Paul's Views on the Nature of Women and Female Homoeroticism," 61–87.

49. See, for example, the conversation between Dante and Brunetto Latini in the realm of the sodomites (*Inferno* 15), and the description of sterile grammar in *De planctu naturae* (Meter 1). See also commentary in Vance, "Differing Seed," and Pequigney, "Sodomy in Dante's *Inferno* and *Purgatorio*." I shall analyze sodomy tropes further in Chapter 6.

50. With regard to the relationship between "female" and "hidden," Irigaray attacks Freud's equation of the hidden and nothingness in terms of female sexuality in "This Sex Which Is Not One": "*the horror of nothing to see*" (26). Irigaray correctly distinguishes between *nothing to see* (the hidden) and *nothing* (absence or lack); the former denotes existence, even if removed from sight and therefore mysterious and unknown.

51. Cixous notes, "Traditionally, the question of sexual difference is treated by coupling it with the opposition: activity/passivity. . . . It is even possible not to notice that there is no place whatsoever for woman in the calculations" ("Sorties," 64).

52. Bakhtin, *Dialogic Imagination*, 276.

53. Delany, "Strategies of Silence," comments, "[T]he Wife of Bath, like the lion she quotes, also speaks against herself, and can only do so in citing this story whose givens—animal versus human—already constrain interpretation, already load the dice" (54); see also Morrison, "Don't Ask, Don't Tell."

54. Kendrick, *Chaucerian Play*, notes: "The Wife both tempts and masters us, making us identify with repressive *female* authority, which knows what is best for us. Even so, the Wife of Bath's and woman's ascendancy is temporary after all; it occurs in the unreal play time and space of the Wife's stories" (126).

55. Hanning, "Maner Glose," 45–46. See also Ferster, *Chaucer on Interpretation:* "By describing women as monsters of sensuality, greed, and deceit, [antifeminists] produce monstrously sensual, greedy, and deceitful women" (124). Gottfried, "Conflict and Relationship," similarly argues, "as long as she continues to work within the system she cannot avoid being co-opted by it" (213); Gottfried chooses the unfortunate label "herstory" to describe the Wife's concern with narrative history.

56. Ellis, "The Merchant's Wife's Tale," 601.

57. Peggy Knapp, "Wandrynge," 157.

Chapter Two: The Text of Criseyde

1. Trevisa, *Dialogus Inter Dominum et Clericum*, 293; I have modernized the yoghs and thorns.

2. See the extensive overview in Windeatt's new *Oxford Guide*; Kaminsky, *Chaucer's Troilus and Criseyde* is useful, though increasingly dated. On the history of story germane to Criseyde, see Mieszkowski, "R. K. Gordon and the Troilus and Criseyde Story"; Donaldson, "Briseis, Briseida, Criseyde, Cresseid, Cressid," 1–12; Suzuki, *Metamorphoses of Helen*, 10–11, 210–57; Muscatine, *French Tradition*, 124–65.

3. I am aware of the irony presented by using the standard, and thus convenient, abbreviation *Troilus:* that Criseyde, the focus of my study and the character whom I shall argue is not taken seriously enough, is deleted from the title.

4. See Dante, *Paradiso* 14.28–33; note Chaucer's contextual transformation: Dante's prayer of praise is reworked as part of a prayer of request.

5. For example, John Fleming, "Deiphoebus Betrayed," describes such arguments as "the vulgar feminist exculpation of Criseyde" (197).

6. Dinshaw, *Chaucer's Sexual Poetics*, chapter 1, "Reading Like A Man: The Critics, the Narrator, Troilus, and Pandarus," 29–64; Hansen, *Fictions of Gender*, chapter 6, "Troilus and Criseyde: 'Beth war of men, and herkneth what I seye!,'" 141–87.

7. On the similarities between the *Troilus* narrator and Pandarus, see Waswo, "The Narrator of *Troilus and Criseyde*"; Carton, "Complicity and Responsibility in Pandarus' Bed"; Dinshaw, *Chaucer's Sexual Poetics*, 47–51.

8. She is therefore not unlike the concept of Woman as set forth by Irigaray in *Speculum of the Other Woman:* "Woman is neither open nor closed. She is indefinite, in-finite, *form is never complete in her.* She is not infinite but neither is she a unit(y), such as letter, number, figure in a series, proper noun, unique object (in a) world of the senses. . . . This incompleteness in her form, her morphology, allows her continually to become something else, though this is not to say that she is ever univocally nothing. No metaphor completes her" (229).

9. Knoespel, in *Narcissus and the Invention of Personal History*, notes, "In antiquity the process of falling in love was conceived as an attraction to an image of the self

seen in the retina of the beloved" (11); see the recent essay by Stanbury, "The Lover's Gaze in *Troilus and Criseyde.*" On this ubiquitous image in the *fin' amors* tradition, see Goldin, *The Mirror of Narcissus*; Hult, *Self-Fulfilling Prophecies.*

10. Margherita, "Originary Fantasies," 133.

11. The solipsistic quality of Troilus's "mirour" speech and the "mere phantasy" of his infatuation are explicated in the well-known reading of D. W. Robertson, Jr., *Preface to Chaucer*, 472–502; though I find a narcissistic quality to Troilus's infatuation, I do not find this to be the stuff of tragedy, even according to Robertson's definition ("to the medieval mind, that hostile world of fortuitous events was an illusion generated by misdirected love" [473]), which leads him to conclude: "When the flesh with its cumbersome desires has been left behind, [Troilus] sees the foolishness of his earthly plight" (500). See the pointed critique of Robertson's reading in Dinshaw, *Chaucer's Sexual Poetics*, esp. 32–36.

12. That the stanzas of Troilus's song are largely derived from Petrarch's eighty-eighth sonnet has long been recognized, but within the narrative it is the narrator who writes the song; thus outside the narrative, Petrarch's influence renders the entire "translating" project even more ironic. On Chaucer's use of Petrarch, see textual notes in the *Riverside Chaucer*, 1028, and Root's edition of *Troilus*; see also discussion in Payne, *Key of Remembrance*, 201–9.

13. On the persona of the narrator, see the recent essay by Bϕrch, "Poet & Persona."

14. Fradenburg, "'Our owen wo to drynke,'" 100; see also Jane Chance, *The Mythographic Chaucer*, 107–67.

15. I refer here to the famous "Galeotto" passage (*Inferno* 5.137–38). On this passage and its connection to Chaucer, see, respectively, Gellrich, *Idea of the Book in the Middle Ages*, 148–50; and Karla Taylor, *Chaucer Reads the Divine Comedy*, 50–77, 228–35.

16. Criseyde describes herself as having been "bought" (5.956); on Criseyde's being "sold," see Shoaf, *Currency of the Word*, 108–9.

17. Jerome, *Adversus Jovinianum* 1.48.

18. Hansen, *Fictions of Gender*, 174.

19. Fradenburg, "'Our owen wo to drynke,'" 106.

20. On the problem of closure and fantasy for readers of *Troilus*, including Robert Henryson's *Testament*-narrator—Henryson turns Chaucer's "invisible" foe into "commoun" spectacle, thereby rendering Cresseid "visible"—see my "Froward Language and Wanton Play."

Chapter Three: "Wreched Engendrynge" and (wo)Mankynde

1. A useful overview of feminist positions related to Chaucer's treatment of women is Green, "Chaucer's Victimized Women."

2. The label originated with Gavin Douglas, who, in his sixteenth-century *Eneados*, describes Chaucer as "euer . . . wemenis frend" (cited by Spurgeon, *Five Hundred Years of Chaucer Criticism*, 72).

3. Diamond, "Chaucer's Women," 82.

4. My argument deals with the G Prologue of the *Legend of Good Women*, which contains the crucial phrase "Wreched Engendrynge" (G.414); line numbers are provided in the text.

5. Hansen, *Fictions of Gender*, 2.

6. Hansen, "Irony and the Antifeminist Narrator," 22.

7. See, for example, lines 1366–67 and 1678–79, where the narrator encourages readers to look elsewhere, 2218 ("What shulde I more telle hire compleynyng? / It is so long"), 2225 ("I wol no more speke of this mateere"), and 2723 ("This tale is seyd for this conclusioun").

8. Mann, *Geoffrey Chaucer*, 33–34. On gender and the creative process of the *Legend*, with an emphasis on politics and art, see Delany, *The Naked Text*, 187–228. For a discussion of the role of the poet as "maker" in relation to the *Legend*, see Kiser, *Telling Classical Tales*, the chapter "'Poesye,' 'Makyng,' and 'Translacioun,'" 132–54.

9. This seems likely given the accuracy of the other reported titles, though there is no extant evidence of Chaucer's having made this work other than hints of Innocent's treatise in Chaucer's Man of Law's Prologue and *Tale* and in the *Pardoner's Tale*. See Lewis, "What Did Chaucer Mean"; see also the debate between Germaine Dempster, who argues for a fairly literal reading—"If words mean anything, 'wretched engendering' means conception and gestation" ("Chaucer's *Wretched Engendering* and *An Holy Medytacion*," 28)—and Beatrice Brown, who argues that the term "wreched engendrynge" may be understood as a metaphor for humanity's fallen state and that Dempster's reading is "narrowly restricted" ("Chaucer's *Wreched Engendrynge*," 331–32).

On the relationship of Chaucer's possible translation to his other work, see Lewis, "Chaucer's Artistic Use," which elucidates the lines on poverty and on merchants, and "Glosses to the *Man of Law's Tale* from Pope Innocent III's *De Miseria Humane Conditionis*." Lewis deals with the historical aspects of the presumed translation in his unpublished dissertation "Chaucer and Pope Innocent III's *De Miseria Humane Conditionis*." My argument here is in no way contingent on a positivist demonstration of the translation; it is the presence of the title in the *Legend of Good Women* with which I am concerned.

10. Lotario dei Segni (Innocent III), *De miseria condicionis humane* 1.3.

11. The word "man" in Middle English is both a nongendered pronoun, used in the sense of "person," and a specifically gendered subject; see also Fyler, "Men, Man, and Woman."

12. "*Pitee*" corresponds to the *pathos* of these tales, of which gendered suffering is the focus. See also Mann's chapter "Suffering Woman, Suffering God," in *Geoffrey Chaucer*, 128–64, on *pitee* as a label for the tales of suffering.

13. Middleton, "*The Physician's Tale* and Love's Martyrs," notes that the tale has been neglected and that "the usual justification is simply that the tale is dull and inferior" (9); Ramsey, "Sentence," notes, "In fact the only thing on which all

commentators agree would seem to be that it is not a particularly good tale" (185); Delany, "Politics and the Paralysis," prefaces her own pointed critique of the tale by noting, "*The Physician's Tale* is generally conceded to be one of Chaucer's least interesting and least successful efforts: flat characters, a rather incompetent narrative flawed by irrelevant digressions, a plot exceedingly improbable and—unlike *The Clerk's* or *The Man of Law's Tales*—without redeeming symbolic depth" (47). While I agree that the tale is inferior, my argument is that its inferiority is part of its reflexive theme, that it is, in fact, a study in the failure of constricted language.

14. The medieval patristic obsession with virginity is documented through the writings of the patristic fathers and their numerous commentators, with Jerome's *Adversus Jovinianum* and *Ad Eustochium* (*Epistola XXII*) widely read; other well-known writings include John Chrysostom's *De virginitate*, Gregory of Nyssa's *De virginitate*, Augustine's *De bono conjugali* and *De sancta virginitate*, and Ambrose's *De virginitate* and *De institutione virginis*, and the pseudo-Jerome *De virginitate*. Thomas Aquinas considers the arguments of Jerome, Augustine, Ambrose, Jovinian (and Aristotle) in his *Summa Theologiae*, 2a.2ae.152.4, and concludes that virginity is admirable but no more important than other virtues. A useful though somewhat brisk survey is provided by McNamara, "Sexual Equality and the Cult of Virginity." See also Alexandre, "Early Christian Women," and the detailed discussion in Bugge, *Virginitas*, esp. the chapter "Sexuality and the Fall of Man," 5–29. See also n.32, below.

15. Bloch, "Chaucer's Maiden's Head," 123.

16. Jerome, *Ad Pacatulam* (*Epistola CXXVIII*).

17. On the relationship of silence and virginity, see Lochrie, *Translations of the Flesh*, 23–27; Salisbury, *Church Fathers*, esp. 35–38. The association of feminine sexuality and necessary covertness is ubiquitous in medieval writings; consider, for instance, that the famous pseudo-Aristotelian/Arabic treatise on sexuality and physiognomy is titled *Secretum secretorum*, the secret of secrets (for Middle English text, see "The Secrete of Secretes," in *Three Prose Versions of the Secreta Secretorum*). A similarly oriented, and more overtly gendered and misogynistic, text is the *De Secretis mulierum*, once attributed to Albertus Magnus (*De secretis mulierum item De virtutibus herbarum lapidum et animalium;* now available as *Woman's Secrets*, ed. Lemay); on the *Secretum secretorum* and *De Secretis mulierum*, see Jacquart and Thomasset, *Sexuality and Medicine*, 127–29.

18. Bloch, "Chaucer's Maiden's Head," 120.

19. Jerome, *Ad Pacatulam*.

20. Peter Brown, *Body and Society*, 61.

21. The concept of women as men's property has a lengthy tradition in Judeo-Christian cultures with strong scriptural origins, and its devastating influence continues to the present day; Moses insists, for instance, that his soldiers consider women the spoils of war—"puellas autem et omnes feminas virgines reservate vobis" [but the girls and all the women that are virgins save for yourselves] (Num.

31.18; cf. Deut. 20.13–14)—in what could be taken as a foreshadowing of the shameful recent situation in the former Yugoslavia, for instance. Gayle Rubin has analyzed patriarchal culture's "traffic" in women, particularly in relation to Claude Levi-Strauss's *The Elementary Structures of Kinship*; see her influential article "The Traffic in Women." My use of the phrase "homosocial economy" echoes the groundbreaking study by Sedgwick, *Between Men*, which posits the argument that men's exchange of women operates within an environment situated along a continuum that includes "homoerotic" as well as the less overtly sexual "homosocial." With regard to the *Physician's Tale*, I would argue that Virginius discards his daughter to avoid a transfer that would validate Appius's superior—and hence figuratively more masculine and virile—social and political position.

22. Jerome, *Ad Pacatulam*.
23. Lomperis, "Unruly Bodies," 23.
24. Ibid., 34.
25. See lines VI.213–55.
26. On the Physician's ill-fitting *moralitas*, see also Ramsey, "Sentence," who notes, "It is a bit of conventional moralizing gone awry" (195).
27. Gratian, *Decretum*, in *Corpus iuris canonici*, C.27, cols 1047–53 and C.36, cols 1288–92. On Gratian's *Decretum* and its commentators, see Makowski, "Conjugal Debt"; Kuttner, *Harmony from Dissonance*; Noonan, "Gration Slept Here"; Brundage, *Law, Sex, and Christian Society*, 229–55. Augustine alone of the Church Fathers overtly condemns suicides motivated by rape in *De civitate Dei* (1.17). On the rape-suicide tradition, see the brief essay by Higonnet, "Speaking Silences."
28. See also Bloch, "Chaucer's Maiden's Head."
29. On other versions of the St. Cecilia legend, see Reames, "Sources." On hagiography in relation to women, including St. Cecilia, see Heffernan, *Sacred Biography*, esp. 250–55. The generic parallels present in the many hagiographic stories point to the singularity of the motif, that all the lives are similar and similarly motivated; in this sense, they would seem to correspond to the famous observation apropos the fathers, made by Gregory of Tours in the Prologue to the *Vitae Patrum*: "Unde manifestum est melius dici Vitae Patrum quam Vitas: quia cum sit diversitas meritorum virtutumque, una tamen omnes vita corporis alit in mundo" [Whence manifest it is better to speak of the Life of the Fathers than the Lives: because although some diversity exists among merits and virtues, nevertheless the life of one body nourished all in the world]. On the relationship between the *Vitae Patrum* and the lives of women saints, see Petroff, *Body and Soul*, 110–36.
30. See the introductory overview by Ridley in *The Riverside Chaucer*, 942–44.
31. Jerome's idea (*Commentariorum in epistolam ad Ephesios* 3.28) is reiterated by Ambrose, whose articulation includes a significant comment on proper names: "nam quae credit occurrit *in uirum perfectum, in mensuram aetatis plenitudinis Christi* carens iam nomine saeculi, corporis sexu, lubrico iuventutis, multiloquio senectutis" [whereas she who believes hastens to meet perfect manliness, the measure of the

age of fulfillment of Christ, doing now without worldly name, sex of body, seductiveness of youth, and garrulousness of old age] (*Expositio evangelii secundum Lucam*, 10.161). Like Ambrose's ideal woman, the Second Nun is known only by her ecclesiastical label. On spiritual gender reassignment, see Miles's chapter "'Becoming Male': Women Martyrs and Ascetic," in *Carnal Knowing*, 53–77, esp. 55; Bullough, "Medieval Medical and Scientific Views of Women," 499–500; and Cameron, "Neither Male nor Female."

32. Although it is beyond the scope of my remarks here to engage fully the issue of voluntary asceticism and its relationship to true piety, I should note here that I do not mean to denigrate the validity of the ascetic life as a choice available to women who desired spiritual closeness with God. On virginity and its valuation in this regard, see Pagels, *Adam, Eve, and the Serpent*, 78–97; Elm, "*Virgins of God*," esp. 1–22.

33. Sherman, "Saints, Nuns, and Speech," 148. See also Collette, "Critical Approaches."

34. Luecke, "Three Faces of Cecilia," 337. See also Beichner, "Confrontation, Contempt."

35. On other versions of the "Griselda" story, see Severs, *Literary Relationships*; and Middleton, "The Clerk and His Tale." On "patience" as topos, see Hanna, "Some Commonplaces of Late Medieval Patience Discussions."

36. A parallel may be drawn owing to the Host's comment—"'Sire Clerk of Oxenford,' oure Hooste sayde, / 'Ye ryde as coy and stille as dooth a mayde / Were newe spoused, sittynge at the bord; / This day ne herde I of youre tonge a word'" (IV.1–4)—which suggests a feminine Clerk. The Clerk responds in language similar to what one might expect of Griselda (and that echoes the Wife of Bath and her *Tale*'s featured character): "'Hooste,' quod he, 'I am under youre yerde; / Ye han of us as now the governance, / And therfore wol I do yow obeisance'" (IV.22–24).

37. With regard to Mariolatry, Bynum notes, "Much more work needs to be done on devotion to the Virgin in the later Middle Ages. The emphasis of Marina Warner, *Alone of All Her Sex*, on Mary as primarily representative woman and model for women seems wrong" (*Holy Feast and Holy Fast*, 409n.43).

38. For an overview of misogamous literature, see Wilson and Makowski, *Wykked Wyves and the Woes of Marriage*.

39. *Hali Meidenhad*, 461–65; I have modernized thorns, eths, and ampersands. Though counseling women to a similar end, the *Ancrene Riwle* focuses less on deterrents and more on reward, often couching its vivid descriptions in emphatically erotic language; see *Ancrene Wisse*, esp. 157–78. On *Hali Meidenhad*, the *Ancrene Riwle*, and similar guides, see Bugge, *Virginitas*, 80–110; Lochrie, *Translations of the Flesh*, 23–55; Elizabeth Robertson, *Early English Devotional Prose*, 44–76, and "Medieval Medical Views of Woman," 142–67; and Barbara Newman, *From Virile Woman*, 19–45.

40. *Hali Meidenhad*, 511–18. The text continues with a description of what

childrearing will be like for the weary and burdened mother, echoing Jerome's *Ad Eustochium* in its emphasis on suffering and toil.

41. Kristeva, *Stabat Mater*, in her *Tales of Love*, 234–63, esp. 259–63.

42. For example, patriarchal culture has rejected the Virgin's material sexuality, insisting that she remains physically a virgin even after giving birth. Such was the stuff of great controversy, fueled by Jovinian's argument that Mary loses her physical virginity in the process of birthing and Ambrose's vehement refutation. Curiously, despite his obsession with virginity, Jerome elected not to refute this particular point in his *Adversus Jovinianum*. On Jerome's omission and on Ambrose's engagement with Jovinian's work, see Hunter, "Resistance to the Virginal Ideal."

43. Kristeva, *Stabat Mater*, 248, 251.

44. Atkinson's chapter "'Mother of Love, Mother of Tears,'" in *The Oldest Vocation*, 144–93, suggests that Griselda's behavior fits the cultural conventions of the period, whereby her prioritizing the marriage—even at the expense of the children—would seem appropriate (see esp. 147–49). But even if Griselda observes decorum in her obedience to her husband, her unemotional response is both curious and indictable. As Stiller observes in *Eve's Orphans*, "[A]lthough the Prioress' anti-Semitism, the Merchant's bitterness, and the Wife of Bath's lust for power yield to a careful explication and become assimilated, Griselda's loyalty to the man she thinks has had her children slain remains beyond imaginative acceptance"(3).

45. This term, used by the Clerk to describe Griselda—"So benigne and so digne of reverence" (IV.411)—is here transferred to Walter by Griselda herself.

46. On the underlying incest motif and its connection to child abandonment in the Griselda stories, see Boswell, *Kindness of Strangers*, 412–13.

47. "Slydyng of corage," as noted in Chapter 2, is the famous description of Chaucer's Criseyde (*Troilus and Criseyde* 5.825), which calls attention to women's alleged fickleness, mutability, and, ultimately, duplicitousness. On Criseyde and "slydyng," see Burnley, "Criseyde's Heart."

48. See lines IV.428–41, where Griselda's behavior is arguably manlike and therefore threatening and unappealing to Walter. She compensates to some degree in the next stanza, which indicates her pregnancy, but it is shown not to be enough.

49. Hansen, *Fictions of Gender*, 191.

50. Longsworth, "Chaucer's Clerk as Teacher," 63. Longsworth's phrase is actually "relentless submissiveness," which I've modified here to use in adjective form.

51. Hawkins, "The Victim's Side," 346.

52. Muscatine comments, "This moral makes so transparently conventional an appeal to Christian piety that it has been a disadvantage to the poem" (*French Tradition*, 191). See also Clasby, "Chaucer's Constance."

53. Delany, "Womanliness in *The Man of Law's Tale*," in her *Writing Woman*, 36.

54. Weissman, "Late Gothic Pathos," 149.

55. On Custance as a constant in relation to language, see Shoaf, "'Unwemmed Custance.'"

56. Readings of the tale concerned with the Man of Law as narrator include Astell, "Apostrophe, Prayer, and the Structure of Satire"; Delasanta, "And of Great Reverence"; Scheps, "Chaucer's Man of Law"; Bestul, "The Man of Law's Tale."

57. Dor, "From the Crusading Virago to the Polysemous Virgin," 140.

58. Consider, for instance, lines II.428–34, where the Sultan and the other Christians are slain; 666–72, where the knight of Satan is killed by the hand; 913–31, the death of the would-be rapist, thrown overboard; 988, Donegild slain for her false messages; 1142–46, the death of Alla.

59. Dinshaw, *Chaucer's Sexual Poetics*, 108. Furrow, "The Man of Law's St. Custance," considers the consummation scene in light of saints'-lives paradigms and notes that this scene, like the marriage to the Sultan, "prevent[s] Custance from being, officially and theoretically, a saint" (229).

Chapter Four: Marks of Womanhood in the Ballades

1. Hansen, *Fictions of Gender* (Berkeley: University of California Press, 1991), 84.

2. "Balade" is the label provided by manuscript copies, and "ballade" is the modernization. A thorough overview of the Middle English ballade is provided by Cohen, *The Ballade*, esp. 233–52. See also Friedman, "The Late Mediaeval Ballade," esp. 98–101, and the introductory matter in Pace and David, eds., *The Minor Poems*. It should be emphasized here that while the French *balade* is strict in form and execution, its Middle English counterpart does not adhere as tightly to convention. I should explain here my use of the label "narrator" to identify the speaker of the ballades: although the ballades are lyrical, rather than narrative, I use "narrator" to emphasize the speaker's presence as a persona.

3. See Derrida, "Plato's Pharmacy," in his *Dissemination*, 61–171, and *Of Grammatology*, esp. 11–14, 30–38 (Spivak supplies a detailed and insightful introduction, esp. lxiv-ii). See also Derrida's critique of gender in relation to Nietzsche's misogyny in *Spurs: Nietzsche's Styles*, esp. 67–70, and "Freud and the Scene of Writing," in *Writing and Difference*, 196–231.

4. Irigaray, *This Sex Which Is Not One*, 26. Irigaray argues, "[Woman's] lot is that of 'lack,' 'atrophy' (of the sexual organ), and 'penis envy,' the penis being the only sexual organ of recognized value. Thus she attempts by every means available to appropriate that organ for herself: through her somewhat servile love of the father-husband capable of giving her one, through her desire for a child-penis, preferably a boy, through access to the cultural values still reserved by right to males alone and therefore always masculine, and so on" (23–24).

5. On "free play," see Derrida, "Structure, Sign and Play in the Discourse of the Human Sciences," in his *Writing and Difference*, 278–93; on *différance*, see "*Différance*," in his *Margins of Philosophy*, 1–27.

6. Aristotle, *Generation of Animals*, 737a and 775a. See also commentary by Dean-Jones, "The Politics of Pleasure"; and Cadden, *Meanings of Sex Difference in the Middle Ages*, esp. chapter 4, 169–227.

7. Galen, *On the Usefulness of the Parts of the Body* 2.299.

8. *Le Seminaire de Jacques Lacan*, cited by Ragland-Sullivan, *Jacques Lacan and the Philosophy of Psychoanalysis*, 286.

9. See, for example, Freud, *Inhibitions, Symptoms, Anxiety*, in the *Standard Edition*, 20.87–156, and "Medusa's Head," *Standard Edition* 18.273–74. See Lacan, "The Meaning of the Phallus," in his *Ecrits: A Selection*, 281–91.

10. See the recent overview of the feminist/phallocrat Lacanian debate in Skura, "Psychoanalytic Criticism."

11. Lacan, "God and the *Jouissance* of the Woman," in *Feminine*, 137–61.

12. See Freud's letter of 21 September 1897 to Wilhelm Fliess in the *Standard Edition*, 1.259. Rather than accept the likelihood that so many respectable men were "pervert[s]," Freud opts to dismiss claims of seduction/incest and interpret them instead as fantasy.

13. 2 Cor 5.6. But see Augustine, *De civitate Dei* 22.17, which rejects the "defect" tradition.

14. The poem variously titled *Against Women Unconstant* and *Newefangelnesse* is not attributed to Chaucer in the manuscripts, and critics disagree as to its authenticity. See, for example, Brusendorff, *The Chaucer Tradition*, esp. 440–42, who argues that "the resemblance in subject and treatment cannot be denied, but the evidence of Chaucerian authorship is even slighter in this case" (441). Pace and David are somewhat skeptical as well, though willing to include the poem in the Variorum Edition; see 187–90. I agree with those who accept the poem as Chaucer's own despite the lack of manuscript authority, particularly owing to its inclusion of the term "newefangelnesse," which the *MED* attributes to Chaucer as its originator—the word appears, for example, in the *Manciple's Tale* ("Flessh is so newefangel" [IX.193]); see discussion, below.

15. Readers have argued that the poem is indebted to a *balade* by Machaut with a similar refrain line—"Qu'en lieu de bleu, dame, vous vestes vert"—though the the idea may be proverbial. See Wimsatt, "Guillaume de Machaut and Chaucer's Love Lyrics," who argues that "with the exception of the Granson-inspired *Complaint of Venus*, all of Chaucer's independent love lyrics are based on poems of Guillaume de Machaut" (66).

16. Cf. line 1 of *To Rosemounde:* "Madame, ye ben of al beaute shryne." Religious imagery is often used in medieval love lyrics to assign value to a desired/desirable woman, though, as I have been arguing throughout this study, these tropes participate insidiously in a culture of Christian misogyny owing to their hegemonic subjugation.

17. The "Boethian lyrics" are so called because of their shared concern with Boethian themes; see, for example, 3.met.9 of the *Boece*. See also commentary by Jordan, *Chaucer and the Shape of Creation*, esp. 10–43; although Jordan's study focuses on the *Troilus* and the *Canterbury Tales*, its introductory matter is useful in situating Chaucer's shorter poems as well.

18. See *Boece* 2.m.5: "Blisful was the first age of men. They heelden hem apayed with the metes that the trewe feeldes broughten forth. They ne destroyeden ne desseyvede nat hemself with outrage." On Boethius and the *prior aetas*, see Jefferson, *Chaucer and the Consolation of Philosophy of Boethius*, esp. 89–93. See also Patch, *Goddess Fortuna*, and *Tradition of Boethius*. Cf. Ovid's *Metamorphoses*, where the Ages are described in language clearly echoed by Chaucer's poem (P. Ovidii Nasonis, *Metamorphoses*), I.89–163.

19. Fyler, "Love and the Declining World," demonstrates a similar intersection of the biblical and the pagan, though he does not find the misogyny that I believe inscribes the conflation.

20. Sartre's succinct phrasing, "Shame is by nature recognition. I recognize that I am as the Other sees me," seems particularly relevant. Cited by Schneider, *Shame, Exposure, and Privacy*, 25. Cf. Paul's famous statement of self-reflexive epistemology: "Videmus nunc per speculum in aenigmate: tunc autem facie ad faciem. Nunc cognosco ex parte: tunc autem cognoscam sicut et cognitus sum" [We see now through a glass in a dark manner: but then face to face. Now I know in part: but then I shall know even as I am known] (1 Cor 13.12). On medieval interpretations and applications of the Pauline epistemology, see Edward Peter Nolan, *Now through a Glass Darkly*.

21. This Genesis account is given fascinating treatment in Tertullian's *De cultu feminarum* 1.2, the notorious "Tu es diabola ianua" [You are the devil's gateway] passage.

22. Carol J. Adams makes a compelling case for feminist-vegetarian critical theory in *The Sexual Politics of Meat*. See also Irigaray, *Je, Tu, Nous*, 27.

23. See Brusendorff, *Chaucer Tradition*, 293; Pace and David, 93–96.

24. Schmidt, "Chaucer's *Nembrot*: A Note on *The Former Age*."

25. The corresponding lines in the *Consolatio* are as follows: "Quodsi rationes quoque non extra petitas sed intra rei quam tractabamus ambitum collocatas agitauimus, nihil est quod ammirere, cum Platone sanciente didiceris cognatos de quibus loquuntur rebus oportere esse sermones." Cf. *General Prologue* I.741–42, and the *Manciple's Tale* IX.207–10. On Chaucer's glossing of the *Consolatio* in his *Boece*, see Minnis, "'Glosyng is a Glorious Thyng,'" 106–24.

26. *Fortune*, like the *Consolation*, is articulated as dialogue, thereby enhancing the text's illusory rhetoric of mimetic conversation between distinct participants. On dialogue in the *Consolation*, see Lerer, *Boethius and Dialogue*. On dialogue in earlier medieval lyrics, see Sigal, *Erotic Dawn Songs of the Middle Ages*, which considers the impact of overtly gendered speakers.

27. Augustine, *De civitate Dei* 11.26.

28. The image of the journey—and hence of erring—is ubiquitous in medieval poetry; consider, for example, the *Canterbury Tales*, *Sir Gawain and the Green Knight*, *Piers Plowman*, the *Commedia*. The episode at the Cave of Errour in Spenser's *Faerie Queene* (I.i.1–28) reflexively glosses the medieval ontological and epistemological

connotations of this trope in medieval texts. On the medieval ontology of pilgrimage and erring, see Holloway, *Pilgrim and the Book*.

29. Texts participating in the *consolatio* tradition return to the governing image of female-teacher, male-pupil. This image, I would argue, reflexively insists on the positive value of the mutability of the feminine—in its metaphoric depiction of instructional scenes—even as it is controlled by a masculine narrator whose status ultimately supersedes that of the feminine abstract to which he ostensibly defers. For an overview of the *consolatio* tradition, see Means, *The Consolatio Genre*.

30. Cicero's notion of *amicitia* in *De amicitia* describes the intense, perhaps narcissistic, bonds of friendship between men: "Verum enim amicum qui intuetur, tamquam exemplar aliquod intuetur sui" [For he who gazes upon a true friend, gazes as if upon a copy of himself] (7.23). Such relationships have come under renewed critical scrutiny owing largely to Sedgwick's groundbreaking study, *Between Men*.

31. Irigaray, *Je, Tu, Nous*, 16 (italics in original).

32. This debate continues; see Pace and David's introduction to *Gentilesse*, 67–68.

33. Pace and David note that "The success of the poem, evidenced by the large number of extant copies [twenty-nine copies without the Envoy, one with], testifies to the popularity of its message. It is the gnomic poem par excellence in which the doctrine of an era has been compressed into a series of memorable commonplaces" (49).

34. Tristam of the Tristam/Isolde romance is of course a ubiquitous figure in medieval love poetry, including Chaucer's; Tristam in named in the *Parliament of Fowles* (290), as is Isolde (who is also named in the *House of Fame* [1796] and the *Legend of Good Women* [G.208]). That the *Rosemounde* narrator entertains fantasies of following Tristam's model underscores the poem's accuracy in its articulation and satirizing of *fin' amors* conventions. On *fin' amors* and the connection to Tristam here, see Lowes, "Illustrations from Chaucer."

35. Gavin Douglas's description has been the subject of much recent debate—is Chaucer "women's friend," and if so, in what way? See Hansen, *Fictions of Gender*, who critiques the concept of a feminist Chaucer and challenges "the bipartite myth of Chaucer's special sympathy or empathy with women and his aesthetic or moral transformation" (36).

36. Indeed the ubiquitous impulse toward codification speaks to a system of patriarchal order. As Murphy, *Rhetoric in the Middle Ages*, notes, "Underlying every medieval rhetorical treatise, whatever its genre, is the assumption that the communication process can be analyzed, its principles abstracted, and methods of procedure written down to be used by others" (363).

Chapter Five: The Jangler's "Bourde"

1. The opening lines of the Parson's Prologue are ostensibly an indication of time passed and distance traveled, but they perhaps highlight as well the lengthy

performance of the Manciple's maxims and the effect of his tedious recitation on his weary audience (X.1–4).

2. Pratt demonstrates the ubiquity and comprehensiveness of commonplace books, particularly John of Wales's *Communiloquium;* see "Chaucer and the Hand That Fed Him." MacDonald makes a case for Chaucer's comic tales as being "used to suggest an unwise dependence on received wisdom," in "Proverbs, *Sententiae,* and *Exempla,*" 465.

3. I have additionally consulted Donald C. Baker's edition of *The Manciple's Tale* in the preparation of this essay and shall refer to it for textual matters. Baker notes that the "My sone" address occurs nine times; however, the omitted "My" of line 325 may be assumed to have existed on the torn leaf of the Hengwrt manuscript, and I include the similar phrase "My deere sone" (line 341) in my count, for a total of eleven.

4. Isidorus Hispalensis (Isidore of Seville), *Etymologiarum sive Originum Libri XX,* 9.5.4–6. Anselm of Canterbury makes a similar argument in explaining the gender identity of Father and Son in his *Monologium* 4.2.

5. Aristotle, *De generatione animalium (Generation of Animals),* 727b–738b.

6. Isidore, *Etymologiarum* 11.2.17–19. Conrad of Hirsau, in his twelfth-century *Dialogus super Auctores,* explicates a similar conflation, 222–28. On Conrad's relation to literary criticism and the Aristotelian *causa,* see Whitbread, "Conrad of Hirsau as Literary Critic." Aquinas takes up the woman-as-matter theory in relation to Aristotelian definition in his *Summa theologiae,* esp. 1a.92.1 and 1a.2ae.81.5. On Aquinas's treatment of women in the *Summa,* see McLaughlin, "Equality of Souls, Inequality of Sexes." A more ambivalent position is set forth by Hildegard of Bingen, *Causa et curae (Liber compositae medicinae),* 2; see also Allen, "Hildegard of Bingen's Philosophy of Sex Identity." Albertus Magnus, *De animalibu,* explicates Aristotelian concepts throughout, with 9, 15, and 16 particularly germane; see also Albertus's *Questiones super De animalibus,* esp. 5.4. An excellent, detailed overview of ancient and medieval perceptions of woman is provided in the recent study by Cadden, *Meanings of Sex Difference in the Middle Ages.* I shall consider further Isidore's and Albertus's distinctions in relation to sexual behaviors and gender identities in Chapter 6.

7. "Lemman," the focus of the Manciple's disclaimer, is used in other medieval texts with ambiguous connotations. See, for instance, *Cleanness:* "In lust and in lecherye and lopelych werkkes, / And hade a wyf for to welde, a worthlych quene, / And mony a lemman, neuer the later, that ladis wer called" (1350–52); in *Pearl,* however, the word is used as a term of endearment corresponding to Christ, the Lamb: "In Jerusalem watz my Lemman slayn / And rent on rode with boyez bolde," "In Jerusalem thus my Lemman swete / Twyez for lombe watz taken thare" (805–6, 829–30). (I have modernized yoghs and thorns.)

8. See, for instance, the *Miller's Tale* I.3278, 3280; the *Reeve's Tale* I.4178, 4317; the Wife of Bath's Prologue III.398, 767. The Monk uses "lemman" without denigration

in his praising of Hercules, VII.2119–20, and the pious Parson, whose tale follows that of the Manciple, uses similarly blunt language, without apology, X.903.

9. The relationship of gender to "public" and "private" categories has recently become an important topic; see, for example, Lochrie, "Women's 'Pryvetees' and Fabliau Politics in the *Miller's Tale*."

10. "Cosin," according to the *MED*, denotes a relative, kinsman, or, as is construed in the modern sense, cousin.

11. The Manciple's evocation of Plato to support his insistence on blunt, literal language assumes an irony if one considers further the polysemy and ambiguity of language that likewise engaged Plato's thinking. See, for example, Derrida, "Plato's Pharmacy," in his *Dissemination*, which critiques the antithetical effects of the Greek word *pharmakon*, an ambiguous term that signifies opposites, "poison" and "cure"; Noonan, *Contraception: A History*, 44–46, also discusses the duality of *pharmakeia* in biblical and medicinal texts. Freud's "The Antithetical Meaning of Primal Words" (*The Standard Edition* 11.153–62), reviews the philologist Karl Abel's exploration of the phenomenon in the language of ancient Egypt and finds these words associated with the bisexual divinities—the words, like the bisexual/hermaphroditic gods, represent a unity of opposites eventually to be divided (155).

12. Augustine rejects the possibility of one-to-one correspondence of words and what is signified (*Confessions* 13.24). But such realizations did not preclude the search for codes and rules that could help promote a sense of certainty; see, for instance, Geoffrey of Vinsauf's *Poetria nova*, 757–60.

13. Wood, "Speech, the Principle of Contraries," argues that the "noght textueel" assertion may be read as a modesty trope. The phrase's reiteration in the Parson's Prologue (X.57)—its only other occasion in the *Canterbury Tales*—helps link the two fragments. Like Wood, Harwood ("Language and the Real") is among those who argue for a connection between the Manciple's and Parson's tales that underscores the contrast rather than the similarities between the two, a position to be reconsidered and challenged by the present discussion.

14. Harwood, "Language and the Real," notes that the most significant reworking is the addition of Phebus's stripping the crow of its song, rendering it silent. On the Manciple's reworking of the Ovidian myth found in *Metamorphoses* 2.531–632, see Work, "The Manciple's Tale," in *Sources and Analogues to Chaucer's Canterbury Tales*; Hazelton, "The Manciple's Tale"; and Baker, 4–11. Cf. John Gower's *Confessio amantis* 3.768–817.

15. Coghill, *The Poet Chaucer*, esp. 128–29; Scattergood, "The Manciple's Manner of Speaking"; Fradenburg, "Servant Tongue." See also Grudin, "Poetics of Guile."

16. See also the passage on "tydynge" in the *House of Fame* 2108–9.

17. Consider, for example, the Manciple's remark to the Cook—"Of me, certeyn, thou shalt nat been yglosed" (IX.34)—which illustrates his discretion in the use of flattery and, through its omission here, calls attention to the likelihood that it has been used elsewhere.

18. Augustine, *Contra mendacium ad Consentium* 10.24.

19. Ibid., 13.28 (at 538). Cf. Isidore, *Etymologiarum* 1.40.1–7; and Boccaccio, *Genealogiae* 14.9 and 14.13.

20. Hansen, *Fictions of Gender*, delineates a connection between submissive, marginal—feminine—voices and the voice/role of the narrator and poet; see esp. 15–25.

21. Innocent's *De miseria* succinctly describes the association of drunken, fetid breath and vulgar speech: "Quid turpius ebrioso, cui fetor est in ore, tremor in corpore; qui promit stulta, prodit occulta; cui mens alienatur, facies transformatur? 'Nullum enim secretum ubi regnat ebrietas'" (2.19) [What is more foul than a drunkard, for whom a fetid stench is in the mouth, a trembling in the body; who utters foolishness, betrays secrets; whose reason is alienated, face transformed? "For nothing is secret where drunkenness reigns"]. Drunkenness as the instigator of vulgar speech is a commonplace trope; see, for instance, the *Parson's Tale* X.607–53; the Miller's Prologue I.3120–86; the words prefacing the Pardoner's Prologue VI.320–328. Cf. *Piers Plowman* B.5.181–87, where Gloton laments his overindulgences and connects them to language. Because the Manciple attacks the Cook's presupposedly vulgar speech, its seems plausible that the "cursed breeth" to which the Manciple refers stands as a trope for foul speech, a position not inconsistent with other readings, including, for example, Pearcy, "Does the Manciple's Prologue Contain a Reference to Hell's Mouth?"

22. The place of the earlier *Cook's Tale* in context is problematic because of the earlier fragment. See Kolve's chapter "The Cook's Tale and the Man of Law's Introduction," in *Chaucer and the Imagery of Narrative*, 257–96.

23. The utility of retraction in practice is not unlike that of Lacan's "unsignifying," his striking through the definite article; see "God and the *Jouissance* of the Woman," in *Feminine*, 137–61.

24. On the penitential motif of the *Parson's Tale* and the *Retractions*, see Robert S. Knapp, "Penance, Irony, and Chaucer's Retraction"; Wurtele, "The Penitence of Geoffrey Chaucer"; Lawler, *One and the Many*, 147–72. In *Currency of the Word*, Shoaf argues that if, as Chaucer claims, "*Al* that is writen is writen for oure doctrine" (X.1083), then the poet's own writings would be included (241–42).

Chapter Six: The Summoner's Subversive Erotics

1. Winterson, *Written on the Body*, 89.

2. Isidorus Hispalensis (Isidore of Seville), *Etymologiarum sive Originum Libri XX*, 11.2.19–20.

3. Boswell, *Christianity*; see esp. 330–32. Though I can only sketch here the sociohistorical contexts of Chaucer's work, my argument is generally informed by Boswell's insightful and extensive study. See also his recent and controversial *Same-Sex Unions in Premodern Europe*; Bullough, "The Sin Against Nature."

4. Boswell, *Christianity*, 207–41.

5. See, for instance, Albertus Magnus, *Summa theologiae* 2.18.122, on *sodomia:* "Sodomia est peccatum contra naturam, masculi cum masculo, vel foeminae cum foemina" [Sodomy is a sin against nature, male with male, or female with female]; and Thomas Aquinas, *Summa theologiae* 2a.2ae.142.4, on the classification of sodomy: "sicut si aliquis delectetur in comestione carnium humanarum, aut in coitu bestiarum aut masculorum" ["for instance, taking pleasure in cannibalism or in bestial or homosexual coition" (trans. Blackfriars)]. Albertus and Aquinas are critiqued in Boswell, *Christianity*, 303–34, which brought these passages to my attention, and in Cadden, *Meanings of Sex Difference in the Middle Ages*, 218–27, also indebted to Boswell's study.

6. For example: "cum ferro plumbarii incense ignito trans tubam ductilem ad egestionis partes secretas applicatam membra spiritalia post intestinas combusserunt" ["with a plumber's iron heated red hot, through a horn applied leading to the privy parts of the bowel, they burned out the respiratory organs past the intestines"]. Geoffrey le Baker, *Chronicon Galfridi le Baker de Swynebroke*, cited and translated by Cuttino and Lyman, "Where is Edward II?," 524. Baker's account is believed to have been written circa 1350, approximately twenty-three years after Edward's death.

7. Foucault, *History of Sexuality Volume I*, 101.

8. Such topics as "difference" and "the other" have become de rigueur, almost cliches of critical controversy. As Dollimore notes in *Sexual Dissidence*, his critique of heterosexist culture's paradoxical insistence on the cultural maintenance of "sexual dissidence," "'Difference' is a fashionable concept. So too is 'the other,' that highly charged embodiment of difference. I propose a distrust of both concepts" (249). These concepts have been, as Sedgwick demonstrates in *Epistemology of the Closet*, "fetishized" (23) by the dominant order. See also Boyd, "On Lesbian and Gay/Queer Medieval Studies."

9. The *MED* defines "geldyng," a gelded horse, figuratively (2[a]) as "a castrated man, a eunuch; a naturally impotent man," and "mare," a riding horse, steed, or mare, figuratively (2[e]) as "a bad woman, a slut." See also Boswell, *Christianity*, 253–54, on "horse," "mule," and related terms in Roman homosexual slang, and Carolyn Dinshaw's discussion of "geldyng," "mare," and their critical implications in the chapter "Eunuch Hermeneutics," *Chaucer's Sexual Poetics*, 156–84.

10. Though the text is vague about the origin of the Pardoner's condition, castration as punishment is listed in criminal codes for a variety of offenses, including homosexual behavior, and although it is unclear whether the punishments were actually carried out, the threat was well known; see Boswell, *Christianity*, 293–302. Abelard's castration, though effected for his heterosexual union with Heloise, underscores the reality of the castration threat and is the subject of great contemporary interest; see, for example, Dronke, *Abelard and Heloise in Medieval Testimonies*. A popular French translation of Abelard's letters appeared in the

thirteenth century and was attributed to Jean de Meun; this text has recently been made available in a dual edition, *La Vie et Les Epistres*. Additionally, a distinction between physical and spiritual eunuchry could be made here, evoking scriptural authority: "Sunt enim eunuchi, qui de matris utero sic nati sunt: et sunt eunuchi, qui facti sunt ab hominibus: et sunt eunuchi, qui seipsos castraverunt propter regnum caelorum. Qui potest capere capiat" (Mt 19.2) [For there are eunuchs, who from their mother's womb so were they born: and there are eunuchs, who were made by men: and there are eunuchs, who have castrated themselves on account of the kingdom of heaven. He who is able to comprehend, let him comprehend]. Origen's self-mutilation, *propter regnum caelorum,* was well known, its merits and faults debated throughout the Middle Ages. Abelard comments on Origen in a letter to Heloise: "In exemplo est magnus ille Christianorum philosophus Origenes qui, ut hoc in se penitus incendium exstigueret, manus sibi inferre veritus non est; ac si illos ad litteram vere beatos intelligeret, qui se ipsos propter regnum coelorum castraverunt.... Culpam tamen non modicam Origines incurrit dum per poenam corporis remedium culpae quaerit, zelum quippe Dei habens, sed non secundum scientam, homicidii incurrit reatum, inferendo sibi manum.... quod miseratione Dei in me est ab alio perpetratum. Culpam evito, non incurro" ["The great Christian philosopher Origen provides an example, for he was not afraid to mutilate himself in order to quench completely this fire within him, as if he understood literally the words that those men were truly blessed who castrated themselves for the Kingdom of Heaven's sake.... Yet Origen is seriously to be blamed because he sought a remedy for blame in punishment of his body. True, he has a zeal for God, but an ill-formed zeal, and the charge of homicide can be proved against him for his self-mutilation.... but in my case, through God's compassion, it was done by another's hand. I do not incur blame, I escape it"]. Text and translation of Letter 4 cited here are, respectively, from "The Personal Letters Between Abelard and Heloise," and *The Letters of Abelard and Heloise,* 148–49. Though Abelard's praises come across as the words of one making the best of a horrible situation, his critique of Origen's excessive literalism locates the blame for both castrations in the flesh: Origen's obsession with the letter, Abelard's with sensual flesh.

On eunuchry in relation to Chaucer's Pardoner, see Curry's influential study "The Secret of Chaucer's Pardoner"; Miller, "Chaucer's Pardoner, the Scriptural Eunuch"; Rowland, "Chaucer's Idea of the Pardoner"; Dinshaw, *Chaucer's Sexual Poetics,* 157–59, 259n.8–11; and, recently, Frantzen, *"The Pardoner's Tale,* the Pervert"; Burger, "Kissing the Pardoner"; Kruger, "Claiming the Pardoner"; and Gross, "Trade Secrets."

11. See McAlpine, "The Pardoner's Homosexuality and How It Matters." A similar conflation is proposed by Karlen, "The Homosexual Heresy," though somewhat generalized.

12. Terms such as "heterosexual" and "homosexual" are recent inventions and can be only anachronistically applied to medieval texts; nonetheless, such termi-

nology is useful for articulating interpretations of sexual representation. (I avoid using the terms "gay" and "queer" because they seem to be so clearly located in a contemporary political context of individuals' self-definition, a concept apparently unknown to Chaucer's time.)

13. *A Chaucer Glossary* (compiled by Davis, Gray, Ingham, Wallace-Hadrell) suggests an "indecent pun" on "burdoun," "accompaniment, ground-bass" and "bourdon," "pilgrim's staff" (19). The MED notes that the word's sense of "a pilgrim's staff; also a walking stick, a club, a spiked staff" (1) may be used figuratively. The MED also notes that an additional usage of "burdoun" corresponds to a mule, and while this sense seems pretty far removed from Chaucer's literal narrative, it could underscore the equine imagery used to describe the Pardoner; in "Chaucer's Puns," Baum suggests a connection between "burdoun" as "a mule between a horse and a she-ass" and the implications of the Pardoner as "mare" (232).

14. See Richardson's overview in *The Riverside Chaucer*, 822–23. Braswell-Means, "A New Look at an Old Patient," provides an insightful overview of physiological connections to psychological and sexual phenomena and aligns Summoner and Pardoner based on an analysis of humors, 272–73. See also Brody, *Disease of the Soul*, 37–47, on the Summoner's symptoms of leprosy, also largely perceived as a sexually related disease.

15. The MED glosses "to pulle a fynch" as "to do something with cunning" ("finch" [b]). In the context of the *General Prologue* the phrase has a twofold sense: to pull a scam over on an unsuspecting victim; to take sexual advantage of someone.

16. The MED notes that the term "girles," of uncertain origin, refers to young people of either sex ([a] a child of either sex—often a boy; [b] a girl, young woman). The feminized implications of the term suggest that the Summoner's "girles" could be catamites, but more likely young yet postpubescent passive males. Boswell, *Christianity*, discusses the relative uses of "youth" and like terms in relation to pederasty and suggests that it may be akin to the use of "girl" by heterosexual men (e.g., "girlfriend") to describe sexual objects other than children (29–31). As for the relationship between pederasty and homosexuality, Greenberg's *The Construction of Homosexuality* has informed my thinking.

17. See MED "gropen" 1.(a), "To feel with the hand or fingers, touch, stroke"; 1.(d), "to touch (sb) something amorously, play with, fondle"; 5.(a), "to examine, ponder, consider"; 5.(b), "question" (sb); (c), "interrogate, test, inquire of . . . probe into."

18. The OED's definition here corresponds to the MED's definition 1.(d) (see note 17).

19. According to the Tatlock and Kennedy *Concordance*, "grope" appears in Chaucer's work three times other than those included in the Summoner's *General Prologue* portrait and *Tale*; "groped" appears once in the *Reeve's Tale*, and "gropeth"

appears twice, once in the *Reeve's Tale* and once in the *Legend of Good Women*. Thus of the word's ten appearances in Chaucer's corpus, four of them belong to the Summoner.

20. The storage of valuables in bodily orifices—and the invitation for a cavity search—perhaps would not seem odd to Chaucer's audience, given its unremarkable acceptance within the text; see also Roy Peter Clark, "Doubting Thomas in Chaucer's *Summoner's Tale*," who speculates that "possibly, bodily orifices served as common hiding places in the Middle Ages" (173), much as they do today for smugglers or prisoners.

21. Readers have often read the tale as an example of wholly scatological fabliau, without sexual content; see, for example, Cooper, *The Canterbury Tales*, 177. Such readings, I would argue, overlook a subtle but real representation of ambiguous sexual expression; consider, for instance, Haldeen Braddy's comment: "This discreditable sort of filth, Chaucer at his worst, figures small in total" ("Chaucer—Realism or Obscenity," cited by Roy Peter Clark, "Doubting Thomas," 178n.45).

22. "Pryvetee," according to the *MED*, denotes not only a sense of "secret" or "private" but also the connotation of "private parts," namely, the genital/anal region. See, for instance, the Miller's Prologue I.3163–64: "An housbonde shal nat been inquisityf / Of Goddes pryvetee, nor of his wyf"; Hanks, "'Goddes Pryvetee' and Chaucer's *Miller's Tale*," provides an insightful critique of the pun. The Wife of Bath uses the double-entendre in describing her close friend: "Hir name was Alisoun. / She knew myn herte, and eek my privetee" (III.530–31); while in context "pryvetee" probably refers to "secrets," the pun reinforces the Prologue's subtext that the Wife prefers the company of women over that of men.

23. The trope of the "finger" as God's power and presence is reiterated throughout Scripture (see, for example, Ex 8.19, 31.18). Though I am not suggesting that it is evoked allegorically in this capacity in the *Summoner's Tale*, the overt attention to "finger" here foregrounds its later, implicit use in the groping episode.

24. Much has been written on the notorious fart, which for many readers is the crux of the story: see, for example, Levitan, "The Parody of Pentecost"; Szittya, "The Friar as False Apostle"; John F. Adams, "The Structure of Irony." The fart is identified by Thomas as a "*thyng . . .* hyd in privetee" (2143, emphasis mine), which perhaps echoes Friar John's earlier insistence that "glosynge is a glorious *thyng*, certeyn" (1793, emphasis mine).

25. Bakhtin, *Rabelais and His World*, 370.

26. I refer here to Dante's *Inferno*, the conclusion of Canto 21 and the beginning of 22, in which Barbariccia gives the signal to rally the troops—"ed elli avea del cul fatto trombetta" ["And he had made a trumpet of his ass"] (21.139)—much to Dante's amazement.

27. Lotario dei Segni (Pope Innocent III), *De miseria condicionis humane*, 2.18.

28. Bakhtin, *Rabelais and His World*, 370.

29. The citation refers to Psalm 44: "Eructavit cor meum verbum bonum; / Dico

ego opera mea regi. / Lingua mea calamus scribae / Velociter scribentis" [My heart has uttered a good word; / I speak my works to the king. / My tongue the pen of the scribe / Swiftly writing]. Jerome uses the same citation to situate a discussion of biblical women and the *sponsa Christi* motif in his *Epistola LXV* ("Ad Principiam virginem sive explanatio Psalmi XLIV").

30. "*Contrapasso*" is used in Dante's *Inferno* to describe the system of punishments. Bertram, damned for his divisiveness, is himself dismembered and remarks: "Cosi s'osserva in me lo contrapasso" ["And thus, in me one sees the law of counter-penalty"] (28.142). Dante's influence on Chaucer in this regard has long been noted; see, for instance, the discussion by Neuse, *Chaucer's Dante*, esp. 201–20, "The Friar and the Summoner: Chaucerian *Contrapasso*."

31. Although it is beyond the scope of my remarks here to engage the deconstructionist debate, suffice it to say that medieval concepts of polysemy (*usurpata translatio, impositio ad placitum*) presuppose some set of parameters. No medieval theorist advocates plurality to the point of a Tower of Babel, nor apparently considers seriously the possibility, given the ubiquitous acceptance of Christian Logocentrism, even if such parameters seem arbitrary. On deconstruction, Derrida, Augustine, and the Word, see the insightful essay by Ferguson, "Saint Augustine's Region of Unlikeness."

32. See Roy Peter Clark, "Doubting Thomas," 164–73.

33. In a discussion of the Lollards, Peggy Knapp suggests, "The Lollards accused users of patristic glosses of obscuring the truth of the Bible, and ecclesiastical authorities accused Lollards of the same thing. . . . In short, 'gloss' had become by the fourteenth century, in Bakhtin's phrase, 'an active participant in the social dialogue'" ("Wandrynge by the Weye," 153). See also Fletcher, "The Topical Heresy of Chaucer's Pardoner," which posits a connection between the Lollard's appropriations and the Pardoner's figurative relationship to heresy.

34. Carruthers, "Letter and Gloss in the Friar's and Summoner's Tales."

35. Reiss, "Biblical Parody"; see also the analysis by Alford in the same volume, "Scriptural Testament in *The Canterbury Tales*." On the ubiquitous concern with letter and gloss in the Middle Ages, see Smalley, *Study of the Bible in the Middle Ages*, 126; Minnis and Scott with Wallace, eds., *Medieval Literary Theory and Criticism*, 65–71.

36. Gluttony is used to identify sins of indulgence; see also lines III.1904–17, where "gluttony" is said to be the sin of Adam. Cf. treatments of gluttony in *De miseria* 2.17–20, *Inferno* 6, and *Piers Plowman* B.5.367–69.

37. See, for instance, *Piers Plowman*'s warning against friars, B.13.67–74.

38. See Beaver, "Homosexual Signs"; Brundage, *Law, Sex, and Christian Society*, 398–400, 472–74; Boswell, *Christianity*, 137–206; Greenberg, *Construction of Homosexuality*, 274–79. See also the treatment of sexual codes apropos penitential handbooks in McNeil and Gamer's *Medieval Handbooks of Penance*, esp. *The Penitential of Cummean*, 102–5; *The Penitential of Theodore*, 184–86; *Penitential Ascribed by Albers to*

Bede, 226–27. On homosexual practices involving women, see Brooten, "Paul's Views on the Nature of Women and Female Homoeroticism."

39. Theologians use as a basis for their arguments Rom 1.26–27: "Propterea tradidit illos Deus in passiones ignominiae. Nam feminae eorum immutaverunt naturalem usum in eum usum qui est contra naturam. Similiter autem et masculi, relicto naturali usu feminae, exarserunt in desideriis suis in invicem, masculi in masculos turpitudinem operantes" [For this God delivered them to disgraceful passions. For their women have changed the natural use into that which is against nature. And similarly the men also, relinquishing the natural use of women, have become exhausted in their desires in turn, men among men working that which is filthy]. Innocent, for example, cites the passage verbatim and appends the comment, "Quid hac turpitudine turpius? Quid hoc crimine criminosius?" [What is more filthy than such filth? What more criminal than this crime?] (*De miseria* 2.24, subtitled "De coitu contra naturam" [Of intercourse against nature]). But the "nature" debate is full of inconsistencies and illogic, since commentators both evoke and ignore the presence of homosexual behaviors in the "natural"—that is, animal—and, for that matter, human world; see Boswell, *Christianity*, 303–32.

We might recall as well Isidore's assumption, cited at the beginning of this chapter, that homoerotic desire is inherent and thus in one sense "natural" for men. In addition, Isidore's definition of "natural law" accommodates his assumption: "Ius naturale est commune omnium nationum, et quod ubique instinctu naturae, non constitutione aliqua habetur; ut viri et feminae coniunctio. . . . Nam hoc, *aut si quid huic simile est*, nunquam iniustum est, sed naturale, aequumque habetur" [Natural law is common to all nations, and is everywhere by natural instinct, and is not had by legislation: (it includes) the joining together of men and women. . . . For this, *or that which is similar*, is never unjust, but natural, and equal] (Isidore, *Etymologiarum,* 5.iv.1–2; emphasis mine).

40. See also commentary in Philo of Alexandria, *Questions and Answers on Genesis* 4.38, who argues that while the Sodomites are literally "pederasts," Lot symbolically offers the feminine (the "inferior") to save the masculine (the "better"). Jerome considers the ambiguity of the Sodomite reference in Sophonias in *Commentarii in prophetas minores: In Sophoniam* 2.8–11. Cf. the explication on the Sodomites in *Cleanness,* where God speaks out, 689–96, and Frantzen's recent analysis, "The Disclosure of Sodomy." Lot's daughters, offered up so willingly by Lot to be "abused," are in the same chapter later implicated in the sexual sin of incest, for the daughters seduce their father and bear his sons; see Gn 19.29–38. The daughters' behavior, while considered a grave sin (see, for example, *Piers Plowman* B.1.25–43), is hardly inexplicable given their twofold identity as sexual objects and their father's property.

41. See Dante's *Inferno* 33.149–50, the Third Ring of the Ninth Circle, where the betrayers of hospitality are frozen; Dante excuses his own rudeness here, suggesting that showing rudeness to the rude is appropriate. On pride as a "general condition of sin" ("conditio generalis omnis peccati"), see Thomas Aquinas, *Summa theologiae* 1a.2ae.84.2.

42. Other texts deal with the trope of sodomy—Alan of Lille's *De planctu Naturae* being the most obvious—but none as overtly linked to textuality, and none so overtly influencing Chaucer's work. On the treatment of sexual tropes in *De planctu*, see Ziolkowski, *Alan of Lille's Grammar of Sex*. Bredbeck's recent *Sodomy and Interpretation*, though concerned largely with Renaissance representations, contains a useful introduction to and history of sodomy as a "scene" of interpretation, 3–30.

43. Vance, "The Differing Seed: Dante's Brunetto Latini," in *Mervelous Signals*, 230–55; see also the discussion by Pequigney, "Sodomy in Dante's *Inferno* and *Purgatorio*"; and Bloch, *Etymologies*, 133–36.

44. The connection is underscored by the similarities in description of Chaucer's "develes ers"—"a tayl / Brodder than of a carryk is the sayl" (1687–88)—and Dante's comment in *Inferno* 34.48, "vele di mar non vid' io mai cotali" ["I've never seen a ship with sails so wide"].

45. See Hanning, "Roasting a Friar," on the frairs-as-fart motif.

46. See, for example, D. W. Robertson, Jr.'s *Preface to Chaucer*, esp. 317–90, 463–503.

47. See also Hanning, "Maner Glose"; Besserman, "'Glosynge is a Glorious Thyng.'"

48. I make this argument in Chapter 1. A useful definition of bisexuality is provided in Cixous's "The Laugh of the Medusa": "the presence . . . of both sexes, nonexclusion either of the difference or of one sex, and, from this 'self-permission,' multiplication of the effects of the inscription of desire" (288). I agree with Dinshaw's assertion that "Chaucer has a deep and acute sense of the differences between the genders in Western patriarchal culture" (*Chaucer's Sexual Poetics*, 193n.14).

49. See, for instance, lines 1772–77, where the Friar "droof awey the cat" in order to take the desired seat for himself; and lines 1838–45, where the Friar asserts his desire for a lavish dinner.

50. On the relationship of public/private to the central/marginal status of homosexuality and homosexual desire, see Sedgwick, *Epistemology of the Closet*, 22.

51. A pun on "ars-metrike" (III.2222) is likely, given the text's obsession with anal imagery. In addition, the suggestion of an *ars metrica*, that is, a method of measuring or assessing, is present in the text's reflexive, or metatextual, attention to figurative construction. A different reading of "ars-metrike" is provided in O'Brien, "'Ars-Metrik,'" who argues that the text uses sophisticated scientific and mechanical metaphors as "satiric participation in the dominant scientific discourse of Chaucer's age" (1).

52. Dinshaw comments on the Pardoner in relation to Paul's ideal in *Chaucer's Sexual Poetics*—"the Pardoner, not-man, not-woman, is the unlikely but best pilgrim for this task [to encourage listeners to think about 'absolute Presence'] on the road to Canterbury; for in the ideal Christian society too, according to Saint Paul, 'non est masculus neque femina' (Gal 3:28)" (183–84)—and, in a recent essay, argues that the Pardoner is "an unwelcome but insistent reminder—get used to it—of heterosexual incompleteness" ("Chaucer's Queer Touches," 92). The Summoner's "groping" episode, I suggest, serves a similar purpose: a vulgar and perhaps unwelcome textual presence, the connotations of which persist nonetheless.

❧ Works Cited

Primary sources

Abelard, Peter. Letters. In "The Personal Letters Between Abelard and Heloise: Introduction, Authenticity, Texts." Edited by J. T. Muckle. *Mediaeval Studies* 15 (1953): 47–94.
———. *The Letters of Abelard and Heloise.* Translated by Betty Radice. New York: Penguin Books, 1974.
———. *La Vie et Les Epistres Pierre Abaelart et Heloys sa Fame, Traduction du XIIIe siecle attribuee a Jean de Meun.* Edited by Eric Hicks. Paris: Honoré Champion, 1991.
Alanus de Insulis (Alan of Lille). *De planctu Naturae.* PL 210.451–82.
Albertus Magnus. *De animalibus.* Edited by Hermann Stadler. Vol. 9, 10, 11 of *Opera omnia.*
———. *Opera omnia.* General editor Bernardus Geyer. Aschendorff: Monasterii Westfalorum, 1950–.
———. *Questiones super De animalibus.* Edited by Ephrem Filthaut, O.P. Vol. 12 of *Opera omnia.*
———. *Summa theologiae sive De mirabili scientia Dei, libri II.* Edited by Dionysius Siedler with Wilhemo Kubel and Henrico Boels. Vol. 35 of *Opera omnia.*
Ps.-Albertus Magnus. *Woman's Secrets: A Translation of Pseudo-Albertus Magnus' De Secretis Mulierum with Commentaries.* Edited by Helen Rodnite Lemay. Albany: State University of New York Press, 1992.
Ambrose, Saint. *De institutione virginis.* PL 16.319–47.
———. *Expositio in evangelii secundum Lucam.* Edited by M. Adriaen. CCSL 14. Turnhout: Brepols, 1957.
———. *De virginitate.* PL 16.197–243.
Ancrene Wisse: The English Text of the Ancrene Riwle Edited from MS. Corpus Christi, Cambridge 402. Edited by J. R. R. Tolkien. EETS 249. London: Oxford University Press, 1962.
Anselm of Canterbury. *De divinitas essentia monologium.* PL 158.141–224.

Aristotle. *Generation of Animals*. Edited and translated by A. L. Peck. Loeb Classical Library. Cambridge: Harvard University Press, 1953.

———. *Metaphysics*. Translated by W. D. Ross. In *The Complete Works of Aristotle*. Edited by Jonathan Barnes. Bollingen Series, no. 71. Vol. 2. Princeton: Princeton University Press, 1984.

Augustine, Saint. *De bono conjugali*. PL 40.373–96.

———. *De civitate Dei*. Edited by Bernardus Dombart and Alphonsus Kalb. CCSL 48. Turnhout: Brepols, 1955.

———. *Confessionum*. PL 32.659–868.

———. *Contra mendacium ad Consentium*. PL 40.517–48.

———. *De doctrina christiana*. Edited by Joseph Martin. CCSL 32. Turnhout: Brepols, 1962.

———. *De sancta virginitate*. PL 40.395–428.

Biblia sacra iuxta vulgatam Clementinam. 4th ed. Edited by Alberto Colunga and Laurentio Turrado. Madrid: Biblioteca de Autores Cristianos, 1965.

Boccaccio, Giovanni. *Genealogiae deorum gentilium, Liber XIV*. Edited by Jeremiah Reedy. Toronto: Pontifical Institute of Medieval Studies, 1978.

Boethius. *Philosophiae consolatio*. Edited by Ludovicus Biehler. CCSL 94. Turnhout: Brepols, 1984.

Chaucer, Geoffrey. *The Book of Troilus and Criseyde by Geoffrey Chaucer*. Edited by Robert Kilburn Root. Princeton: Princeton University Press, 1926.

———. *The Manciple's Tale*. Edited by Donald C. Baker. A Variorum Edition of the Works of Geoffrey Chaucer. General editor Paul G. Ruggiers. Vol. 2. Norman: University of Oklahoma Press, 1984.

———. *The Minor Poems*. Edited by George B. Pace and Alfred David. A Variorum Edition of the Works of Geoffrey Chaucer. General editor Paul G. Ruggiers. Vol. 5, part 1. Norman: University of Oklahoma Press, 1982.

———. *The Riverside Chaucer*. 3d ed. Edited by Larry D. Benson. Boston: Houghton Mifflin Company, 1987.

Cicero. *De amicitia*. Edited by L. Laurand. Paris: Societe D'edition Les Belles Lettres, 1928.

Cleanness. In *Poems of the Pearl Manuscript*, 111–84.

Conrad of Hirsau. *Dialogus super auctores*. In *Accessus ad auctores, Bernard D'Utrecht, Conrad D'Hirsau*. Edited by R. B. C. Huygens. Leiden: E.J. Brill, 1970.

Dante Alighieri. *Dantis Alagherii Epistolae*. 2d ed. Edited by Paget Toynbee. Oxford: Clarendon Press, 1966.

———. *The Divine Comedy of Dante Alighieri: Inferno*. Edited and translated by Allen Mandelbaum. 1980. Reprint, New York: Bantam Books, 1982.

———. *The Divine Comedy of Dante Alighieri: Paradiso*. Edited and translated by Allen Mandelbaum. 1984. Reprint, New York: Bantam Books, 1986.

———. *De vulgari eloquentia*. Edited by Pier Vincenzo Mengaldo. Padua: Editrice Antenore, 1968.

Dunbar, William. *Lament for the Makars.* In *The Oxford Book of Late Medieval Verse and Prose.* Edited by Douglas Gray. 316–18. Oxford: Clarendon Press, 1985.
Galen. *On the Usefulness of the Parts of the Body.* Translated by Margaret Tallmadge May. Ithaca: Cornell University Press, 1968.
Geoffrey of Vinsauf. *Poetria nova.* Edited by Ernest Gallo. In *The Poetria nova and Its Sources in Early Rhetorical Doctrine.* The Hague: Mouton, 1971.
Gower, John. *Confessio amantis.* In *The English Works of John Gower.* Edited by G. C. Macaulay. EETS e.s. 82. 1900. Reprint, Oxford: Oxford University Press, 1957.
Gratian. *Decretum.* In *Corpus iuris canonici.* Edited by Aemilius Friedberg. 1879. Reprint, Graz: Akademische Druck, 1955.
Gregory of Nyssa. *De virginitate.* PG 46.324–452.
Gregory of Tours. *Vitae Patrum, seu Liber de Vita quorumdam feliciosorum.* PL 71.1009–96.
Guillaume de Lorris and Jean de Meun. *Le Roman de la rose.* Edited by Félix Lecoy. 3 vols. Paris: Honoré Champion, 1966–74.
Hali Meidenhad: An Alliterative Homily of the Thirteenth Century from MS. Bodley 34, Oxford. Edited by F. J. Furnival. EETS o.s. 18. 1922. Reprint, New York: Greenwood Press, 1969.
Henryson, Robert. *Testament of Cresseid.* Edited by Denton Fox. London: Nelson, 1968.
Heraclitus of Ephesus. *Heracliti Ephesii Reliquiae.* Edited by I. Bywater. 1877. Reprint, Chicago: Argonaut, 1969.
Hildegard of Bingen. *Causa et curae (Liber compositae medicinae).* Edited by Paul Kaiser. Leipzig: B.G. Teubner, 1903.
Isidorus Hispalensis (Isidore of Seville). *Etymologiarum sive Originum Libri XX.* Edited by W. M. Lindsay. Oxford: Oxford University Press, 1911.
Jerome, Saint. *Adversus Jovinianum.* PL 23.221–352.
———. *Commentarii in prophetas minores: In Sophoniam.* Edited by M. Adriaen. CCSL 76A. Turnhout: Brepols, 1970.
———. *Commentariorum in epistolam ad Ephesios.* PL 26.467–590.
———. *Epistolae.* PL 22.325–1197.
Ps.-Jerome. *De virginitate.* PL 30.163–75.
John Chrysostom, Saint. *De virginitate.* PG 48.533–96.
Langland, William. *The Vision of Piers Plowman: A Complete Edition of the B-Text.* Edited by A. V. C. Schmidt. London: J.M. Dent, 1978.
Lotario dei Segni (Innocent III). *De miseria condicionis humane.* Edited by Robert E. Lewis. The Chaucer Library. Athens: University of Georgia Press, 1978.
Migne, J. P., editor. *Patrologiae cursus completus: series graeca.* Paris, 1857–94, and reprints.
———, editor. *Patrologiae cursus completus: series latina.* Paris, 1844–83, and reprints.
Parmenides of Elea. *Parmenides of Elea: Fragments.* Edited and translated by David Gallop. Phoenix Pre-Socratics, no. 1. Toronto: University of Toronto Press, 1984.
Pearl. In *Poems of the Pearl Manuscript,* 53–110.

Penitential of Theodore, The. In *Medieval Handbooks of Penance: A Translation of the Principle libri poenitentiales and Selections from Related Documents.* Edited and translated by John T. McNeill and Helena M. Garner. 1938. Reprint, New York: Columbia University Press, 1990.

Philo of Alexandria. *Questions and Answers on Genesis.* Edited and translated by Ralph Marcus. Loeb Classical Library. Cambridge: Harvard University Press, 1953.

Poems of the Pearl Manuscript, The. Edited by Malcolm Andrew and Ronald Waldron. York Medieval Texts. 2d series. Berkeley: University of California Press, 1978.

Publius Ovidii Nasonis (Ovid). *Metamorphoses.* Edited by William S. Anderson. Bibliotheca Scriptorum Graecorum et Romanorum Teubneriana. Leipzig: BSB B.G. Turner, 1977.

Quintilian. *Institutio oratoria.* Edited by H. E. Butler. Loeb Classical Library. Cambridge: Harvard University Press, 1969.

Quintus Septimus Florens Tertullian. *De cultu feminarum.* Edited by Aemili Kroymann. CCSL 1. Turnhout: Brepols, 1954.

Secrete of Secretes, The. In *Three Prose Versions of the Secreta Secretorum.* Edited Robert Steele. 1–39. EETS e.s. 74. London: Kegan Paul, 1898.

Sir Gawain and the Green Knight. In *Poems of the Pearl Manuscript,* 207–300.

Spenser, Edmund. *The Faerie Queene.* Edited by Thomas Roche, Jr., with Patrick O'Donnell, Jr. New Haven: Yale University Press, 1981.

Thomas Aquinas, Saint. *Summa Theologiae.* Edited and translated by Blackfriars. General editor Thomas Gilbey, O.P. New York: McGraw-Hill, 1963–.

Trevisa, John. *Dialogus inter dominum et clericum.* Edited by Ronald Waldron. In "Trevisa's Original Prefaces on Translation: A Critical Edition." In *Medieval Studies Presented to George Kane.* Edited by Edward Donald Kennedy, Ronald Waldron, and Joseph S. Wittig. 285–99. Suffolk: D.S. Brewer, 1988.

Secondary Sources

Adams, Carol J. *The Sexual Politics of Meat: A Feminist-Vegetarian Critical Theory.* New York: Continuum, 1990.

Adams, J. N. *The Latin Sexual Vocabulary.* London: Duckworth, 1982.

Adams, John F. "The Structure of Irony in the *Summoner's Tale.*" *Essays in Criticism* 12 (1962): 126–32.

Aers, David. *Chaucer, Langland, and the Creative Imagination.* London: Routledge and Kegan Paul, 1980.

Alexandre, Monique. "Early Christian Women." In *A History of Women in the West, Vol. 1: From Ancient Goddesses to Christian Saints.* Edited by Pauline Schmidtt Pantel. Translated by Arthur Goldhammer. 409–44. Cambridge: Belknap/Harvard University Press, 1992.

Alford, John A. "The Grammatical Metaphor: A Survey of Its Use in the Middle Ages." *Speculum* 57 (1982): 728–60.

---. "Scriptural Testament in *The Canterbury Tales:* The Letter Takes Its Revenge." In Jeffrey, 197–203.
Allen, Prudence, R.S.M. *The Concept of Woman: The Aristotelian Revolution, 750 B.C.–1250 A.D.* London: Eden Press, 1985.
---. "Hildegard of Bingen's Philosophy of Sex Identity." In *Gender and the Moral Order in Medieval Society.* Edited by Thelma Fenster. Spec. issue *Thought* 64 (1989): 231–41.
Anapolous, Anna. "Writing the Mystic Body: Sexuality and Textuality in the *Ecriture-feminine* of Saint Catherine of Genoa." In Grosz, *Feminism,* 185–207.
Astell, Ann. "Apostrophe, Prayer, and the Structure of Satire in *The Man of Law's Tale.*" *Studies in the Age of Chaucer* 13 (1991): 81–97.
Atkinson, Clarissa W. *The Oldest Vocation: Christian Motherhood in the Middle Ages.* Ithaca: Cornell University Press, 1991.
Baer, Richard A. *Philo's Use of the Categories Male and Female.* Leiden: E.J. Brill, 1970.
Bakhtin, Mikhail M. *The Dialogic Imagination: Four Essays.* Edited by Michael Holquist. Translated by Caryl Emerson and Michael Holquist. Austin: University of Texas Press, 1981.
---. *Rabelais and His World.* Translated by Helene Iswolsky. Bloomington: Indiana University Press, 1984.
Bal, Mieke. *Lethal Love: Feminist Literary Readings of Biblical Love Stories.* Bloomington: Indiana University Press, 1987.
Baron, Dennis. *Grammar and Gender.* New Haven: Yale University Press, 1986.
Barr, Jane. "The Vulgate Genesis and St. Jerome's Attitudes to Women." In *Equally in God's Image: Women in the Middle Ages.* Edited by Julia Bolton Holloway, Constance S. Wright, and Joan Bechtold. 122–43. New York: Peter Lang, 1990.
Baum, Paull F. "Chaucer's Puns." *PMLA* 71 (1956): 225–46.
---. "Chaucer's Puns: A Supplementary List." *PMLA* 73 (1958): 167–70.
Beaver, Harold. "Homosexual Signs (In Memory of Roland Barthes)." *Critical Inquiry* 8 (1981): 99–119.
Beichner, Paul E., C.S.C. "Confrontation, Contempt of Court, and Chaucer's Cecilia." *Chaucer Review* 8 (1974): 198–204.
Bennett, Paula. "Gender as Performance: Shakespearean Ambiguity and the Lesbian Reader." In *Sexual Practice/Textual Theory.* Edited by Susan J. Wolfe and Julia Penelope. 94–109. Cambridge: Blackwell, 1993.
Benson, Larry D., editor. *The Learned and the Lewed: Studies in Chaucer and Medieval Literature.* Harvard English Studies, no. 5. Cambridge: Harvard University Press, 1974.
Benstock, Shari. *Textualizing the Feminine: On the Limits of Genre.* Norman: University of Oklahoma Press, 1991.
Besserman, Laurence. "Glosynge is a Glorious Thyng: Chaucer's Biblical Exegesis." In Jeffrey, 65–73.

Bestul, Thomas H. "*The Man of Law's Tale* and the Rhetorical Foundation of Chaucerian Pathos." *Chaucer Review* 9 (1975): 216–26.

Biddick, Kathleen. "Gender, Bodies, Borders: Technologies of the Visible." In *Studying Medieval Women: Sex, Gender, Feminism*. Edited by Nancy F. Partner. Spec. issue *Speculum* 68.2 (1993): 389–418.

Blamires, Alcuin. "The Wife of Bath and Lollardy." *Medium AEvum* 58 (1989): 222–42.

Bloch, R. Howard. "Chaucer's Maiden's Head: 'The Physician's Tale' and the Poetics of Virginity." *Representations* 28 (1989): 113–34.

———. *Etymologies and Genealogies: A Literary Anthropology of the French Middle Ages*. Chicago: University of Chicago Press, 1983.

———. *Medieval Misogyny and the Invention of Western Romantic Love*. Chicago: University of Chicago Press, 1991.

Blumenfeld-Kosinski, Renate, and Timea Szell, editors. *Images of Sainthood in Medieval Europe*. Ithaca: Cornell University Press, 1991.

Børch, Marianne. "Poet & Persona: Writing the Reader in *Troilus*." *Chaucer Review* 30 (1996): 215–28.

Boswell, John. *Christianity, Social Tolerance, and Homosexuality: Gay People in Western Europe from the Beginning of the Christian Era to the Fourteenth Century*. Chicago: University of Chicago Press, 1980.

———. *The Kindness of Strangers: The Abandonment of Children in Western Literature from Late Antiquity to the Renaissance*. New York: Vintage, 1988.

———. *Same-Sex Unions in Premodern Europe*. New York: Villard Books, 1994.

Boyd, David Lorenzo. "On Lesbian and Gay/Queer Medieval Studies." *Medieval Feminist Newsletter* 15 (1993): 12–15.

Braswell-Means, Laurel. "A New Look at an Old Patient: Chaucer's Summoner and Medieval Physiognomia." *Chaucer Review* 25 (1991): 266–75.

Bredbeck, Gregory. *Sodomy and Interpretation: Marlowe to Milton*. Ithaca: Cornell University Press, 1991.

Brody, Saul Nathaniel. *The Disease of the Soul: Leprosy in Medieval Literature*. Ithaca: Cornell University Press, 1974.

Brooten, Bernadette J. "Paul's Views on the Nature of Women and Female Homoeroticism." In *Immaculate and Powerful: The Female In Sacred Image and Social Reality*. Edited by Clarissa W. Atkinson, Constance H. Buchanan, and Margaret R. Miles. 61–87. Boston: Beacon, 1985.

Brown, Beatrice. "Chaucer's *Wreched Engendrynge*." *Modern Philology* 35 (1938): 325–33.

Brown, Peter. *The Body and Society: Men, Women, and Sexual Renunciation in Early Christianity*. New York: Columbia University Press, 1988.

Brundage, James A. *Law, Sex, and Christian Society in Medieval Europe*. Chicago: University of Chicago Press, 1987.

Brusendorff, Aage. *The Chaucer Tradition*. Gloucester, Mass.: Peter Smith, 1965.

Bugge, John. *Virginitas: An Essay in the History of a Medieval Ideal.* The Hague: Martinus Nijhoff, 1975.
Bullough, Vern L. "On Being a Male in the Middle Ages." In Lees, 31–45.
———. "Medieval Medical and Scientific Views of Women." *Viator* 4 (1973): 485–501.
———. "The Sin Against Nature and Homosexuality." In *Sexual Practices and the Medieval Church.* Edited by Vern L. Bullough and James Brundage. 55–71. Buffalo: Prometheus Books, 1982.
Burger, Glenn. "Kissing the Pardoner." *PMLA* 107 (1992): 1143–56.
Burnley, J. D. "Criseyde's Heart and the Weakness of Women: An Essay in Lexical Interpretation." *Studia Neophilologica* 54 (1982): 25–38.
Burns, E. Jane. *Bodytalk: When Women Speak in Old French Literature.* Philadelphia: University of Pennsylvania Press, 1993.
———. "Knowing Women: Female Orifices in Old French Farce and Fabliau." In Straus, *Skirting,* 81–104.
———. "This Prick Which Is Not One." In Lomperis and Stanbury, 188–212.
Butler, Judith. *Bodies That Matter: On the Discursive Limits of "Sex."* New York and London: Routledge, 1993.
———. *Gender Trouble: Feminism and the Subversion of Identity.* New York: Routledge, 1990.
Bynum, Caroline Walker. *Fragmentation and Redemption: Essays on Gender and the Human Body in Medieval Religion.* New York: Zone, 1991.
———. *Holy Feast and Holy Fast: The Religious Significance of Food to Medieval Women.* Berkeley: University of California Press, 1987.
———. *Jesus as Mother: Studies in the Spirituality of the Middle Ages.* Berkeley: University of California Press, 1982.
———. *The Resurrection of the Body in Western Christianity, 200–1336.* New York: Columbia University Press, 1995.
Cadden, Joan. *Meanings of Sex Difference in the Middle Ages: Medicine, Science, Culture.* Cambridge History of Medicine. Cambridge: Cambridge University Press, 1993.
Cameron, Averil. "Neither Male Nor Female." In *Women in Antiquity.* Edited by Ian McAuslan and Peter Walcot. Greece and Rome Studies 3. 26–35. Oxford: Oxford University Press, 1996.
Carruthers, Mary. "Letter and Gloss in the Friar's and Summoner's Tales." *Journal of Narrative Technique* 2 (1972): 208–14.
———. "The Wife of Bath and the Painting of Lions." *PMLA* 94 (1979): 209–22.
Carton, Evan. "Complicity and Responsibility in Pandarus' Bed and Chaucer's Art." *PMLA* 94 (1979): 47–61.
Chance, Jane. *The Mythographic Chaucer: The Fabulation of Sexual Politics.* Minneapolis: University of Minnesota Press, 1995.
Chenu, Marie-Dominique, O.P. *Nature, Man, and Society in the Twelfth Century: Essays on New Theological Perspectives in the Latin West.* Edited and translated by

Jerome Taylor and Lester K. Little. Chicago: University of Chicago Press, 1968.

Cixous, Hélène. "The Laugh of the Medusa." Translated by Keith Cohen and Paula Cohen. In *The Signs Reader: Women, Gender, Scholarship*. Edited by Elizabeth Abel and Emily K. Abel. 279–97. Chicago: University of Chicago Press, 1983.

Cixous, Hélène, and Catherine Clément. *The Newly Born Woman*. Translated by Betsy Wing. Minneapolis: University of Minnesota Press, 1986.

Clark, Elizabeth A. "'Adam's Only Companion': Augustine and the Early Christian Debate on Marriage." In Edwards and Spector, 15–31.

———. *Jerome, Chrysostom, and Friends: Essays and Translations*. Studies in Women and Religion, no. 2. New York: Edwin Mellen, 1979.

Clark, Roy Peter. "Doubting Thomas in Chaucer's *Summoner's Tale*." *Chaucer Review* 11 (1976): 164–78.

Clasby, Eugene. "Chaucer's Constance: Womanly Virtue and the Heroic Life." *Chaucer Review* 13 (1979): 221–33.

Coghill, Nevill. *The Poet Chaucer*. 2d ed. Oxford: Oxford University Press, 1967.

Cohen, Helen Louise. *The Ballade*. New York: Columbia University Press, 1915.

Cohen, Jeremy. *"Be Fertile and Increase, Fill the Earth and Master It": The Ancient and Medieval Career of a Biblical Text*. Ithaca: Cornell University Press, 1989.

Colish, Marcia L. *The Mirror of Language: A Study in the Medieval Theory of Knowledge*. Revised ed. Lincoln: University of Nebraska Press, 1968.

Collette, Carolyn. "Critical Approaches to the *Prioress's Tale* and the *Second Nun's Tale*." In *Chaucer's Religious Tales*. Edited by C. David Benson and Elizabeth Robertson. Chaucer Studies XV, 95–107. Cambridge: D.S. Brewer, 1990.

Cooper, Helen. *Oxford Guides to Chaucer: The Canterbury Tales*. Oxford: Oxford University Press, 1989.

Cox, Catherine S. "Froward Language and Wanton Play: The 'Commoun' Text of Henryson's *Testament of Cresseid*." *Studies in Scottish Literature* 29 (1996), forthcoming.

———. "Langland's Christian Narcissus: Self-Reflexive 'Mesure' in *Piers Plowmn B*." *Christianity and Literature* 42 (1992): 5–23.

Crane, Susan. *Gender and Romance in Chaucer's Canterbury Tales*. Princeton: Princeton University Press, 1994.

Culianu, Ioan. "A Corpus for the Body." Review essay. *Journal of Modern History* 63 (1991): 61–80.

Curry, W. C. *Chaucer and the Mediaeval Sciences*. Revised ed. New York: Barnes and Noble, 1960.

———. "The Secret of Chaucer's Pardoner." *Journal of English and Germanic Philology* 19 (1919): 593–606.

Cuttino, G. P., and Thomas W. Lyman. "Where is Edward II?" *Speculum* 53 (1978): 522–44.

Dallery, Arleen B. "The Politics of Writing (The) Body: *Ecriture Feminine*." In *Gender, Body, Knowledge: Feminist Reconstructions of Being and Knowing*. Edited by

Alison M. Jagger and Susan R. Bordo. 52–67. New Brunswick: Rutgers University Press, 1989.

Damrosch, David. "*Non Alia Sed Aliter:* The Hermeneutics of Gender in Bernard of Clairvaux." In Blumenfeld-Kosinski and Szell, 181–95.

Davis, Norman, et al. *A Chaucer Glossary.* Oxford: Oxford University Press, 1979.

Dean-Jones, Lesley. "The Politics of Pleasure: Female Sexual Appetite in the Hippocratic Corpus." In *Discourses of Sexuality: From Aristotle to AIDS.* Edited by Domna C. Stanton. 48–77. Ann Arbor: University of Michigan Press, 1992.

Delany, Sheila. "Anatomy of a Resisting Reader: Some Implications of Resistance to Sexual Wordplay in Medieval Literature." In Straus, *Skirting,* 7–34.

———. *The Naked Text: Chaucer's Legend of Good Women.* Berkeley: University of California Press, 1994.

———. "Politics and the Paralysis of Poetic Imagination in *The Physician's Tale.*" *Studies in the Age of Chaucer* 3 (1981): 47–60.

———. "Strategies of Silence in the Wife of Bath's Recital." In Hahn, 49–69.

———. *Writing Woman: Women Writers and Women in Literature, Medieval to Modern.* New York: Schocken, 1983.

Delasanta, Rodney. "And of Great Reverence: Chaucer's Man of Law." *Chaucer Review* 5 (1971): 288–310.

de Lauretis, Teresa. "The Violence of Rhetoric: Considerations on Representation and Gender." In *The Violence of Representation: Literature and the History of Violence.* Edited by Nancy Armstrong and Leonard Tennenhouse. 239–58. London: Routledge, 1989.

Dempster, Germaine. "Chaucer's *Wretched Engendering* and *An Holy Medytacion.*" *Modern Philology* 35 (1937): 27–29.

Derrida, Jacques. *Dissemination.* Translated by Barbara Johnson. London: Athlone Press, 1981.

———. *Of Grammatology.* Translated by Gayatri Chakravorty Spivak. Baltimore: Johns Hopkins University Press, 1976.

———. "The Law of Genre." Translated by Avital Ronell. *Critical Inquiry* 7 (1980): 55–81.

———. *Margins of Philosophy.* Translated by Alan Bass. Chicago: University of Chicago Press, 1982.

———. *Memoires for Paul de Man.* New York: Columbia University Press, 1986.

———. *Spurs: Nietzsche's Styles.* Translated by Barbara Harlow. Chicago: University of Chicago Press, 1979.

———. *Writing and Difference.* Translated by Alan Bass. Chicago: University of Chicago Press, 1978.

Diamond, Arlyn. "Chaucer's Women and Women's Chaucer." In Diamond and Edwards, 60–83.

Diamond, Arlyn, and Lee R. Edwards, editors. *The Authority of Experience: Essays in Feminist Criticism.* Amherst: University of Massachusetts Press, 1977.

Dinshaw, Carolyn. "Chaucer's Queer Touches / A Queer Touches Chaucer." *Exemplaria* 7 (1995): 75–92.

———. *Chaucer's Sexual Poetics*. Madison: University of Wisconsin Press, 1989.

Doane, Mary Ann. *The Desire to Desire: The Woman's Film of the 1940's*. Bloomington: Indiana University Press, 1987.

Dollimore, Jonathan. *Sexual Dissidence: Augustine to Wilde, Freud to Foucault*. Oxford: Clarendon Press, 1991.

Donaldson, E. Talbot. "Briseis, Briseida, Criseyde, Cresseid, Cressid: Progress of a Heroine." In *Chaucerian Problems and Perspectives*. Edited by Edward Vasta and Z. P. Thundy. 1–12. Notre Dame: University of Notre Dame Press, 1970.

———. *Speaking of Chaucer*. New York: Norton, 1970.

Dor, Juliette. "From the Crusading Virago to the Polysemous Virgin: Chaucer's Constance." In *A Wyf Ther Was*. Edited by Juliette Dor. 128–40. Liege: Universite de Liege, 1992.

Dronke, Peter. *Abelard and Heloise in Medieval Testimonies*. W. P. Ker Lecture, no. 26. Glasgow: University of Glasgow Press, 1976.

DuBois, Page. *Sowing the Body: Psychoanalysis and Ancient Representations of Women*. Chicago: University of Chicago Press, 1988.

Ebin, Lois A. *Illuminator, Makar, Vates: Visions of Poetry in the Fifteenth Century*. Lincoln: University of Nebraska Press, 1988.

Edwards, Robert R., and Stephen Spector, editors. *The Olde Daunce: Love, Friendship, Sex, and Marriage in the Medieval World*. Albany: State University of New York Press, 1991.

Ellis, Deborah. "The Merchant's Wife's Tale: Language, Sex, and Commerce in Margery Kempe and in Chaucer." *Exemplaria* 2 (1990): 595–626.

Elm, Susanna. *"Virgins of God": The Making of Asceticism in Late Antiquity*. Oxford: Clarendon Press, 1996.

Ferguson, Margaret W. "Saint Augustine's Region of Unlikeness: The Crossing of Exile and Language." *Georgia Review* 29 (1975): 842–64.

Ferster, Judith. *Chaucer on Interpretation*. Cambridge: Cambridge University Press, 1985.

Finke, Laurie A. *Feminist Theory, Women's Writing*. Reading Women Writing Series. Ithaca: Cornell University Press, 1992.

Finke, Laurie A., and Martin B. Shichtman, editors. *Medieval Texts and Contemporary Readers*. Ithaca: Cornell University Press, 1987.

Fleming, John V. "Deiphoebus Betrayed: Virgillian Decorum, Chaucerian Feminism." In *A Volume of Essays in Memory of Judson Boyce Allen (1932–85)*. Edited by R. A. Shoaf. Spec. issue *Chaucer Review* 21.2 (1986): 182–99.

Fletcher, Alan J. "The Topical Heresy of Chaucer's Pardoner." *Chaucer Review* 25 (1990): 110–26.

Foucault, Michel. *The History of Sexuality, Volume 1: An Introduction*. Translated by Robert Hurley. 1978. Reprint, New York: Random House/Vintage, 1990.

Fradenburg, Louise O. "The Manciple's Servant Tongue: Politics and Poetry in *The Canterbury Tales.*" *ELH* 52 (1985): 85–118.

———. "'Our owen wo to drynke': Loss, Gender, and Chivalry in Troilus and Criseyde." In Shoaf, *Chauer's Troilus,* 88–106.

———. "'Voice Memorial': Loss and Reparation in Chaucer's Poetry." In Hahn, 169–202.

———. "The Wife of Bath's Passing Fancy." *Studies in the Age of Chaucer* 8 (1976): 31–58.

Frantzen, Allen J. "The Disclosure of Sodomy in *Cleanness.*" *PMLA* 111 (1996): 451–64.

———. "*The Pardoner's Tale,* the Pervert, and the Price of Order in Chaucer's World." In *Class and Gender in Early English Literature: Intersections.* Ed. Britton J. Harwood and Gillian R. Overing. 131–47. Bloomington: Indiana University Press, 1994.

Freccero, John. *Dante: The Poetics of Conversion.* Edited by Rachel Jacoff. Cambridge: Harvard University Press, 1986.

Frese, Delores Warwick. *An Ars Legendi for Chaucer's Canterbury Tales: Re-Constructive Reading.* Gainesville: University of Florida Press, 1991.

Freud, Sigmund. *The Standard Edition of the Complete Psychological Works of Sigmund Freud.* Edited and translated by James Strachey. 24 vols. London: Hogarth, 1953–74.

Friedman, Albert B. "The Late Medieval Ballade and the Origin of Broadside Balladry." *Medium AEvum* 27 (1958): 95–110.

Fries, Maureen. "'Slydyng of Corage': Chaucer's Criseyde as Feminist and Victim." In Diamond and Edwards, 45–59.

Furrow, Melissa. "The Man of Law's St. Custance: Sex and the *Saeculum.*" *Chaucer Review* 24 (1990): 223–35.

Fuss, Diana. "Reading Like a Feminist." *differences* 1.2 (1989): 77–92.

Fyler, John. "Love and the Declining World: Ovid, Genesis, and Chaucer." *Mediaevalia* 13 (1987): 295–307.

———. "Man, Men, and Women in Chaucer's Poetry." In Edwards and Spector, 154–76.

Gallacher, Patrick J. "Chaucer and the Rhetoric of the Body." *Chaucer Review* 28 (1994): 216–36.

Garbaty, Thomas J. "*Troilus* V, 1786–92 and V, 1807–27: An Example of Poetic Process." *Chaucer Review* 11 (1977): 299–305.

Gellrich, Jesse M. *The Idea of the Book in the Middle Ages: Language Theory, Mythology, and Fiction.* Ithaca: Cornell University Press, 1985.

Goldin, Frederick. *The Mirror of Narcissus in the Courtly Love Lyric.* Ithaca: Cornell University Press, 1967.

Gottfried, Barbara. "Conflict and Relationship, Sovereignty and Survival: Parables of Power in the Wife of Bath's Prologue." *Chaucer Review* 19 (1985): 202–24.

Gottfried, Robert S. *Doctors and Medicine in Medieval England, 1340–1530*. Princeton: Princeton University Press, 1986.

Green, Richard Firth. "Chaucer's Victimized Women." *Studies in the Age of Chaucer* 10 (1988): 3–21.

Greenberg, David F. *The Construction of Homosexuality*. Chicago: University of Chicago Press, 1988.

Gross, Gregory W. "Trade Secrets: Chaucer, the Pardoner, the Critics." *Modern Language Studies* 25.4 (1995): 1–33.

Grosz, Elizabeth. "The Body of Signification." In *Abjection, Melancholia, and Love: The Work of Julia Kristeva*. Edited by John Fletcher and Andrew Benjamin. 80–103. New York: Routledge, 1990.

———. *Volatile Bodies: Toward a Corporeal Feminism*. Bloomington: Indiana University Press, 1994.

———, editor. *Feminism and the Body*. Spec. issue *Hypatia* 6.3 (1991).

Grudin, Michaela Paasche. "Chaucer's *Manciple's Tale* and the Poetics of Guile." *Chaucer Review* 25 (1991): 329–42.

Hahn, Thomas, editor. *Reconceiving Chaucer: Literary Theory and Historical Interpretation*. Spec. issue *Exemplaria* 2.1 (1990).

Hanks, D. Thomas, Jr. "'Goddes Pryvetee' and Chaucer's *Miller's Tale*." *Christianity and Literature* 33.2 (1984): 7–12.

Hanna, Ralph, III. "Some Commonplaces of Late Medieval Patience Discussions: An Introduction." In *The Triumph of Patience: Medieval and Renaissance Studies*. Edited by Gerald J. Schiffhorst. 65–87. Orlando: University Presses of Florida, 1978.

Hanning, Robert W. "'I Shal Finde It in a Maner Glose': Versions of Textual Harassment in Medieval Literature." In Finke and Shichtman, 27–50.

———. "Roasting a Friar, Mis-taking a Wife, and Other Acts of Textual Harassment in the *Canterbury Tales*." *Studies in the Age of Chaucer* 7 (1985): 3–22.

Hansen, Elaine Tuttle. *Chaucer and the Fictions of Gender*. Berkeley: University of California Press, 1992.

———. "Irony and the Antifeminist Narrator in Chaucer's *Legend of Good Women*." *Journal of English and Germanic Philology* 82 (1983): 11–31.

Harwood, Britton J. "Language and the Real: Chaucer's Manciple." *Chaucer Review* 6 (1972): 268–79.

Hawkins, Harriet. "The Victim's Side: Chaucer's *Clerk's Tale* and Webster's *Duchess of Malfi*." *Signs* 1 (1975): 339–61.

Hazelton, Richard. "*The Manciple's Tale*: Parody and Critique." *Journal of English and Germanic Philology* 62 (1963): 1–31.

Heffernan, Thomas J. *Sacred Biography: Saints and Their Biographers in the Middle Ages*. New York: Oxford University Press, 1988.

Higonnet, Margaret. "Speaking Silences: Women's Suicide." In *The Female Body in Western Culture: Contemporary Perspectives*. Edited by Susan Rubin Suleiman. 68–83. Cambridge: Harvard University Press, 1985.

Holloway, Julia Bolton. *The Pilgrim and the Book: A Study of Dante, Langland, and Chaucer*. New York: Peter Lang, 1987.
Hopper, Vincent Foster. *Medieval Number Symbolism: Its Sources, Meaning, and Influence on Thought and Expression*. New York: Cooper Square Publishers, 1969.
Hult, David F. *Self-Fulfilling Prophecies: Readership and Authority in the First Roman de la Rose*. Cambridge: Cambridge University Press, 1986.
Hunter, David G. "Resistance to the Virginal Ideal in Late-Fourth-Century Rome: The Case of Jovinian." *Theological Studies* 48 (1987): 45–64.
Irigaray, Luce. *Je, Tu, Nous: Toward a Culture of Difference*. Translated by Alison Martin. New York: Routledge, 1993.
———. *Speculum of the Other Woman*. Translated by Gillian C. Gill. Ithaca: Cornell University Press, 1985.
———. *This Sex Which Is Not One*. Translated by Catherine Porter with Carolyn Burke. Ithaca: Cornell University Press, 1985.
Jacquart, Danielle, and Claude Thomasset. *Sexuality and Medicine in the Middle Ages*. Translated by Matthew Adamson. Princeton: Princeton University Press, 1988.
Jager, Eric. *The Tempter's Voice: Language and the Fall in Medieval Literature*. Ithaca: Cornell University Press, 1993.
Jefferson, Bernard L. *Chaucer and the Consolation of Philosophy of Boethius*. Princeton: Princeton University Press, 1917.
Jeffrey, David Lyle, editor. *Chaucer and Scriptural Tradition*. Ottawa: University of Ottawa Press, 1984.
Jordan, Robert M. *Chaucer and the Shape of Creation: The Aesthetic Possibilities of Inorganic Structure*. Cambridge: Harvard University Press, 1967.
Kaminsky, Alice. *Chaucer's Troilus and Criseyde and the Critics*. Athens: Ohio University Press, 1980.
Karlen, Arno. "The Homosexual Heresy." *Chaucer Review* 6 (1971): 44–63.
Kendrick, Laura. *Chaucerian Play: Comedy and Control in the Canterbury Tales*. Berkeley: University of California Press, 1988.
Kiser, Lisa J. *Telling Classical Tales: Chaucer and the Legend of Good Women*. Ithaca: Cornell University Press, 1983.
———. *Truth and Textuality in Chaucer's Poetry*. Hanover: University Press of New England, 1991.
Knapp, Peggy A. "Wandrynge by the Weye: On Alisoun and Augustine." In Finke and Shichtman, 142–57.
Knapp, Robert S. "Penance, Irony, and Chaucer's Retraction." *Assays* 2 (1983): 45–67.
Knoespel, Kenneth. *Narcissus and the Invention of Personal History*. New York: Garland, 1985.
Kolve, V. A. *Chaucer and the Imagery of Narrative: The First Five Canterbury Tales*. Stanford: Stanford University Press, 1984.
Kooper, Erik. "Loving the Unequal Equal: Medieval Theologians and Marital Affection." In Edwards and Spector, 44–56.

Kraemer, Ross Shepard. *Her Share of the Blessings: Women's Religions Among Pagans, Jews, and Christians in the Greco-Roman World.* Oxford: Oxford University Press, 1992.

Kristeva, Julia. *Desire in Language: A Semiotic Approach to Literature and Art.* Edited by Leon S. Roudiez. Translated by Thomas Gora, Alice Jardine, and Leon S. Roudiez. New York: Columbia University Press, 1980.

———. *Tales of Love.* Translated by Leon S. Roudiez. New York: Columbia University Press, 1987.

———. "Women's Time." Translated by Alice Jardine and Harry Blake. In *Feminist Theory: A Critique of Ideology.* Edited by Nannerl O. Keohane, Michelle Z. Rosaldo, and Barbara C. Gelpi. 39–53. Chicago: University of Chicago Press, 1982.

Kruger, Steven F. "Claiming the Pardoner: Toward a Gay Reading of Chaucer's Pardoner's Tale." *Exemplaria* 6 (1994): 115–39.

Kundera, Milan. *The Unbearable Lightness of Being* (Novel). Translated by Michael Henry Heim. New York: Harper/Perennial, 1985.

Kuttner, Stephan. *Harmony from Dissonance: An Interpretation of Medieval Canon Law.* Latrobe: Archabbey Press, 1960.

Lacan, Jacques. *Ecrits: A Selection.* Translated by Alan Sheridan. New York: Norton, 1977.

———. *Feminine Sexuality: Jacques Lacan and the Ecole Freudienne.* Edited by Juliet Mitchell and Jacqueline Rose. New York: Norton, 1985.

———. *The Four Fundamental Concepts of Psycho-Analysis.* Edited by Jacques-Alain Miller. Translated by Alan Sheridan. New York: Norton, 1978.

Laqueur, Thomas. *Making Sex: Body and Gender from the Greeks to Freud.* Cambridge: Harvard University Press, 1990.

Lawler, Traugott. *The One and the Many in the Canterbury Tales.* Hamden, Conn.: Archon Books, 1980.

Lawton, David. *Chaucer's Narrators.* Cambridge: D.S. Brewer, 1985.

Lees, Clare A., editor. *Medieval Masculinities: Regarding Men in the Middle Ages.* Minneapolis: University of Minnesota Press, 1994.

Leicester, H. Marshall, Jr. *The Disenchanted Self: Representing the Subject in the Canterbury Tales.* Berkeley: University of California Press, 1990.

———. "Of a Fire in the Dark: Public and Private Feminism in the *Wife of Bath's Tale.*" In *Women in the Middle Ages.* Edited by Hope Phyllis Weissman. Spec. issue *Women's Studies* 11 (1984): 157–78.

Lemay, Helen. "Women and the Literature of Obstetrics and Gynecology." In *Medieval Women and the Sources of History.* Edited by Joel T. Rosenthal. 189–209. Athens: University of Georgia Press, 1990.

Lerer, Seth. *Boethius and Dialogue: Literary Method in the Consolation of Philosophy.* Princeton: Princeton University Press, 1985.

Leupin, Alexandre. *Barbarolexis: Medieval Writing and Sexuality.* Translated by Kate M. Cooper. Cambridge: Harvard University Press, 1989.

Levitan, Alan. "The Parody of Pentecost in Chaucer's *Summoner's Tale.*" *University of Toronto Quarterly* 40 (1971): 236–46.

Lewis, Robert Enzer. "Chaucer and Pope Innocent III's *De Miseria Humane Conditionis*." Unpublished dissertation. University of Pennsylvania, 1964.
———. "Chaucer's Artistic Use of Pope Innocent III's *De Miseria Humane Conditionis* in the Man of Law's Prologue and Tale." *PMLA* 81 (1966): 485–92.
———. "Glosses to the *Man of Law's Tale* from Pope Innocent III's *De Miseria Humane Conditionis*." *Studies in Philology* 64 (1967): 1–16.
———. "What Did Chaucer Mean by *Of the Wreched Engendrynge of Mankynde*?" *Chaucer Review* 2 (1968): 139–58.
Lindley, Arthur. "'Vanysshed Was This Daunce, He Nyste Where': Alisoun's Absence in the *Wife of Bath's Prologue* and *Tale*." *ELH* 59 (1992): 1–21.
Lochrie, Karma. "The Language of Transgression: Body, Flesh, and Word in Mystical Discourse." In *Speaking Two Languages: Traditional Disciplines and Contemporary Theory in Medieval Studies*. Edited by Allen J. Frantzen. 115–40. Albany: State University of New York Press, 1991.
———. *Margery Kemp and Translations of the Flesh*. Philadelphia: University of Pennsylvania Press, 1991.
———. "Women's 'Pryvetees' and Fabliau Politics in the *Miller's Tale*." *Exemplaria* 6 (1994): 287–304.
Lohr, Charles H., S.J. "Medieval Latin Aristotelian Commentaries." *Traditio* 23 (1967): 313–413; 24 (1968): 149–245; 26 (1970): 135–216; 27 (1971): 251–351; 28 (1972): 281–396; 29 (1973): 93–197.
Lomperis, Linda. "Unruly Bodies and Ruling Practices: Chaucer's *Physician's Tale* as Socially Symbolic Act." In Lomperis and Stanbury, 21–37.
Lomperis, Linda, and Sarah Stanbury, editors. *Feminist Approaches to the Body in Medieval Literature*. Philadelphia: University of Pennsylvania Press, 1993.
Longsworth, Robert. "Chaucer's Clerk as Teacher." In Benson, 61–66.
Lowes, John L. "Illustrations from Chaucer Drawn Chiefly from Deschamps." *Romanic Review* 2 (1911): 113–28.
Luecke, Janemarie, O.S.B. "Three Faces of Cecilia: Chaucer's *Second Nun's Tale*." *American Benedictine Review* 33 (1982): 335–47.
MacDonald, Donald. "Proverbs, Sententiae, and Exempla in Chaucer's Comic Tales: The Function of Comic Misapplication." *Speculum* 41 (1966): 453–65.
Maclean, Ian. *The Renaissance Notion of Woman: A Study in the Fortunes of Scholasticism and Medical Science in European Intellectual Life*. Cambridge: Cambridge University Press, 1980.
Mahoney, John. "Alice of Bath: Her 'secte' and 'gentil text.'" *Criticism* 6 (1964): 144–55.
Makowski, Elizabeth. "The Conjugal Debt and Medieval Canon Law." *Journal of Medieval History* 3 (1977): 99–114.
Malvern, Marjorie. "'Who peyntede the leon, tel me who?': Rhetorical and Didactic Roles Played by an Aesopic Fable in the *Wife of Bath's Prologue*." *Studies in Philology* 80 (1983): 238–52.
Mann, Jill. *Geoffrey Chaucer*. Feminist Readings. Atlantic Highlands, N.J.: Humanities Press International, 1991.

Margherita, Gayle. "Originary Fantasies and Chaucer's *Book of the Duchess*." In Lomperis and Stanbury, 116–41.

Mazzotta, Giuseppe. *Dante, Poet of the Desert: History and Allegory in the Divine Comedy*. Princeton: Princeton University Press, 1979.

McAlpine, Monica. "The Pardoner's Homosexuality and How It Matters." *PMLA* 95 (1980): 8–22.

McLaughlin, Eleanor Commo. "Equality of Souls, Inequality of Sexes." In Ruether, *Religion*, 213–66.

McLeod, Glenda. *Virtue and Venom: Catalogs of Women from Antiquity to the Renaissance*. Ann Arbor: University of Michigan Press, 1991.

McNamara, Jo Ann. "Sexual Equality and the Cult of Virginity in Early Christian Thought." *Feminist Studies* 3 (1976): 145–58.

Means, Michael. *The Consolatio Genre in Medieval English Literature*. Humanities Monograph, no. 36. Gainesville: University of Florida Press, 1972.

Michie, Helena. *The Flesh Made Word: Female Figures and Women's Bodies*. Oxford: Oxford University Press, 1987.

Middle English Dictionary. Edited by Hans Kurath and Sherman Kuhn, et al. Ann Arbor: University of Michigan Press, 1954–.

Middleton, Anne. "The Clerk and His Tale: Some Literary Contexts." *Studies in the Age of Chaucer* 2 (1980): 121–50.

———. "*The Physician's Tale* and Love's Martyrs: 'Ensamples Mo Than Ten' as a Method in the *Canterbury Tales*." *Chaucer Review* 8 (1973): 9–32.

Mieszkowski, Gretchen. "R. K. Gordon and the Troilus and Criseyde Story." *Chaucer Review* 15 (1980): 127–37.

Miles, Margaret R. *Carnal Knowing: Female Nakedness and Religious Meaning in the Christian West*. Boston: Beacon Press, 1989.

Milhaven, J. Giles. "A Medieval Lesson on Bodily Knowing: Women's Experience and Men's Thought." Review essay. *Journal of the American Academy of Religion* 57 (1989): 341–72.

Miller, Robert P. "Chaucer's Pardoner, the Scriptural Eunuch, and *The Pardoner's Tale*." *Speculum* 30 (1955): 180–99.

Minnis, A. J. "'Glosyng is a Glorious Thyng': Chaucer at Work on the 'Boece.'" In *The Medieval Boethius: Studies in the Vernacular Translations of De Consolatione Philosophae*. Edited by A. J. Minnis. 106–24. Suffolk: D.S. Brewer, 1987.

Minnis, A. J., and A. B. Scott with David Wallace, editors. *Medieval Literary Theory and Criticism c. 1100-c. 1375: The Commentary-Tradition*. Revised editon. Oxford: Clarendon Press, 1988.

Moi, Toril. *Sexual/Textual Politics: Feminist Literary Theory*. London: Methuen, 1985.

Morrison, Susan Signe. "Don't Ask, Don't Tell: The Wife of Bath and Vernacular Translations." *Exemplaria* 8 (1996): 97–123.

Mosse, Fernand. *A Handbook of Middle English*. Baltimore: Johns Hopkins University Press, 1952.

Mulvey, Laura. "Visual Pleasure and Narrative Cinema." In *Women and Cinema.* Edited by Karyn Kay and Gerald Peary. 412–28. New York: Dutton, 1977.

Murphy, James J. *Rhetoric in the Middle Ages: A History of Rhetorical Theory from St. Augustine to the Renaissance.* Berkeley: University of California Press, 1974.

Muscatine, Charles. *Chaucer and the French Tradition.* Berkeley: University of California Press, 1964.

Neuse, Richard. *Chaucer's Dante: Allegory and Epic Theater in The Canterbury Tales.* Berkeley: University of California Press, 1991.

Neuss, Paula. "Double-Entendre in *The Miller's Tale.*" *Essays in Criticism* 24 (1974): 325–39.

Newman, Barbara. *From Virile Woman to WomanChrist: Studies in Medieval Religion and Literature.* Philadelphia: University of Pennsylvania Press, 1995.

Nicholls, Stephen G. *Romanesque Signs: Early Medieval Narrative and Iconography.* New Haven: Yale University Press, 1983.

Nichols, John A. "Female Nudity and Sexuality in Medieval Art." In *New Images of Medieval Women: Essays Toward a Cultural Anthropology.* Edited by Edelgard DuBruck. 165–76. Lewiston, New York: Edwin Mellen, 1989.

Nims, Margaret. "*Translatio:* 'Difficult Statement' in Medieval Poetic Theory." *University of Toronto Quarterly* 43 (1974): 215–30.

Nolan, Barbara. "'A Poet Ther Was': Chaucer's Voices in the General Prologue to the *Canterbury Tales.*" *PMLA* 101 (1986): 154–69.

Nolan, Edward Peter. *Now through a Glass Darkly: Specular Images of Being and Knowing from Virgil to Chaucer.* Ann Arbor: University of Michigan Press, 1990.

Noonan, John T., Jr. *Contraception: A History of its Treatment by the Catholic Theologians and Canonists.* Cambridge: Harvard University Press, 1965.

———. "Gration Slept Here: The Changing Identity of the Father of the Systematic Study of Canon Law." *Traditio* 35 (1979): 145–72.

Nyquist, Mary. "Ever (wo)Man's Friend: A Response to John Fyler and Elaine Tuttle Hansen." In Hahn, 37–47.

O'Brien, Timothy. "'Ars-Metrik': Science, Satire, and Chaucer's Summoner." *Mosaic* 23.4 (1990): 1–22.

O'Meara, Dominic J. *Pythagoras Revived: Mathematics and Philosophy in Late Antiquity.* Oxford: Clarendon Press, 1989.

Oliver, Kelly. *Reading Kristeva: Unraveling the Double-bind.* Bloomington: University of Indiana Press, 1993.

Olson, Glending. "Making and Poetry in the Age of Chaucer." *Comparative Literature* 31 (1979): 272–90.

Oxford English Dictionary. Oxford: Oxford University Press, 1971.

Pagels, Elaine. *Adam, Eve, and the Serpent.* New York: Random House, 1988.

Pardes, Ilana. *Countertraditions in the Bible: A Feminist Approach.* Cambridge: Harvard University Press, 1992.

Parker, Patricia. *Literary Fat Ladies: Rhetoric, Gender, Property.* London: Methuen, 1987.

Patch, Howard R. *The Goddess Fortuna in Mediaeval Literature.* Cambridge: Harvard University Press, 1927.

———. *The Tradition of Boethius: A Study of His Importance in Mediaeval Culture.* New York: Oxford University Press, 1935.

Patterson, Lee. "Ambiguity and Interpretation: A Fifteenth-Century Reading of *Troilus and Criseyde.*" *Speculum* 54 (1979): 297–330.

———. "'For the Wyves love of Bath': Feminine Rhetoric and Poetic Resolution in the *Roman de la Rose* and the *Canterbury Tales.*" *Speculum* 58 (1983): 656–95.

———. *Negotiating the Past: The Historical Understanding of Medieval Literature.* Madison: University of Wisconsin Press, 1987.

Payne, Robert O. *The Key of Remembrance: A Study of Chaucer's Poetics.* New Haven: Yale University Press, 1963.

Pequigney, Joseph. "Sodomy in Dante's *Inferno* and *Purgatorio.*" *Representations* 36 (1991): 22–42.

Percy, Roy J. "Does the *Manciple's Prologue* Contain a Reference to Hell's Mouth?" *English Language Notes* 11 (1974): 167–75.

Petroff, Elizabeth Alvilda. *Body and Soul: Essays on Medieval Women and Mysticism.* Oxford: Oxford University Press, 1994.

Pratt, Robert A. "Chaucer and the Hand That Fed Him." *Speculum* 41 (1966): 619–42.

Probyn, Elspeth. "This Body Which Is Not One: Speaking an Embodies Self." In Grosz, *Feminism,* 111–24.

Radcliff-Umstead, Douglas. "Erotic Sin in the *Divine Comedy.*" In *Human Sexuality in the Middle Ages and Renaissance.* Edited by Douglas Radcliff-Umstead. Pittsburgh: University of Pittsburgh Center for Medieval and Renaissance Studies, 1978.

Ragland-Sullivan, Ellie. *Jacques Lacan and the Philosophy of Psychoanalysis.* Urbana: University of Illinois Press, 1987.

Ramsey, Lee C. "'The Sentence of It Sooth Is': Chaucer's *Physician's Tale.*" *Chaucer Review* 6 (1971): 185–97.

Reames, Sherry L. "The Sources of Chaucer's *Second Nun's Tale.*" *Modern Philology* 76 (1978): 111–35.

Reiss, Edmund. "Biblical Parody: Chaucer's Distortions of Scripture." In Jeffrey, 47–61.

Rich, Adrienne. "Compulsory Heterosexuality and Lesbian Existence." *Signs* 5 (1980): 631–60.

Riehle, Wolfgang. *The Middle English Mystics.* Translated by Bernard Standring. London: Routledge and Kegan Paul, 1981.

Robertson, D. W., Jr. *A Preface to Chaucer: Studies in Medieval Perspectives.* Princeton: Princeton University Press, 1962.

Robertson, Elizabeth. *Early English Devotional Prose and the Female Audience.* Knoxville: University of Tennessee Press, 1990.

———. "Medieval Medical Views of Woman and Female Spirituality in the *Ancrene Wisse* and Julian of Norwich's *Showings.*" In Lomperis and Stanbury, 142–67.

Ross, Thomas W. "Taboo Words in Fifteenth-Century England." In *Fifteenth Century Studies*. Edited by Robert F. Yeager. 137–60. New York: Archon, 1984.
Rowland, Beryl. "Chaucer's Idea of the Pardoner." *Chaucer Review* 14 (1979): 140–54.
Rubin, Gayle. "The Traffic in Women: Notes on the 'Political Economy' of Sex." In *Toward an Anthropology of Women*. Edited by Rayna R. Reiter. 157–210. New York: Monthly Review Press, 1975.
Ruether, Rosemary Radford. "Misogynism and Virginal Feminism in the Fathers of the Church." In Ruether, *Religion*, 150–83.
———, editor. *Religion and Sexism: Images of Woman in the Jewish and Christian Traditions*. New York: Simon and Shuster, 1974.
Salisbury, Joyce E. *Church Fathers, Independent Virgins*. New York: Verso, 1991.
Scattergood, V. J. "The Manciple's Manner of Speaking." *Essays in Criticism* 24 (1974): 124–46.
Scheps, Walter. "Chaucer's Man of Law and the Tale of Constance." *PMLA* 89 (1974): 285–95.
Schmidt, A. V. C. "Chaucer's Nembrot: A Note on *The Former Age*." *Medium AEvum* 47 (1978): 304–7.
———. *The Clerkly Maker: Langland's Poetic Art*. Cambridge: D.S Brewer, 1987.
Schneider, Carl D. *Shame, Exposure, and Privacy*. Boston: Beacon, 1979.
Schor, Naomi. "This Essentialism Which Is Not One: Coming to Grips with Irigaray." *differences* 1.2 (1989): 38–58.
Schor, Naomi, and Elizabeth Weed, eds. *The Essential Difference*. Bloomington: Indiana University Press, 1994.
Sedgwick, Eve Kosofsky. *Between Men: English Literature and Male Homosocial Desire*. New York: Columbia University Press, 1985.
———. *Epistemology of the Closet*. Berkeley: University of California Press, 1990.
Severs, J. Burke. *The Literary Relationships of Chaucer's Clerkes Tale*. 1942. Reprint, Hamden, Conn.: Archon, 1972.
Shahar, Shulamith. *The Fourth Estate: A History of Women in the Middle Ages*. Translated by Chaya Galai. 1983. Reprint, New York: Routledge, 1990.
Sherman, Gail Berkeley. "Saints, Nuns, and Speech in the *Canterbury Tales*." In Blumenfeld-Kosinski and Szell, 136–60.
Shoaf, R. A. *Dante, Chaucer, and the Currency of the Word: Money, Images, and Reference in Late Medieval Poetry*. Norman, Okla.: Pilgrim, 1983.
———. "'Unwemmed Custance': Circulation, Property, and Incest in the *Man of Law's Tale*." In Hahn, 287–302.
———, editor, with Catherine S. Cox. *Chaucer's Troilus and Criseyde "Subgit to alle Poesye": Essays in Criticism*. Binghamton: Medieval and Renaissance Texts and Studies, 1991.
Sigal, Gale. *Erotic Dawn-Songs of the Middle Ages: Voicing the Lyric Lady*. Gainesville: University Press of Florida, 1996.
Siraisi, Nancy G. *Medieval and Early Renaissance Medicine: An Introduction to Knowledge and Power*. Chicago: University of Chicago Press, 1990.

Skura, Meredith. "Psychoanalytic Criticism." In *Redrawing the Boundaries: The Transformation of English and American Studies*. Edited by Stephen Greenblatt and Giles Gunn. 349–73. New York: Modern Language Association, 1992.

Smalley, Beryl. *The Study of the Bible in the Middle Ages*. Notre Dame: University of Notre Dame Press, 1964.

Speirs, John. *Chaucer the Maker*. London: Faber and Faber, 1951.

Spelman, Elizabeth. *Inessential Woman: Problems of Exclusion in Feminist Thought*. Boston: Beacon, 1988.

Spurgeon, Caroline F. E., editor. *Five Hundred Years of Chaucer Criticism and Allusion, 1357–1900*. Vol. 1. Cambridge: Cambridge University Press, 1925.

Stanbury, Sarah. "The Lover's Gaze in *Troilus and Criseyde*." In Shoaf, *Chaucer's Troilus*, 224–38.

———. "The Virgin's Gaze: Spectacle and Transgression in Middle English Lyrics of the Passion." *PMLA* 106 (1991): 1083–93.

Stiller, Nikki. *Eve's Orphans: Mothers and Daughters in Medieval English Literature*. Westport, Conn.: Greenwood Press, 1980.

Stokes, Michael C. *One and Many in Presocratic Philosophy*. Washington, D.C.: Center for Hellenic Studies, 1971.

Straus, Barrie Ruth. "The Subversive Discourse of the Wife of Bath: Phallocentric Discourse and the Imprisonment of Criticism." *ELH* 55 (1988): 527–54.

———, editor. *Skirting the Texts: Feminisms' Re-readings of Medieval and Renaissance Texts*. Spec. issue of *Exemplaria* 4.1 (1992).

Suzuki, Mihiko. *Metamorphoses of Helen: Authority, Difference, and the Epic*. Ithaca: Cornell University Press, 1989.

Szittya, Penn R. "The Friar as False Apostle: Antifraternal Exegesis and the *Summoner's Tale*." *Studies in Philology* 71 (1974): 19–46.

Tatlock, J. S. P. "The Epilog of Chaucer's *Troilus*." *Modern Philology* 18 (1921): 631–32.

Tatlock, John, and Arthur G. Kennedy. *A Concordance to the Complete Works of Geoffrey Chaucer and to the Romaunt of the Rose*. Washington, D.C.: Carnegie Institute, 1927.

Taylor, Karla. *Chaucer Reads the Divine Comedy*. Stanford: Stanford University Press, 1989.

Taylor, Mark C. *Erring: A Postmodern A/theology*. Chicago: University of Chicago Press, 1985.

Tuana, Nancy. *The Less Noble Sex: Scientific, Religious, and Philosophical Conceptions of Woman's Nature*. Bloomington: Indiana University Press, 1993.

Turner, James Grantham. *One Flesh: Paradisal Marriage and Sexual Relations in the Age of Milton*. Oxford: Clarendon Press, 1987.

Vance, Eugene. *Mervelous Signals: Poetics and Sign Theory in the Middle Ages*. Lincoln: University of Nebraska Press, 1986.

Vitz, Evelyn Birge. *Medieval Narrative and Modern Narratology: Subjects and Objects of Desire*. New York: New York University Press, 1989.

Warner, Marina. *Alone of All Her Sex: The Myth and Cult of the Virgin Mary.* New York: Alfred A. Knopf, Inc., 1976.
Waswo, Richard. "The Narrator of *Troilus and Criseyde.*" *ELH* 50 (1983): 1–25.
Weissman, Hope Phyllis. "Late Gothic Pathos in *The Man of Law's Tale.*" *Journal of Medieval and Renaissance Studies* 9 (1979): 133–53.
Whitbread, Leslie G. "Conrad of Hirsau as Literary Critic." *Speculum* 47 (1972): 234–45.
Wilson, Katharine M., and Elizabeth M. Makowski. *Wykked Wyves and the Woes of Marriage: Misogamous Literature from Juvenal to Chaucer.* Albany: State University of New York Press, 1990.
Wimsatt, James I. "Guillaume de Machaut and Chaucer's Love Lyrics." *Medium AEvum* 47 (1978): 66–87.
Windeatt, Barry. *Oxford Guides to Chaucer: Troilus and Criseyde.* Oxford: Oxford University Press, 1992.
Winterson, Jeanette. *Written on the Body* (Novel). London: Jonathan Cape, 1992.
Wood, Chauncey. "Speech, the Principle of Contraries, and Chaucer's Tales of the Manciple and the Parson." *Mediaevalia* 6 (1980): 209–29.
Work, James A. *"The Manciple's Tale."* In *Sources and Analogues to Chaucer's Canterbury Tales.* Edited by W. F. Bryan and Germaine Dempster. 699–722. 1941. Reprint, New York: Humanities Press, 1958.
Wurtele, Douglas. "The Penitence of Geoffrey Chaucer." *Viator* 11 (1980): 335–61.
Ziolkowski, Jan. *Alan of Lille's Grammar of Sex: The Meaning of Grammer to a Twelfth-Century Intellectual.* Cambridge: Medieval Academy of America, 1985.

Index

Abelard, Peter, 159n.10
Adams, Carol J., 154n.22
Adams, J. N., 140n.11
"Adam Scriveyn" (Chaucer), 1–2
Aers, David, 133n.2
Against Women Unconstant (Chaucer), 79–81
Alan of Lille, 12, 136n.29, 142n.31, 144n.49, 165n.42
Albertus Magnus, Saint, 114, 148n.17, 156n.6, 159n.5
ambiguity, 19–20, 45, 57, 66–67, 116–17, 156n.7
ambivalence: cultural, 53–55, 62, 66–67, 97, 114–15; narrative, 19, 37–38, 52, 130; textual, 19, 40–41, 64, 66–67, 72, 130
Ambrose, Saint, 137n.37, 148n.14, 149n.31, 151n.42
amicitia, 87–88, 155n.30
Ancrene Riwle, 150n.39
androgyny, 10, 64–66, 131, 165n.52
Anselm of Canterbury, 156n.4
antifeminism. *See* misogyny
appropriation: and hermeneutics, 2, 12–14; narrative, 17, 20, 93, 97; and performance, 31–35, 62–64, 72, 104–5, 108, 110, 122–24

Aristotle, 8, 78, 99, 113, 131, 136n.30, 137n.46, 156n.6
asceticism, 65–66, 150n.32
Atkinson, Clarissa, 142n.32, 151n.44
audience, 21–23, 34, 27, 62–63, 97, 107–9, 124, 142n.30. *See also* readers
Augustine, Saint, 13, 28–29, 101, 121, 157n.12; *Confessions*, 139n.59, 157n.12; *Contra mendacium*, 12–13, 105–6; *De bono conjugali*, 148n.14; *De civitate Dei*, 7, 87, 137, 149n.27, 153n.13; *De doctrina christiana*, 7, 137n.51; *De sancta virginitate*, 148n.14
autoeroticism, 26, 34, 35, 124, 126, 142n.29

Babel, Tower of, 84–85, 163n.31
Baker, Donald C., 156n.3
Bakhtin, Mikhail, 16, 31, 35, 101, 120, 143n.43
Bal, Mieke, 135n.24
ballade, 77–96, 152n.2
Barr, Jane, 136n.36
Baum, Paul, 161n.13
Bennett, Paula, 134n.19
Bernard of Clairvaux, Saint, 143n.41

Bible. *See* individual titles
Biddick, Kathleen, 134n.21
bisexuality, 20, 128, 139n.7, 157n.11, 165n.48
Blamires, Alcuin, 144n.47
Bloch, R. Howard, 8–9, 10, 34, 58, 59, 142n.41
Boccaccio, Giovanni, 51
body, female: attitudes toward, 6–8, 30, 33, 40, 42–43, 50, 59–60, 73, 82–83, 98–99, 113, 131, 141n.25, 152n.4; commodification of, 60–63, 148n.21, 149n.21, 164n.40; representations of, 12, 19, 22, 24–26, 40–43, 61–65, 78–79, 135n.25, 138n.54, 141n.24, 143n.41. *See also* essentialism; feminine; gender and sexual difference
body, male: attitudes toward, 78–79, 82–83, 98–99, 113, 127–28, 130–31, 152n.4; representations of, 19, 33, 118–19, 121, 122–24, 162n.20. *See also* castration; gender and sexual difference; masculine
Boece (Chaucer), 86, 89, 154n.18
Boethius, 81, 89, 153n.17, 154n.25
boredom, 55, 147n.7
Boswell, John, 114, 151n.46, 158n.3, 159n.5, 161n.16
Braddy, Haldeen, 162n.21
Braswell-Means, Laurel, 161n.14
Bredbeck, Gregory, 165n.42
Brody, Saul N., 161n.14
Brooten, Bernadette, 144n.48, 164.38
Brown, Beatrice, 147n.9
Brown, Peter, 60
Brundage, James, 142n.39
Brusendorff, Aage, 153n.44
Bugge, John, 148n.14
Burns, E. Jane, 25, 136n.35
Butler, Judith, 134n.19, 134n.21
Bynum, Caroline Walker, 9, 141n.22, 141n.25, 150n.37

Cadden, Joan, 156n.6, 159n.5
Canterbury Tales (Chaucer). *See* individual characters and titles
captatio benevolentiae, 23
caricature, 23, 30, 38
Carruthers, Mary, 123, 139n.3
castration, 78, 115, 159n.10
Chenu, Marie-Dominique, 138n.49
childbirth, 16, 56–57, 70, 79, 150n.40, 151n.44, 151n.48; patristic attitudes toward, 6–7, 10, 27, 29–30, 42, 57, 65, 67, 137n.39, 151n.42. *See also* conception
Christ, 7, 16, 89
Chrysostom, Saint John, 148n.14
Cicero, 155n.30
Cixous, Helene, 9, 34, 139n.7, 144n.51, 165n.48
Clark, Roy Peter, 122, 162n.20
Cleanness, 134n.12, 156n.7
Clerk, The, 5
Clerk's Prologue, 150n.36
Clerk's Tale, 57, 66–73, 76, 92, 151n.45
closure, 52, 72, 94, 95, 146n.20
Coghill, Neville, 103
Cohen, Jeremy, 143n.39
communiloquia, 156n.2
conception, 4–5, 67–68, 124; and biology, 98–99, 142n.32, 143n.41, 157n.6; patristic attitudes toward, 27, 29–30, 56–57, 65, 142n.31, 142n.32, 143n.36, 143n.39, 143n.41
Conrad of Hirsau, 156n.6
consolatio, 87, 155n.29
contrapasso, 120, 121, 127, 163n.30
Cook, The, 106–8
Cook's Tale, 157n.22
Corinthians: First, 135n.23, 154n.20; Second, 123
corruption, 2, 117–19, 122–24
Cox, Catherine S., 143n.41, 146n.20
Crane, Susan, 134n.17
Criseyde, 39–52, 53, 76, 151n.47

cross-gendering, 29, 32, 98, 131, 149n.31, 151n.48

Dante: *De vulgari eloquentia*, 138n.51; Epistle to Con Grande, 133n.4; *Inferno*, 45, 125–6, 140n.10, 141n.22, 142n.26, 144n.49, 162n.26, 163n.30, 164n.41, 165n.44; *Paradiso*, 39, 145n.4
David, Alfred, 153n.14, 155n.33
decorum. *See signum proprium*
Delany, Sheila, 72, 144n.53, 147n.8, 148n.13
Dempster, Germaine, 147n.9
Derrida, Jacques, 15–17, 24, 77, 109, 157n.11
desire, 43, 59, 77–79, 84, 100, 113–14, 124, 140n.7, 141n.17, 164n.39, 165n.48; and narrative performance, 22–23, 35, 91–92, 94, 141n.17, 142n.30
Deuteronomy, 149n.21
Diamond, Arlyn, 53
differance, 77
Dinshaw, Carolyn, 12, 26, 31, 42, 43, 48, 74, 134n.17, 139n.7, 165n.48, 165n.52
diversity, 1–2
Doane, Mary Anne, 22
Dollimore, Jonathan, 134n.18, 159n.8
Donaldson, E. Talbot, 139n.56
Dor, Juliette, 73
Douglas, Gavin, 146n.2, 155n.35
drunkenness, 24–25, 107–8, 158n.21
Dunbar, William. *See Lament for the Makars*

ecriture feminine, 10, 12, 138n.54. *See also* feminist literary theory
Eden, 81–85, 88, 94. *See also* Eve
Edward II, 114, 159n.6
Ellis, Deborah, 37
essentialism, 11–12, 19, 86, 131, 137n.44

eunuchry. *See* castration
Eve, 6, 64, 82–84, 111, 129, 134n.22
Exodus, 162n.23

Faerie Queene, 154n.28
fantasy object. *See* fetish
father-daughter relationships, 40, 42, 48, 58–63, 70, 72–73, 125, 164n.40. *See also* incest
father-son relationships, 44
feminine, 4, 42, 82, 94; and carnal, 7–8, 30–31, 58, 84, 95, 128, 143n.41; and Christianity, 7, 40, 114, 135n.24; and epistemology, 19, 42, 51–52, 57, 81, 86, 102, 103–4, 137n.46. *See also* gender
feminist literary theory, 10–11, 77–79, 135n.24, 137n.43, 137n.45, 139n.3, 146n.1, 153n.10, 154n.22. *See also* individual authors
Ferguson, Margaret, 163n.31
Ferster, Judith, 145n.55
fetish, 40, 43, 48, 51, 52, 64–65, 74, 91
fin'amors, 44, 48, 79, 80, 91, 96–97, 153n.16, 155n.34
Finke, Laurie, 134n.17
flattery, 20–21, 25–26, 80, 103–4, 139n.5, 141n.26, 157n.17
flatulence, literary representations of, 120–1, 124, 126–7, 162n.24, 162n.26
Fleming, John V., 145n.5
flesh. *See* body
Fletcher, Alan, 163n.33
Former Age, The (Chaucer), 81–85
Fortune (Chaucer), 87–89
Foucault, Michel, 114–15
Fradenburg, Louise O., 24, 45, 50, 103, 138n.52
Freccero, John, 138n.51
Freud, Sigmund, 77–79, 144n.50, 153n.12, 157n.11
Friar's Tale, 119, 130
Fries, Maureen, 139n.3

Furrow, Melissa, 152n.59
Fyler, John, 154n.19

Galatians, 66, 131, 165n.52
Galen, 78
Garbaty, Thomas, 133n.6
gender: categories, 4–6, 42, 57, 76–77, 93, 94, 113, 131–2, 134n.19, 137n.43; identity, 5–10, 55, 70–71, 72–73, 100, 113–17, 128–32, 131–32, 134n.17, 149n.21; in medieval culture, 4–6, 53, 60, 86, 93, 103, 131–2; in medieval theology, 6–8, 128; and sexual difference, 4–5, 54, 74, 78, 79, 82–84, 131–2, 134n.17, 137n.39, 139n.7, 144n.50, 152n.4. *See also* feminine; masculine
General Prologue, 1, 15, 24, 110, 110–19, 140n.8
Genesis, 82–85, 125, 143n.39, 154n.21, 164n.40
Gentilesse (Chaucer), 89–90
Geoffrey le Baker, 114, 159n.6
Geoffrey of Vinsauf, 13, 138n.51, 157n.12
gift-giving, 49, 103, 119, 126–27
glossing, 20, 32, 123–24, 139n.5, 163n.33, 163n.35; as erotic metaphor, 20–21, 25, 27, 128, 131, 139n.5, 140n.11
gluttony, 24–25, 82–83, 124, 141n.22, 158n.21, 163n.36
go-between. *See* mediation
Gottfried, Barbara, 145n.55
Gower, John, 157n.14
Gratian, 63
Gregory of Nyssa, 148n.14
Gregory of Tours, 149n.29
grief. *See* mourning
Griselda, 66–73, 76, 92
Guillaume de Machaut, 153n.15

hagiography, 54, 59, 64–66, 72, 74, 97, 149n.29, 152n.59
Hali Meidenhad, 67–69
Hanning, Robert, 37
Hansen, Elaine, 18, 42, 48, 55, 71, 76, 155n.35, 157n.14, 158n.20
Harwood, Britton, 157n.13, 157n.14
Hawkins, Harriet, 71
Hebrews, 52
Helen of Troy, 47
Henryson, Robert. *See Testament of Cresseid*
Heffernan, Thomas, 149n.29
Heraclitus, 139n.59
heterosexual orthodoxy, 73, 116–17, 123, 127–28, 135n.27, 160n.12
Hildegard of Bingen, 156n.6
Holloway, Julia Bolton, 155n.28
homosexuality, 160n.12, 161n.16; and Christianity, 114–18, 144n.48, 164n.39; and female homoeroticism, 36, 142n.30, 144n.48, 162n.22; as metaphor, 114, 123–32, 165n.42; and sodomy, 114–15, 123–26, 144n.48, 159n.5, 164n.39
Host, The, 63, 115, 130
House of Fame (Chaucer), 4, 155n.34
Hugh de Despenser, 114

incest, 48, 60–61, 70, 79, 151n.46, 153n.12, 164n.40
infidelity, 40–41, 44, 46–48, 51, 99–100
impositio ad placitum, 13, 31, 130–31, 140n.15, 163n.31
Innocent III, Pope, 56, 65, 107–8, 120, 147n.9, 158n.21, 164n.39
Irigaray, Luce, 10–11, 25, 26, 38, 77, 90, 137n.44, 141n.24, 144n.50, 145n.8, 152n.4
Isidore of Seville, Saint, 13, 98–99, 113–14, 164n.39

Jean de Meun, 137n.43, 142n.31
Jerome, Saint, 136; *Ad Eustochium*, 28, 141n.26, 148n.14, 151n.40; *Ad Furiam*, 28; *Ad Pacatulam*, 60; *Ad Principiam*, 163n.29; *Adversus Jovinianum*, 23–24, 47, 142n.36, 148n.14, 151n.42; *Commentariorum Ephesios*, 10, 64–65; *In Sophoniam*, 164n.40
Jordan, Robert, 153n.17
jouissance, 22, 79, 141n.15
Judas, 104

Kendrick, Laura, 145n.54
Kiser, Lisa, 3
Knapp, Peggy, 38
Knoespel, Kenneth, 145n.9
Kristeva, Julia, 69, 141n.15
Kundera, Milan, 16

Lacan, Jacques, 77–79, 109, 141n.17, 158n.23
lack, 14–15, 24, 77–79, 85–87, 115, 144n.50, 152n.4
Lak of Stedfastnesse (Chaucer), 85–87
Lament for the Makars, 3
Langland, William. *See Piers Plowman*
Laqueur, Thomas, 134n.19
Legend of Good Women (Chaucer), 3, 54–56, 93, 147n.7, 155n.34
Leicester, H. Marshall, Jr., 18, 133n.7, 138n.55, 144n.46
leprosy, 161n.14
Lerer, Seth, 154n.26
Leupin, Alexandre, 136n.29
Lewis, Robert Enzer, 147n.9
Lochrie, Karma, 135n.25, 148n.17, 157n.9
Lollardy, 122, 144n.47, 163n.33
Lollius, 39, 44, 51

Lomperis, Linda, 61
Longsworth, Robert, 71, 151n.50
Lot, and daughters, 125, 164n.40. *See also* incest
Luecke, Janemarie, 66

MacDonald, Donald, 156n.2
Mahoney, John, 143n.39
makyng: and gender, 4–5; and narrative voice, 43–44; and poetry, 2–4, 56, 74, 96, 130, 133n.8
Malvern, Marjorie, 139n.3
Manciple's Prologue, 107–108, 157n.17
Manciple's Tale, 97–112
Mann, Jill, 56, 147n.12
Man of Law's Tale, 5, 57, 72–75, 152n.58
Margherita, Gayle, 14–15, 43
Mariolatry, 67, 69, 80, 97, 150n.37
marriage, 21, 28–29, 140n.14, 151n.44. *See also* misogamy
masculine, 4, 42, 44, 54, 78, 82; and Christianity, 114; and epistemology, 8, 18–19, 38, 57, 102, 128, 131. *See also* gender
mater, 98–99, 104, 137n.46, 156n.6
Mater dolorosa, 70
Matthew, Gospel of, 88, 160n.10
McAlpine, Monica, 115
McLaughlin, Eleanor, 156n.6
McNamara, Jo Ann, 148n.14
Means, Michael, 155n.29
mediation, 20–21, 44–45, 48, 140n.10, 146n.15
memory, 15–17
Merchant's Tale, 68–69, 151n.44
metatextuality. *See* narrative reflexivity
Middleton, Anne, 147n.13
Miles, Margaret, 150n.31
Miller, The, 101

Miller's Prologue, 140n.8, 162n.22
Miller's Tale, 120, 156n.8
Minnis, A. J., 154n.25
misogamy, 28–29, 37, 67–69
misogyny: classical origins of, 6, 8–9, 42, 78; in literature, 19–21, 27, 31–32, 36–38, 46–48, 54–57, 63, 75, 81, 92–95, 97, 100–111, 129, 143n.40; patristic origins of, 6–7, 9–10, 27–28, 30–31, 42, 79, 82–84, 135n.34, 136n.36, 137n.39
Moi, Toril, 9
Monk, The, 101, 156n.8
Moses, 119, 148n.21
mother-child relationships, 70, 151n.44; with daughter, 60; with son, 64, 70, 97–99, 102, 104–6
mourning, 14–15, 77, 82, 138n.52
Mulvey, Laura, 141n.17
Murphy, James J., 155n.36
Muscatine, Charles, 151n.52
mysticism, 135n.25, 142n.28

narcissism, 43, 146n.11, 155n.30
narrative reflexivity: metaphoric, 63–64, 77, 81, 95, 118, 130–32, 148n.13, 154n.20, 155n.29, 165n.51; thematic, 1–5, 39–40, 51, 55–57, 133n.6
Narrator, *Canterbury Tales*, 1, 15–16
Narrator, *Legend of Good Women*, 16, 54–55
Narrator, *Troilus and Criseyde*, 3–5, 16, 39–52
Neuse, Richard, 163n.30
Newefangelnesse (Chaucer). See *Against Women Unconstant*
Nichols, John A., 141n.25
Nolan, Edward Peter, 154n.20
Noonan, John, 157n.11
Numbers, 148n.21

O'Brien, Timothy, 165n.51
Olson, Glending, 133n.8

Origen, 160n.10
origin, 14–15, 104
Ovid, 102, 154n.18, 157n.14

Pace, George B., 153n.14, 155n.33
Pagels, Elaine, 150n.32
Pandarus, 44–45
Pardes, Ilana, 135n.24
Pardoner, The, 33, 63, 110, 115–18, 159n.10
Parliament of Fowls (Chaucer), 155n.34
Parson, The, 115, 157n.8
Parson's Prologue, 155n.1
Parson's Tale, 98, 109, 111, 157n.8, 158n.24
patriarchy: and ideology, 29, 31, 71, 73, 78–79, 95–96; and social order, 32, 42, 51, 54, 60, 75, 88–89, 100
Patterson, Lee, 134n.21, 138n.51, 143n.40
Paul, Saint, 6–7, 10, 65–66, 79, 101, 123, 128, 131, 134n.22, 135n.23, 135n.24, 165n.52. See also specific titles
Pearl, 3, 134n.12, 156n.7
penitential handbooks, 144n.48, 163n.38
Petrarch, 3, 146n.12
Petroff, Elizabeth, 149n.29
Philo of Alexandria, 134n.22, 137n.37, 164n.40
Physician's Tale, 57, 58–63, 149n.21
Piers Plowman, 3–4, 104, 124, 134n.12, 141n.22, 158n.21
platitudes, 106, 111
Plato, 16, 86, 100–101, 157n.11
polysemy: defined, 1, 133n.4; and literary criticism, 14, 30–32, 58, 111, 122, 157n.11, 163n.31; metaphoric, 34–36, 38, 58, 73, 95, 102, 120. See also ambiguity; glossing; *signum translatum*; unisemy
power relationships, social, 60–63, 93–95, 149n.21

Prioress, The, 151n.44
promiscuity, 13–14, 21, 29–31, 36, 38
propriety. *See signum proprium*
Proverbs, 8, 23, 135n.28
Psalms, 121, 163n.29
psychoanalytic theory, 11–12, 77–79, 153n.9. *See also* individual authors
Pythagoras, 8, 131, 136n.30

Quintilian, 13

Ramsey, Lee C., 147n.13, 149n.26
rape, 45, 54, 55, 73, 119, 125, 148n.21, 149n.27, 164n.40
readers: external, 1–3, 27, 38, 39, 41, 43, 48, 51, 53, 75, 92–93, 162n.21; internal, 18, 20–21, 27, 39, 42–45, 52, 143n.36, 147n.7. *See also* glossing
Reeve, The, 1, 101
Reeve's Tale, 156n.8
Reiss, Edmund, 123
renunciation, 60, 101, 108–11, 158n.23
Retractions, 98, 108–109, 111–12, 158n.24
Rich, Adrienne, 135n.27
Robertson, D.W., Jr., 146n.11
romance. *See fin'amors*
Romans, 164n.39
Rubin, Gayle, 149n.21

Sartre, Jean Paul, 154n.20
Scattergood, V.J., 103
Schmidt, A.V.C., 84
Second Nun, The, 115–19
Second Nun's Prologue, 64
Second Nun's Tale, 57, 64–66, 76
Secretum secretorum, 148n.17
Sedgwick, Eve Kosofsky, 4, 149n.21, 155n.30, 159n.8, 165n.50
self-pity, 35, 38, 47–49, 61, 72, 102–3
sexual difference. *See* gender
Sherman, Gail Berkeley, 66

Shoaf, R. A., 140n.15, 146n.16, 158n.24
Sigal, Gale, 154n.26
signum proprium, 12–13, 43, 51, 86, 106
signum translatum, 13, 43
Sir Gawain and the Green Knight, 134n.12
Sophonias (Zephaniah), 125
Spelman, Elizabeth, 137n.44
Stanbury, Sarah, 141n.17
Stiller, Nikki, 151n.44
Stokes, Michael, 136n.30
Straus, Barrie Ruth, 139n.3, 140n.8
subjectivity: defined, 15; and textuality, 2, 5, 52, 133n.7
substitution, 20–24, 26, 41, 44–45
suicide, 54, 55, 63, 149n.27
Summoner's Prologue, 126
Summoner's Tale, 115–132
syphillis, 116–117

Tatlock, John, 3
Taylor, Mark C., 143n.41, 143n.45
tears, 69–70, 151n.44
temptress, 8, 82, 135n.28
Tertullian, 154n.21
Testament of Cresseid, 3, 146
Thomas Aquinas, Saint, 114, 148n.14, 156n.6, 159n.5, 164n.41
Timothy, 6–7
To Rosemounde (Chaucer), 91
translatio, 13–14, 43, 51
translation, 39–40, 43–45, 48, 51, 56–57, 146n.12
Trevisa, John, 39
Troilus, 43–52
Troilus and Criseyde (Chaucer), 2–3, 5, 39–52, 151n.47. *See also* individual characters
Truth (Chaucer), 90–91
Turner, James, 135n.24, 135n.35

unisemy, 34–35, 121–22

unisexuality. *See* androgyny; bisexuality

Vance, Eugene, 17, 21, 126
victimization, 33, 40–42, 47–48, 51–53, 57–63, 71–75
virginity, 33–35, 65; Christian ideal of, 27, 59, 62, 64, 148n.14, 151n.42 (*see also* asceticism); and misogyny, 58, 62, 67
Virgin Mary, 40, 64, 69, 151n.42
vision, 39–40, 46, 52, 59–60, 141n.17, 145n.9, 146n.20
voyeurism, 44–45

Warner, Marina, 150n.37
Weissman, Hope, 72
Whitbread, Leslie, 156n.6
widows, 28, 42, 48, 54
Wife of Bath, The, 18–38, 42, 53, 67, 76, 100–101, 128, 151n.44, 162n.22
Wife of Bath's Prologue, 19–38, 128–30, 140n.11, 142n.30, 156n.8, 162n.22
Wife of Bath's Tale, 23, 129–30, 150n.36
Wimsatt, James, 153n.15
Winterson, Jeanette, 113
Woman: absence of, 10, 76, 82, 90, 95; and ideology, 6, 14, 33–34, 40, 51, 97, 103–4, 145n.8. *See also* essentialism; gender
Womanly Noblesse (Chaucer), 91–92
Wood, Chauncey, 157n.13

Ziolkowski, Jan, 140n.11, 165n.42

www.ingramcontent.com/pod-product-compliance
Lightning Source LLC
Chambersburg PA
CBHW032252150426
43195CB00008BA/425